To Martin

with Best Wishes
from a fellow Chadsian

J M Menzie-Hall
Herstmonceux
15 September 2021.

Lost Child of Empire

The Life of
Squadron Leader
John M'Kenzie-Hall
M.V.O.

by John M'Kenzie-Hall
edited by James M'Kenzie-Hall (son)

Edited and published by James M'Kenzie-Hall
Email: jmkenziehall@yahoo.com

Acknowledgements:
My father (John) would like to thank his niece Annabella Schiffer for typing his memoirs, and to his now departed colleagues Jacko Jackson Smith, Peter Wilson and Michael Hickey for their comments and suggestions.
The editor (son James) thanks Bruce Winslade for putting the book together (graphic design and editing), and the input of Sam Parry, Alasdair Clayre, Stephen Burris (for research and fact checking in the USA), Marcus Bicknell, Caroline Gray, Andrew Hillier and Julie Collie (the daughter of Michael Welch).

Printed by Mixam, Hertfordshire, United Kingdom.

Typeset in 11-point Warnock Pro
Design by Winslade Graphics, Stroud, UK
Image scanning and refinement by Winslade Graphics, Stroud, UK

ISBN: 978-1-9997784-1-5

Contents

The beginning of my flying career. Aviation Cadet John M'Kenzie-Hall,
Initial Training Wing (ITW), Paignton, Devon, 1941. Note 'Australia' on shoulder.

Introduction

Over a period of time I have made notes on various incidents and highlights that have occurred during the course of my life which I thought my son might be interested to read at some time in the future. However, as these began to mount up, I realised that in a narrative form they were disconnected and needed linking together in some type of time frame. My early life in Australia, Malaysia and Africa coincided with the last gasp and then ultimate decline of the British Empire. By the British Empire I mean the dominions, colonies, protectorates, mandates and other territories ruled or administered by the United Kingdom. By 1920, three years before I was born, the British Empire represented 24% of the Earth's total land area. It is not my intention to eulogise or defend this empire (all empires fade away anyway) but I grew up in it, and witnessed it from its zenith, right through to the period of post-war decolonisation and decline ending with the humiliation of the Suez Crisis in 1956 in which I participated. Putting my life experience in this context: I am that 'Lost Child of Empire'. I am conscious that today's readers are likely to view certain types of behaviour described here quite differently to the way we saw them all those years ago.

At first the idea of writing an autobiography did not appeal to me. I had always considered this type of work should be restricted to those whose status and success in life warranted publication as either historically or politically important. Eventually it was pointed out to me that these days it is not necessary to have been academically successful, been an international film star or a footballer or to have made a fortune (preferably in a dubious manner) to warrant the telling of one's personal story. That should have been self-evident to me and I now accept that, if the contents and interest of one's life adds anything of merit to our changing society, it should be recorded; if not for a wider posterity at least for the interest of one's descendants whether it be history from the top down or from the bottom up.

This then is the justification for my attempt to put clothes on the skeleton of my life, and my temerity in writing my autobiography.

My ambitions have never been to become famous in war or peace, and I certainly recoil from being considered eligible to join the millionaires' club. I do not think I had any aim at all other than to achieve the inevitable small boy's dream to become an engine driver or, in my case, an 'aeroplane driver'! My only over-riding obsession throughout my stop-and-start progress through life has been to focus on understanding the essentials and priorities of any project I have undertaken, to acquire the highest standard of expertise to see it through. This has not always been easy, and I must admit failure on several occasions; in particular during my early days in Africa, just after the end of World War Two, when the introduction to a new way of life temporarily led me along paths where self-discipline and integrity were demoted to second place. I was 22 years old at the end of the war, the job was done and I was a demobbed fighter pilot looking for adventure.

I like to think that now in 2018, having reached the age of 95 years, I can summarise my flying career as follows:

> Over 14,000 flying hours logged as both a service and civilian pilot from 1942–1964.

> Categorisation as a transport and VIP pilot and instructor has remained as 'exceptional' over many years.

> I had the honour of being appointed Personal Pilot and Instructor to Prince Philip, Duke of Edinburgh, during the seven years of my final appointment in The Royal Air Force as Commander of the First Helicopter Section of The Queen's Flight at RAF Benson in Oxfordshire.

> I think I can claim that my chosen career as an 'aeroplane driver' has been a modest success!

Family history can be rather tiresome except to the immediate family. In these first two decades of the 21st century it has become a lot easier to look it up on the internet. I am immensely proud of my ancestors and their place in our island history. I feel no shame in giving a brief description of my parents and their antecedents who contributed to the making of the British Empire. Recently Douglas Murray wrote in *The Strange Death of Europe* (2017) about the European tyranny of guilt, judging ourselves by our worst moments and everyone else by their best. Europe has twice lost a generation of its young men

My grandfather Cecil Percy Hall
(1853–1927), owner of the Lily Tea Estate,
India.

My grandmother, Alice May Hall.

in World War One and World War Two. My own Father was injured at Gallipoli in the first and captured by the Japanese at the Fall of Singapore in the second.

An account of both my parents' lives is necessarily brief as most of the papers and documents, giving details of both their families, were destroyed by the Japanese during the invasion and occupation of Malaysia in World War Two.

I begin our family story in India. My great-grandfather Arthur Hall (1809–1879) served in India in the 3rd/5th Bengal Light Cavalry and the 21st Hussars and retired as a major general. He had married Anne Mackenzie, the second daughter of a fellow officer, John Mackenzie of Hilton and Brae, at Ghazipur on 3 October 1842 and this is no doubt where the M'Kenzie-Hall name originates (though why the apostrophe crept in instead of a 'C' is a mystery which I put down to a clerical error somewhere along the way). My grandfather Cecil Percy Hall (1845–1927) was a tea planter in India at The Lily Tea Estate in the Nelliampathy Hills (Western Ghats) in the state of Kerala (southwest India) about 60 kilometres (37 miles) from Palakkad (Palghat). The hill station was located at an altitude of 4,000 feet above sea level up a series of about ten twisting and turning hairpin bends. The tropical hill resort is known for orange, cardamom, coffee and tea plantations. Tea took over from coffee planting in the 1870s. Cecil Percy Hall, was born in India and, like many Victorian colonials, was extremely hard and unforgiving. This is due partly to the low survival rate because of disease, primitive living conditions, isolation and lack of amenities. He had four sons: Arthur, Byng, Jack and Charlie. They were all sent to England for their education. However, on their return to India, he expected each son to take up a position on the tea estate. If any of them wanted to see him, they were expected to make an appointment.

My Father, also John but known as Jack, is listed as born at Bangalore, India on 11 October 1893. Jack M'Kenzie-Hall (1893–1949) had an unlucky life and was often in the wrong place at the wrong time especially in both World Wars. He was wounded at Gallipoli in 1915 and captured by the Japanese at the fall of Singapore in 1942 and imprisoned at the notorious Changi-Sime Road internment camp.

Jack M'Kenzie-Hall in 1912, aged 19, at The Lily Tea Estate, Nilgiri Hills, South India.

The Lily Tea Estate, India, where Jack Hall spent his early years.

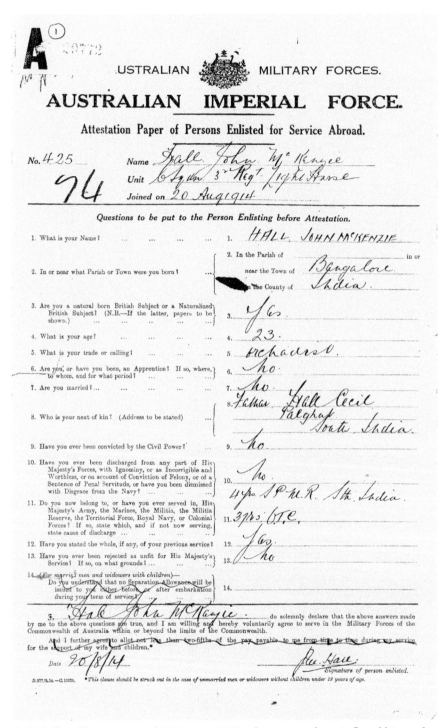

Jack Hall's enlistment record, 20 August 1914 – he seems to have inflated his age by two years as he was born in 1893.

My father,
Jack M'Kenzie-Hall
(1893–1949)

Jack's adult life began with an argument with his authoritarian father Cecil. He therefore quit India to seek his fortune in Australia. He ended up in Tasmania in 1912, where he became an 'orchardist' farming apples. The next year the entire apple crop was destroyed by frost and my Father could not continue. On the outbreak of the First World War, Jack immediately enlisted on 20 August 1914 with the Australian Imperial Force. His enlistment papers (number 425) show that he joined C Squadron 3rd Regiment of Light Horse at Pontville in Tasmania. The 3rd Australian Light Horse embarked for Egypt on 20 October 1914 and from there were sent to Gallipoli in 1915. The Gallipoli campaign lasted ten months from 17 February 1915 to 9 January 1916. My Father was wounded in the head and his wound was severe enough to be trepanned. I was told that there was heavy fire as they got out of the trenches. Jack was discharged in Egypt on 5 July 1915 and documents state he returned to Australia. However on 26 September 1915, Jack M'Kenzie-Hall, occupation Planter, is listed as being

M'Kenzie-Hall family house in Kerala, India.

a first class passenger on the Bibby Lines' ship *Gloucestershire* sailing from Liverpool to Colombo [Editor's note: in 1915 the *Gloucestershire* was converted to an armed merchant cruiser as *HMS Gloucestershire*]. The reason for this journey may have been that Jack sought medical care for his head wound.

He married Grace Hay Edwards in 1916. At the end of the First World War, Jack and his wife Grace travelled from Australia to visit his father in India. My parents seem to have stayed in India for some time as his war medals were sent to Nelliampathy in 1922, signed for by Jack and witnessed by Grace. Sometime during their visit to India, Grace was injured when she was thrown from her horse and lay unconscious until she was found. Again bad luck struck when, on their return from India to Australia, somewhere in the middle of the Indian

The author, John M'Kenzie-Hall, at 17 months.

Ocean, in calm seas, the boat caught fire and started to sink. To lighten the load their possessions were thrown overboard and the passengers took to the lifeboats. My elder sister Joanna (born 1918) was a baby at the time and was separated from her parents and put into a different lifeboat. It was some time before they were all reunited.

My story begins five years later in Australia.

A young John M'Kenzie-Hall looking whimsical. Photo taken during his time as a schoolboy in Melbourne between 1931 and 1934.

Chapter One

Australia and Malaya (Part I)

Australia

In 1804 Lord Hobart, who was Secretary of State for War and the Colonies in England, sent a Colonel Collins to Tasmania to found a new settlement which became known, after His Lordship, as Hobart. Shortly afterwards a colonising party was sent to form another new settlement on the banks of the Tamar river and this became Launceston. My mother, Grace Hay-Edwards, was born in Hobart in 1892 and I was born in Launceston on 7 June 1923.

I am told that from my birth I was allergic to milk and there was great concern for my survival. However, with some concoction like 'extract of beef' in water and many prayers, by a local group of Christian Scientists, I struggled through. Why the latter were involved I have never understood, since my mother was strictly Church of England and her cousins, the Rt. Rev. Henry Hutchinson Montgomery, who was the Bishop of Tasmania, lived close by. My mother and her two sisters had been brought up in their early years by the Bishop's wife Maud, along with her own family as my grandmother had died. Also, my grandfather, George Hay Edwards III (1845–1918), was absent for long periods due to his work as a chartered engineer and surveyor.

I am always amused at the story my mother told of 'little Monty' (the future Field Marshal Bernard Law Montgomery, 1st Viscount Montgomery of El Alamein) as my mother described him as they grew up together. He was "a very naughty little boy who was always pulling my pig-tails and letting off fire crackers under my chair on my birthday" (Guy Fawkes Day, 5 November). I recall this aggressive trait re-manifesting itself later in North Africa when he was confronted by the Germans in 1942.

I have no recollections of Tasmania, since we moved to Perth in Western Australia in either 1924 or 1925, and then to Melbourne.

I have given a great deal of thought to my earliest memories but only snatches of scenes come back clearly. There is a vivid recollection of a house in Perth, Western Australia, which had an enormous tiled Victorian conservatory, filled in every direction with flowering shrubs and rare orchids. It was all overhung by masses of exotic ferns and several small tropical trees. In the centre of this glass jungle stood a raised marble fountain with a waterspout that, when in full flow, seemed to disappear in to the heights before cascading back in to a marble break-barrier and spreading downwards in silvery fingers to join the oversized golden carp. It was through these doors into the garden that I experienced my first love.

There was a hole in the boundary fence to the next door property and I can still distinctly recall the little girl, whom I watched enraptured and longed to join, playing by herself on the lawn. I must have been about 3 years old. My father was fortunate in having one of the few Model T Fords and as a special treat he used to drive me to the coast for a picnic and a swim. The road for miles consisted of short rises and falls and at speed (about 30mph) one experienced the delicious childish sensation of continuous switchback, watching the adults begin to regret their last meal.

When I was about four years old we apparently decided to relocate to Melbourne and my father took the unprecedented step to drive us from Perth, via Adelaide. This was a somewhat hazardous journey in 1927 of some 2,000 miles, skirting the Nullarbor Plain and rounding the Spencer Gulf before reaching Adelaide and heading south for Melbourne.

Apart from our family of four, we were loaded down with petrol cans, food and giant canvas water bottles strapped on the front, jerry cans on the rear. My sister and I were jammed in the back with the luggage and gradually covered in various coloured dust, the non-existent road surfaces being of dry earth. It was Easter time and I am told that due to these rough roads my Easter Egg was inadvertently bounced out of the car. My Father refused to go back and look for it and I was apparently inconsolable and cried for hours. When we eventually arrived in Melbourne everyone was amazed by our epic journey and a mechanic even more so, when he discovered that most of the engine was, by now, suspended by only one bolt.

During the period in Melbourne we went to stay with friends, or possibly cousins of my mother, who had a large sheep farm in the north of Victoria. I have vague memories of vast open spaces, sheep, wallabies and dust. I do, however, have a very specific memory of a dog.

The son of the owner of the farm was about my age and we played happily together until he produced the model of a boat. Naturally we both wanted it and a tug o' war ensued, which became quite noisy. The dog, thinking the master's son was in jeopardy, leapt to his defence and bit me on my left upper arm, dragging me away. My wound was quite deep and so was my shock. To add to my suffering, iodine was poured in the punctures. The wound healed but the unfortunate incident left me with a stammer until I was well in to my teens. There was no speech therapy in those days and psychological effect led to a lack of confidence which was not helped by the other boys when I went to school. I had the horror of being picked on by the teacher to stand up and speak, aware that the giggles and remarks from the rest of the class would only make the situation worse. The stuttering diminished as I grew older but was still apparent on occasions of stress for many years.

Malaya

It must have been around 1926 when my father decided to take on the work of rubber planting in the Straits settlements of the Malay Peninsula, now called Malaysia. His experience of tea planting in India served him well and he began to re-build his life. As the price of rubber was high and with the trade beginning to prosper he sent for my mother, my sister and me in 1927. My sister, aged 9, was later sent back to Australia to attend Ruyton Girls' School in Melbourne.

By the time we arrived in Malaya my father had resigned from the rubber company which had employed him and had taken on a more senior job with a Danish firm, Perak Oil Palms Ltd. This was a massive pioneer project to open up a vast acreage of primary jungle to plant Nipah palms and produce vegetable oils for commercial use. These palms, first grown in cultivation in South America, grew up to 30 feet in height and produced clusters of bulbous, fatty fruit. Having cleared over a thousand acres of jungle, inter-connecting canals were dug between, which were planted with the palms. In addition to irrigation, these waterways enabled the harvested fruit to be loaded into small floating containers which were despatched to irregular collection points. Here they were loaded onto wagons of an internal railway system which criss-crossed the estate, ultimately arriving at the factory. The fruit was then crushed to produce the oil, rich in protein and fat. It has the appearance and consistency of coconut oil, and is used industrially as an edible fat in margarine. It can also produce oil for the manufacture of a type of sugar and soap. My father used to distil some of the liquid and produce petrol of medium octane, which he used in his own car. Since its properties had a high alcohol content he had quite a problem preventing his labourers from illicit distilling and drinking to excess.

In the early days of settlement in Malaya, the bungalows were fairly primitive. In general they were primarily made of wood, with a thatched roof

Drawing room inside the first bungalow at Perak Oil Palms Estate, Bernam River, Malaya.

of palm leaves or similar waterproof material. Corrugated metal sheeting was often used, but in monsoon weather the noise inside was almost indescribable; comparable perhaps with the drumming cadence of contemporary pop music. A wide veranda surrounding the living accommodation, and the whole bungalow, was usually built on stilts for protection against flooding as well as against large, curious animals. The space underneath allowed the passage of cooling breeze but, if built too low, could harbour many nasty creepy-crawlies! Full length green canvas and wood blinds, known as 'chits', were fitted to the outside of the veranda and were fully lowered during the day to keep out the heat of the sun. The sitting room was large, with a smaller dining area to the rear. Behind a wooden serving screen, steps led down to the kitchen area at ground level. Our food, having been prepared by the 'cook', then arrived via the 'houseboy', who served it from behind the screen. My mother had a hand-bell which she used to summon the next course. The houseboy invariably did not hear the bell or rather said he had not. My father, an inventive man, was thus challenged and we witnessed the appearance of a long length of rubber tubing which started from the kitchen, suspended perilously above our dining table and was 'operated' by a rubber bulb. The summoner would squeeze this bulb and the propelled air would in turn operate a bell in the kitchen. This was considered quite a modern invention before electricity arrived. Lighting was by candles, or kerosene lamps, which were eventually replaced by Tilley lamps. I remember being told of two events which illustrate and underline the difficulties of living in isolation and in somewhat primitive conditions.

Father had hunted a great deal in India, in and around his father's estate, and in Malaya it was a pleasure for him to get away from the day-to-day routine on the plantation and spend some time in the surrounding jungle. Apart from elephant, buffalo, wild boar, leopard, panther and deer, to name but a few, there were also rhino. Black and white rhino were few and far between in our district, and only occasionally caused havoc among the crops. The main culprit to create damage was 'dear old Jumbo' the elephant, who not only flattened crops, devastated vegetable patches, felled and debarked trees but also kept us a awake on many nights by using the wooden supports of our bungalow as 'rubbing posts'. Father used to bring a gong to chase them away but the shaking of the whole bungalow was quite frightening while it lasted.

One day Father heard that an expedition was shortly coming in to his area in search of the rare white rhino which, it was rumoured, had recently been seen locally. A launch duly arrived up the Bernam River to our landing stage and, after refreshments, the party set off with one of father's trackers as a guide. Father had to remain behind because of some trouble at the factory but promised to catch up with them later. Having cleared up his problem, later in the day he hurried to catch them up and some hours later heard them moving a little way ahead. He was just about to call out to them when he heard a movement to his right. In a patch of light about 20 feet away he saw a rhino, which appeared to be pursuing the hunters rather than being hunted by them! He very carefully moved downwind (as he thought away from the party), and stopped behind a small bush to listen for movement. All of a

Wide verandahs at the old bungalow, Perak Oil Palms Estate, Malaya.

With my mother Grace and sister Joanna, holidaying in Cameron Highlands, Malaya.

sudden, there was a loud explosion. His hat flew off and the rhino charged past him going flat out. The white rhinoceros is not really white but a dirty grey, with dark areas fading in to what is generally found to be dried mud. The marksman swore he saw a clear picture of the head and shoulders of the beast before he fired but my father came to two conclusions; he had been wearing a hat called a 'double terrai' (a double felted hat with a wide brim) which, in the subdued light of the jungle floor, did appear a muddy grey. The over-excited hunter had failed to work downwind and had mistaken my father for the rhino. It was plain that he had failed to carry out the fundamental principle of big game hunting; that of 'certain identification'. Second, and this seemed the more likely explanation, he had totally mis-aimed and by a very lucky chance the bullet went high into the crown of father's hat! There followed a heated exchange of 'compliments', some sound advice was given and the rhino was finally caught up with and despatched the next day. My Father always said it was not exactly professionalism that allowed a very rare white rhino's head to be mounted over the door of the British Museum instead of his head!

Nowadays the killing of animals is much frowned upon and I certainly lost my appetite for the 'sport' in East Africa many years later. However, it must be remembered that 60 or 70 years ago the various species were not as yet accepted as endangered. Big game hunting was recognised and practised throughout the world as a man's way of proving himself, and of protecting others from the constant fear of being attacked as they pushed the undeveloped world further and further into what we now call civilisation.

Christmas is always an exciting time for children and when they are aged about six or seven the thrill of expectation is usually fostered by adults and over-exposed by catalogues and newspapers. At P.O.P. (Perak Oil Palms) my sister and I were the only children, and one Christmas we had been scanning the magazines and catalogues for weeks, writing the usual letters to Father Christmas. Apart from another air gun, more powerful than the Daisy air gun I already had, it had been suggested to me that certain books, games and perhaps another gun might be possible if I remained good and did not complain when having to take senna pods every evening (parents can be devious, can they not!). I had no reason to expect what my parents had in store for me.

My father had several assistants working for him and their bungalows were generally some two or three miles apart on the estate. Since there were no proper roads, and therefore no cars, everything was carried by hand, bicycle or wagon. During the day little railway engines puffed up and down a network of lines, drawing the loaded wagons to and fro, but at night the engines were put in to their sheds. Since railway lines criss-crossed the entire estate, including passing close to the bungalows, the empty wagons were always on call but now pushed by coolie power. The afternoon of this particular Christmas Eve my sister and I were sent over to an assistant's bungalow for the night and were awakened at 5.00 am for the return home trip. The morning was cold and dark, with just a glimmer of light from a brilliant, starry sky. The trolley wagon, with its wooden platform floor, was waiting for us but as there was no engine to pull it there were three Tamil coolies ready to push us. On the trolley were three chairs, a table, on which there was a hurricane lamp and around which we sat with our *amah* (a nursemaid employed to look after young children). The labourers, in those days called 'coolies', pushed the trolley until it reached a good speed and then they all jumped on until it slowed down. There were no steep inclines but several long downward slopes and we must have accelerated to 10 or 20 mph for some inclines; with brilliant stars above, the cold exhilarating air of dawn rushing past, adding to the chill of excitement! The sides of the track were lit by millions of yellow/green/white fireflies and from a distance the calls of the awakening monkeys and other weird jungle noises rising above the clickety-clack of the trolley wheels made it all seem like a dream. Every now and then a nightjar, with its glowing orange eyes, would be disturbed from its resting on the tracks and suddenly fly up, with a great whir of wings as if gesticulating furiously at being run down. As

With my mother Grace and father Jack M'Kenzie-Hall.

First bungalow at Perak Oil Palms Estate on Bernam River.

we neared the bungalow the dawn was breaking but the beauty of this was ignored in our anticipation of the surprises in store.

Even today I can recall the tremendous feeling of joy and disbelief when I saw, sitting in all its glory just by the steps on the veranda, the pedal car I had been wanting all summer! It proudly shone in its blue and silver paintwork, equipped with windscreen, horn and instrument panel. I had little thought but to spend the rest of my life pedalling all over the estate and on in to an adventurous world. I did not, at that tender age, appreciate the fact that my father had had to widen numerous bridges over the canals and to erect safety barriers on the sides to prevent me from falling in. It was not long before I discovered my area was confined to the endurance of my legs and the bridges nearer home. This particular Christmas was one example when anticipation and realisation were not only equal but also equally outstanding.

I am told I had an *amah* and a tutor, neither of whom unfortunately was a success. After a couple of years my parents heard that a new convent was just opening in the Cameron Highlands and were willing to take me as a boarder. My parents drove up to the convent and left me in the charge of the Sisters while they repaired to a nearby hotel to wait for me to settle in. At just turned seven I was the oldest child there but was put to bed with the four-year-olds at 5.00 pm. I was quite unused to such discipline, hated the large newly built, prison-like building and had no confidence in the women who wore robes, white caps and hissed down at one. The long arched colonnades spread deep shadows, contrasting terrifyingly with the dazzling new, white-washed walls. Myriads of black shadowed windows seemed to hover threateningly above me. Stone washed floors led on to further stone washed floors leading on again to the dormitory, with its rows of beds like choir stalls. I found the whole atmosphere terrifying and I ran away at the first opportunity, soon after being put to bed.

The distance from the convent to the hotel was about three miles, down a valley, and there was no habitation whatsoever between the two, only jungle. My absence was not noticed for some little time and, when it was, dusk was already setting in before my parents were notified by telephone. What a night they must have spent! For most of the night search parties were out and, to add to their nightmare, it appears that there had been recent warnings of a man-eating tiger in that area! I only vaguely remember feeling lost and waking up beside a tree next morning to find a couple of the search party calling out as they stood looking at me. I was to recall this incident 24 years later while sitting in the same jungle in Malaya waiting for a couple of Chinese communist terrorists to approach; I shall expand on this encounter later when recalling 1953. Having brought me back to the hotel I was left to the tender mercies of my mother and not-so-tender father. They had had an awful shock but I was not sent back to the convent.

It appears that from here I went to lodge with family friends in the capital, Kuala Lumpur. They were called Harrison and the husband was the general manager of the Kuala Lumpur racecourse. They had a son, Edgar, the same age as me and, to my delight, I had a playmate for the first time and we spent most of our time pedalling our bicycles in and around the racecourse. I do remember clearly noticing the difference between their bungalow and ours on the estate. The Harrisons' bungalow was built in stone and it had a polished staircase upon which was patterned carpet. It ascended between glistening white walls to a landing leading to bedrooms, each of which actually had their own bathrooms as well as hot and cold running water! They had electricity and even the cupboards had lights installed to provide gentle heat needed to prevent the clothes from turning green with mildew, owing to the high humidity during the rainy season. It seemed all so bright and new and exciting, until I had to go to school every day, when the joy faded and I longed to be back on the estate where freedom now seemed so much more important than luxuries. However, I have jumped too far ahead and would like to go back to the earlier period of my first arrival in the Malay States.

One of my more pleasant memories of living in the middle of the jungle was the occasional picnic. This was primarily laid on for the adults and I no doubt missed a great deal of the goings-on. There were, however, still exciting things for a child to experience which leave a lasting impression. My father's assistants were invited to join us together with any visitors who happened to be staying at the time. On this particular occasion the motor launch was loaded early in the morning, before the sun became too hot. There was cold roast chicken, salad, green peas, lots of fruit and of course beer, spirits, as well as my favourite drink 'American ice cream soda'. A suitable spot had been chosen to moor and land for our picnic and with gramophone wound up and, the party in high spirits, we set off. The river was about 400 yards wide and made its way slowly in a muddy flow through unbroken jungle. The trees on either side rising to some 100 feet or more in eerie silence, except for the cries of monkeys and the calling of birds. We travelled on the shady side and, at two or three knots, the temperature was wonderfully cool. The river was teeming with crocodile and our hands were kept well inboard! Towards mid-day we moored at a little natural harbour and some of the party tried their hand at fishing, some stretched their legs while others prepared lunch and yet others kept the gramophone well wound. I can remember asking for the empty bottles which, when floating, provided excellent target practice for my air gun. Returning at just about dusk, with the sun going down rapidly and the incessant chug-chug of the launch as background, I remember records such as *Red Sails in the Sunset* and *There's a Rainbow Round my Shoulder* as, full of food and drink, we arrived tired and contented at the jetty.

What was general life like for adults living so far away from civilisation? My mother did her shopping once a month. She went down river by motor launch (there were no roads) for about four hours to the nearest riverbank village for the basic foodstuffs. If more sophisticated shopping was required she rowed across the river by sampan (a flat-bottomed boat) with her chauffeur (a 'syce', originally used for a person who takes care of horses) where the car was kept. From there to Taiping or Ipoh was some 30 miles further on. After a night stop at a hotel or Government Rest House she would make the return journey. Amongst the goods we looked forward to on her return was the occasional toy, chosen previously, with much longing, from a Whiteaway Laidlaw & Co. catalogue, along with bars of rather soggy, melted Cadbury's chocolate and some European manufactured sweets. We were never allowed any native sweets. The launch brought back large blocks of ice wrapped in sacking and stored in sawdust boxes which were tipped in to large lead-lined crates and were our only means of keeping food and drink cool. When it melted, which often occurred before the next scheduled shopping trip, so did we!

All our water was boiled and each night, before going to sleep under mosquito nets, we had to drink a concoction made up of senna pods. Each morning before breakfast it was mandatory to swallow a tablespoonful of cod liver oil and sometimes, to help make it more palatable, castor oil on a sugar cube. I can never remember an occasion when I was ill.

Because of white ants and other creepy-crawlies, all the legs of the furniture were placed in glass jars of water which prevented the ascent of these unwanted creatures. The roof, thatched in *atap* (nipa palm leaves), leaked in places and, since it was not lined, other animals and insects made their home in it; especially geckos who had the unfortunate habit of dropping down on one when least expected, creating a diversion at mealtimes. There were also snakes and the odd adventurous rat which always sent the whole family in to a frenzied chase, usually fruitless. The bungalow stood at the convergence of two rivers, the Perak and the Bernam, with a peninsula garden running down to the wooden pier where the launch was berthed. The garden was supervised by my Mother between 4.00 pm and 5.30 pm. We were only allowed out in the sun without our 'topees' after 4.00 pm. The area was alive with colour, bougainvilleas, kannas, frangipani, allemandes, hibiscus and, always my favourite, the exotic moonflower. There were large blue and white trumpet flowers grown over a number of wooden arches. They glowed bright white in the moonlight and were generally covered in myriads of little green flashing

Crocodiles – an ever-present menace. My father Jack had shot the one below.

fireflies. Father had made a badminton court for us and my sister Joanna and I were very often in confrontation; being five years my senior she usually won both on and off the court! My Father also hacked a nine-hole golf course out of the jungle which was rough, covered in ant-hills and inhabited by snakes. I was always told that his handicap depended on how many animal intruders he managed to shoot on the way round rather than the holes he sank!

From the pier a set of wide wooden steps ran down to the water for getting on or off the motor launch. These steps were also used by the *dhobi* woman (washerwoman) to beat our clothes and rinse them in water. One day she just vanished, leaving most of the clothes behind. Sometime later my father shot an annoying crocodile that was constantly cruising around outside our swimming pool. This was a cleaned area of water on one side of the pier and protected by a palisade of strong wooden poles and was regularly inspected for damage. Later on, while examining the crocodile, a number of bangles and bracelets were found and identified by the washerwoman's husband.

We had four gardeners, they were 'coolie' (Tamil) women and they used long handled metal sickles. We called them the 'swing sisters' because they spent all day working in a line and swinging their sickles in a circle to cut the grass. They were very proficient and the lawns always looked immaculate. Our main staff consisted of an Indian cook, two Chinese houseboys, a Chinese *amah*, an Indian or Chinese syce and an Indian water carrier, who often supervised the swing sisters in various tasks in the garden.

Household incidents were legion but I can only remember a few. Staff were difficult to find, difficult to train and once trained would either demand higher wages or be 'stolen' by other Europeans who had lost theirs. All food and drink was locked away and my mother had a huge bunch of keys which she swore never left her side. Each evening whisky and gin bottles were marked at the point of last pouring. Sugar and flour were measured and issued each day as were many types of stored food. It was not unusual to find alcohol bottles topped up with water to their proper levels or ridiculous excuses made for shortages in dried goods. My mother was fully aware of all this but not of how to deal diplomatically with the problem or consequence of losing a trained member of staff, followed by the inevitable time taken in the hiring and retraining of a replacement. She therefore allowed a percentage of 'wastage' for thieving and pilfering and philosophically turned a blind eye in most cases. It must have been a very lonely life for her since there were no other women to engage with. All the European staff were bachelors. Very occasionally my parents took the long journey to a large town and were able to socialise at the club or hotel for a few days.

I have previously described our bungalow and given a rough diagram of its layout. At the back and on both sides, small wooden steps ran up to the primitive

John is holding the rifle that Jack used to shoot the crocodile.

washrooms attached to the bedrooms, what would be called ensuite today. The bathrooms were simply furnished with a 4' x 3' wooden slat upon which one stood. To one side stood a very large earthen jar (*coujar*), which held 40–50 gallons of water. In one corner was a wide wooden seat with a hole in it and which had a bucket suspended immediately beneath it and below the floor. This particular apparatus was somehow never enquired about or referred to in our family. The water-carrier would appear in the morning, or whenever necessary, with two kerosene cans filled with water and fastened by rope to each end of a wooden pole, balanced over his shoulder. It took him four or five trips to fill the coujar, and then, duty done, he would disappear until the next day. An Aunt of mine from Australia came to stay with us and, in need of freshening herself, decided to take a shower. She entered the bathroom, disrobed and commenced to use the 'dipper', a small receptacle attached to the *coujar* used to dip in to it and pour the water over one's head. She had just started when the door opened and in, purposefully, walked the water-carrier, carrying his two cans of water. She was horrified and shouted the only word she had picked up in Tamil, 'Ingiva, ingiva... you fool... ingiva!!' He completely ignored her and calmly continued in his allotted task, emptied the cans in to the *coujar*, turned on his heel and left the bathroom, only to return some moments later to my now apoplectic aunt who screamed, promptly threw the dipper at the astonished man and fled the bathroom.

Later, on relating this unnerving event to my father, he was able to throw some light on the apparent insolence and insensitivity of his employee. He rather drily explained to my Aunt, much to her chagrin, 'My dear Edith, I am not in the least surprised. You bade him 'Enter' or 'Come in' and he did but comply. I wonder what he thought of the dipper being hurled at him?'

We did not employ local

Mother Grace, sister Joanna and John at the old bungalow, Perak Oil Palms Estate.

Malays as domestic staff. They kept very much to their own *kampongs* where they cultivated their rice and other foodstuffs essential to their diet or they fished in the rivers or coastal waters. The carpenters or '*fundis*' I came across were Sikhs and better workers it would be hard to find.

Our bedrooms had mosquito nets over the beds and every night it was a practice before getting in to bed to inspect the netting for any insects or reptiles such as centipedes or scorpions.

All the areas were then sprayed with a Flit gun before tucking the netting in all around the mattress and climbing in. We were forbidden to leave the room at night for any reason but were instructed to call out or bang on the wall if we needed to attract attention.

We were also forbidden, for the sake of our own safety, to go nearer than six feet to the riverbank unless accompanied by an adult. The snatching by a crocodile of our *dhobi* woman being a fine deterrent! However, I was allowed to play in an old abandoned motor launch, discarded alongside a narrow, muddy estuary, away from the river and well within sight of the bungalow. It was while playing here one evening at dusk that I got quite a fright. I had lingered too long and was on my way back to the bungalow when I saw a pair of green eyes looking at me alongside a bush. I let out a yell and ran for my life for about 50 yards, to reach the safety of the bungalow steps, up which I tore. My father did investigate and came to the conclusion that it had been a black panther. A watch was kept for some time afterwards, but it was never seen again; the creature probably having been just as shocked as I!

Father rose at 4.30 every morning, had a cup of tea and then went down to the coolie lines, where the daily workers were mustered around 5.00 am. He would then go on to the estate office where he would work until 8.00 am returning home for a breakfast of cereal with tinned milk, followed by fish or eggs, toast with marmalade and percolated coffee. A tin of 'Craven A – Black Cat' cigarettes always stood on the table and he would solemnly count each one to see if there were any missing since the previous night. After breakfast he toured the estate, went to the factory, or back to the office, until 'tiffin', lunch, at 1.00 pm. He stayed at home then until 3.30 when he returned to the office to work again until 6.30–7.00 pm.

There were several assistants on the estate, one of whom, a Eurasian, had made himself extremely unpopular with the estate workers; going out of his way to bully and insult them. One morning my father discovered his mangled body on one of the estate roads. In the early hours the man had been dragged from his slumber, bound, then tied to a car and dragged along the bumpy road surface until very dead.

On another occasion a Tamil foreman had stolen equipment from the factory and not only lied about it but was both sarcastic and rude to my father when summarily dismissed. This so infuriated my father that he took his walking stick and beat the man down the steps and had him marched off the estate and put on the next boat to call. He did not, though, send him to prison. On father's return from a trip to England some years later this man had somehow heard of his return and was waiting on the dock in Singapore begging him to take him on again. He turned out to be a loyal and reliable worker.

I was now approaching eight years old and was without a tutor as the last one left as he was unable to take the isolation of our estate. My parents decided to send me to school in Australia, England being so much further and the journey there being much longer and more difficult. My mother sailed to

Melbourne with me on a Blue Funnel steamer and on arrival we went to stay with old friends of my father's, a barrister and future prime minister of Australia, called Menzies, and his wife Pattie (at 10 Howard Street?). They had two sons at Trinity Grammar School and it seemed perfectly sensible to send me there too. Initially I went as a day-boy (home address: 65 Wellington Street, Kew) but, after a while, my mother needed to return to Malaya and I was enrolled as a boarder. In 1931 I began as a boarder in Merritt House and continued until 1934 (year four).

As a day-boy it was not too bad, but as a boarder I found it difficult to integrate. Having spent most of my childhood on my own, I had developed a level of independence, and I found it difficult to conform to what was, to me, such an alien way of life and distorted language. I was teased, both for my spoken English as well as my lack of knowledge of subjects that had been taught in the lower forms. I was placed in a class well below my age and picked on constantly by the teachers for not knowing the answers. I also stammered badly, from the dog bite I had received during my baby days in Australia, and this was manna from heaven to the bullies. I was therefore quite unready to become a boarder and have never lost my hatred of schools and school life. Menzies' son, Ian, was older than I was and so was given the task of looking after me. As a day-boy, Ian, his brother and I used to play happily in the garden of their parents, and Aunt Pattie used to join in our games of cowboys and Indians. I regret to say that at school Ian turned out to be a vicious bully to all the younger boarders, and he seemed to derive great satisfaction from the punishment doled out to us, having instigated our 'sins' himself then 'snitched' to the teacher.

I no longer went to the Menzies' house and, on short holidays, was boarded out to a family called Urquart. They provided food and bed but otherwise ignored me. They had an outside privy which had a very wide wooden seat and it was too high for me to manage properly. Unfortunately I then sometimes dribbled on this seat, resulting in a telling-off and threats of punishment to such an extent that I was almost relieved to return to school. The longer holidays were just as unpleasant, but in a different way.

When school broke up everyone, except me, went home. I was left kicking my heels in a very empty school for several days before I was picked up and driven to a so-called 'holiday home'. My guardian for the holidays was a thin, tall, prim spinster called Miss Gawler. She ran a house-cum-farm and took in several children for the holidays. The farm was situated in the Dandenong Hills (approximately 22 miles or 35km east of Melbourne) and was a perfect paradise. We were surrounded by leafy forest that had kookaburras, kangaroo and exotic birds of all sizes and colours and acres of safe areas of forest where we could play. However, we all had a strict routine to follow; up early each

Jack M'Kenzie-Hall and his wife Grace.

morning to feed the chickens and pigs and clean out the sties and the runs before breakfast. After breakfast we made our beds and tidied up and were each given a task which took us up to lunchtime. We were allowed some playtime in the afternoon until tea-time when there were more allotted chores. Mine was to go and feed the pigs with buckets of swill at just about dusk, and then collect the eggs on my way back. It was, however, a very welcome break from school and each Saturday we were allowed to walk the two miles to the nearest sweet shop and spend our pocket money. I do hope that before she died Miss Gawler, having benefitted from the hard work of her little charges, found it in herself to have a kind word for them.

I always seemed to return to school several days before the others, spending the days wandering the grounds and the empty classrooms and eating with matron. Our headmaster, Mr Bird (*'Oiseau'* to us), was high church and I found Sundays particularly tedious. It seemed to be spent continually at prayer, either at school or at the Church. Our school song ended with the words, 'For the green and the gold and the mitre…', hence our caps were deep green, embellished with three cords of yellow and embroidered with a white symbol of a mitre. Wearing these with a grey suit and stiff white wing collars, we all commenced the day by assembling in the hall for early morning prayers. After breakfast we assembled in the common room for Bible studies, before marching off in crocodile fashion to church. Following lunch we again assembled for a Crusaders meeting and, to cap it all, we attended a further church service in the evening.

During my whole time at School I only recall two nice things happening to me. The first was sport. I was good at all field events and won the *Victor Ludorum* twice for running, hurdles and high jump [Editor's note: in the Trinity Grammar School history book it lists John M'Kenzie-Hall as being Merritt House Captain in the prep school]. The second was receiving the news that I was to spend one of the long school holidays visiting my parents in Malaya. I sailed to Singapore on a Blue Funnel steamer called the *MS Centaur II* [Editor's note: built 1924, later acted as an Australian hospital ship in WWII and was torpedoed by a Japanese submarine 30 nautical miles east of the southern tip of Moreton Island, Brisbane, 14 April 1943, with loss of 268 lives]. I was placed in the care of the captain, who indulged me and gave me the free run of the ship. I spent most of the time on the bridge or accompanying the captain ashore at the various ports of call. The journeys to and fro were too long for more than a short visit to my parents but it was a great adventure to a small boy. The inevitable return to school was a hateful experience and I was never able to settle down again. There was one highlight during this period that I must mention; a young Don Bradman, in his early cricketing days, actually came to coach at Trinity College and I have both bowled and batted with him!

Things at this time had not been going well for my father. Although it was my mother's intention to visit us in Australia after a short period, once again fate stepped in. Having worked extremely hard to build up the Perak Palm Oil Estate and perhaps not taking enough rest, my father became ill. It seems that one day on a tour of the fields he was bitten by a flea from a rat. This developed in to what was known as 'Japanese river fever', an extremely virulent and dangerous disease for which, at that time, there was no known cure. He was not expected to live and for several weeks it was touch and go. It was several months before he was strong enough to consider working once more. He was still weak and was sensibly advised to seek a less strenuous or stressful post. He therefore resigned from the Danish company and took the post of manager of a rubber plantation just outside the capital, Kuala Lumpur. This was with Harrison & Crossfields, who were well thought of in the rubber trade. Up until this time my mother had spent a great deal of time and thought on having a new bungalow, with electricity and proper drainage, plus the planning and execution of the surrounding garden built at Perak Oil Palm Estate. She had endured much privation previously and all was becoming much more comfortable for them, when everything changed. It must have been very hard. There was the dreadful anxiety of my father's illness, followed by his having to relinquish an established and secure position and take a post elsewhere, as well as accept a lower income. I was of course unaware of what my parents must have had to go through at the time. My concern was my undying hate of school but, to my utter relief, they relented and brought me back to Malaya where I attended a school in the nearby city of Kuala Lumpur.

So, in 1935, aged 12, I returned to Malaya and started school again. I had almost forgotten my Malay and by this time had a slightly confused Australian accent. How I loved to be back in what I considered home, although it was sad that I would never see Perak Oil Palms Estate again. However, I had come back just as the world slump occurred and rubber, tin and most other products fell dramatically in price. Companies went out of existence or contracted to keep alive. My Father was made redundant and took the decision to return to England, find a job and put me to school.

Chapter Two

England (Part I)

For the second time since the loss of all his possessions in the Indian Ocean my father sold up, apart from a few family heirlooms and silver, and took passage with all of us from Singapore to Tilbury in a Japanese ship, called the *Terukuni Maru*, a most comfortable Japanese passenger liner (built 1929–1930 with air conditioning for the fortnightly scheduled European service, an 11,931 ton steel-hulled vessel, 505 feet long; it could carry 121 first-class passengers, 68 second-class passengers, and 60 third class passengers, with a crew of 177). In the four weeks' sailing we enjoyed all the onboard entertainment, such as deck games, swimming, fancy dress balls and delicious deck servings of copious cups of beef tea each morning, while relaxing in deck chairs. On many evenings dinner was served Japanese style, squatting on cushions on deck and having food cooked in front of one under candlelight and bright stars.

Leaving Singapore, we crossed the Indian Ocean to Colombo in Ceylon. We stayed overnight in the Galle Face Hotel (the 'best hotel East of Suez') where I remember having bought a model catamaran about two feet long. I never assembled it and somewhere, when we arrived in England, it got lost. Then on to Massawa in Eritrea where I was dragged through a dusty town to a museum where it was said a Mermaid was displayed. It turned out to be an ugly fish with a tail, or something like that depicted as a mermaid. Not worth the journey!

Our next port of call was Suez where we were intrigued by the myriad of 'bum boats' selling souvenirs and alcohol of dubious origin. It was great fun for the children to be entertained by the 'Gully Gully Man' with his display of conjuring using baby chicks. I have now been through the Suez Canal several times but the first was the most spectacular, apart from the nasty and often revolting habits of the Egyptians on each bank. We witnessed incredibly clear mirages and the colour miracles of the Red Sea including a sand storm just before reaching Port Said.

We then steamed North to Kalamata and Greece and then on to Taranto and Naples, passing the Isle of Capri. This was the period when the Italians were about to invade Abyssinia, and Mussolini was very much in power. We were warned before leaving the ship that anyone making disparaging remarks, or even joking about, the fat dictator would be arrested and almost certainly spend some time in gaol. We escaped by keeping our mouths firmly shut and sailed on to Marseille.

At that time Marseille appeared very run-down with areas of slum housing, and it seemed very dirty. Due to its dry heat that was very different from the steamy Far East, we soon abandoned our visit. The only excitement there for me was a motorboat trip out to the Château D'If and crawling through the passageway where Alexander Dumas' *Count of Monte Cristo* was said to have made his escape. To round off the story of this voyage, it is sad to relate that the very comfortable *Terukuni Maru* sank off the English coast near Harwich on 21 November 1939 after striking a German magnetic mine.

Arriving at Tilbury Docks in England in 1936, we entrained directly to Birmingham and rented a house in Sutton Coldfield. My father started looking for a job and a school for me. Of course he had jumped from a slump in overseas markets to a worse slump in England where he had no experience. He finally found a job as a salesman for industrial ventilator fans. I remember accompanying him in a rather battered Wolseley car around the grimy industrial areas of the Midlands on a number of occasions and seeing his despair as each visit came to nothing. It became obvious that there was no future whatsoever in England for him and in any case he could not reconcile himself either to the climate or the way of life.

It was inevitable that he should return to the Far East, and in 1937 he returned to the Malay States, as they were then called, as manager of the Lambak Rubber Estate at Mengkibol in Johor. It is strange that I was nearly killed in an ambush close to that estate some sixteen years later. He quickly established himself and was about to have my mother to join him when in 1941 the Japanese army invaded in the North. As the Japanese soldiers worked their way South, mostly on bicycles in those early days, most people thought they would be stopped. Since our forces were totally unprepared and concentrated in the South, the Japanese progress was so swift that my father had little time to blow up the factory, burn what he could, disable the vehicles and evacuate over the causeway to Singapore where he joined the Malay Volunteer Force. He had refused a passage on the last ship to leave Singapore, which was fortunate, since it was almost immediately sunk. He was captured while driving an ambulance with casualties from the pitifully small contingent of mixed forces trying to defend the causeway between Johor and Singapore. He was sent to Sime Road Prison and then incarcerated in Changi gaol where he laboured as a coolie for the duration of the war on the construction of runways for the airfield at Changi Creek. He is listed in the Changi Internment Camp Register under card index no. 959 as Hall. J. M., planter, British, aged 50, and in the camp register as no. 820 (Cambridge University Library, RCMS 103/12/22, June 1942).

He spoke little of his internment except to tell how, at one point, he lost his upper set of false teeth and had to pay almost all he had to get them back. This may be why he used the voucher system or in some cases bartered his few possessions for food or medicine. He was also in an early escape plan which failed and, as a result, he underwent what he called the squatting torture. This meant squatting in full sun with a post between the back of the knees. Every time he fell over he was beaten in the ribs and back by a rifle butt. Seven or eight hours in a static squatting position is some measurement of what was considered fairly light punishment.

When he was released and recuperating in England during 1946 he received a demand from a fellow prisoner who, with others, had been running a 'black market' in prison. It seemed that most of the Red Cross parcels were rarely received by the recipients but were diverted. Prisoners were able to buy essential food or other items from this clique by giving vouchers at outrageous prices to these unscrupulous people. On receiving this demand for some hundreds of pounds my father took immediate action. He wrote a very polite letter to the writer suggesting that if he would care to present himself in person he was sure that some accommodating solution could be found. The inference was clear and he never heard another word.

For the third time in his lifetime he had lost everything in the material sense. He was 14 stone when captured and weighed just six stone when released. He was physically and mentally weakened, and he arrived in England with no funds. There was no compensation forthcoming from the Government for civilian internees except a once only payment of £40. The only thing that enabled him to survive once he had partly recovered his health was the small disability war pension from the 1914–1918 war awarded him by the Australian Government for his severe wounds whilst in the 3rd Australian Light Horse at Gallipoli. I was also able to contribute a small sum which I had been making to my mother throughout the war, once I had been commissioned.

This was hardly enough to live on and my mother was persuaded by Norah, Viscountess Torrington to rent a small cottage next to her house at Buckfastleigh in Devon. Norah was the second wife of 9th Viscount

Torrington. The family connection was my great-great-grandfather Charles Henry Hall (1763–1827), Dean of Christ Church Oxford and Dean of Durham, who married, on 3 September 1794, Anna Maria Bridget Byng (1771–1852), daughter of John Byng, 5th Viscount Torrington. All this occurred just at the time when my own income was severely reduced and I was greatly relieved

Charles Henry Hall (1763–1827), Dean of Christ Church Oxford, Dean of Durham, and my great-great-grandfather.

For a biography of Charles Hall see appendix pp275–276.

Memorial to Charles Henry Hall at Durham Cathedral.

Jack M'Kenzie-Hall's house, Moshi, 1947, when he was Custodian of Enemy Property.

when my Mother contacted me in London with the news that my Father had been offered a post overseas. He was appointed as 'Custodian of Enemy Property' in Tanganyika, British East Africa. The Germans had occupied Tanganyika in the 1880s during the so-called 'Scramble for Africa', but by 1920 it was under British mandate.

By 1946, Tanganyika was a trustee territory under the jurisdiction of the newly formed United Nations but administrated by the UK. The task outlined to my father was to take over all the property previously confiscated from Germany and its allies and allocate it to existing or new settlers and to assist in opening up new areas in the task of post-war development. He flew out to Kenya by Sunderland flying boat, landing on Lake Victoria, and stayed on a little time with my mother's cousin Brian Montgomery, brother of Bernard. This was at Lake Elmenteita, the Soysambu estate of Lord Delamere in Kenya, where Brian was the manager. My mother joined my father in Moshi, Tanganyika, after he had settled in, and she once again furnished a bungalow.

I will always regret that I was not able to take advantage of the little time I had with my father, to know him better. I admired him, sometimes feared him, but looked up to him as a role model. I cannot honestly say I loved him. We never had any long personal conversations about his past or how he felt after each setback in his life. I was too young before he went to Malaya in

1937, and I was away in the Fleet Air Arm when he returned in 1945. I cannot have been with him, in between his absence abroad, for much more that a total of a few months to a year during his lifetime. In the formative years of childhood and young adulthood I believe it is very important to have a steady and stable father and son relationship to give one confidence in the future and a framework on which to judge standards. I am proud of his indomitable spirit in the many setbacks he faced and overcame and will always remember his wicked sense of humour which appeared boundless. Jack M'Kenzie-Hall died in 1949, aged 56 years old.

During the period from our arrival in England I had encountered a stop-go education at a number of schools in the Birmingham area. None of these made much of an impression on me, either educationally or emotionally. I can recall the daily journey to one to which I travelled every day by tram on a five-penny ticket. I finally ended up at a technical college for engineering in some industrial area of Bordesley Green, an inner city area of Birmingham. I had hardly had a constant or rounded education by the time war broke out in 1939.

I have previously mentioned my desire to fly, and I spent all my spare time making models of aeroplanes. Early in 1939, a cousin visited us and commented on my strong wish to be a pilot. He was Squadron Leader Tudor Evans, and he had come to Castle Bromwich airfield to pick up a Fairey Battle (a not-very-successful light bomber) for his squadron. He took me to the airfield, showed me the aircraft, sat me in the navigator's seat while he started and ran up the engine and left me overwhelmed with excitement as I watched him take off. My career choice was decided from that moment and it did not change even when, shortly afterwards, we learnt that he had been shot down and killed over France [Editor's note: I cannot find any trace of a Squadron Leader Tudor Evans. In May 1940, during 'The Battle for France' the Fairey Battles suffered very high casualties: 60 out of 118 of them were lost within four days as they were used in a frontline role and were shot down in vast numbers by superior German BF 109 fighters that flew 100 mph faster than the slow Fairey Battles].

The Outbreak of War

When war broke out in September 1939 we had moved to a small cottage above the harbour in Paignton in Devon. I applied to join the Royal Air Force but I was of course too young, at 16 years old, to be accepted in HM Forces at that time. To fill the gap I joined the Local Defence Volunteers on the first day it was formed. I was enrolled as a private in the Paignton Platoon under the command of a Mr Walters who had been a harbour master at Port Dickson in Malaya before retirement. I marched with the other broomstick brigade and spent nights looking out to sea for the imminent invasion. Eventually, because

John M'Kenzie-Hall – despatch rider in Home Guard uniform on his Levis motorcycle.

John M'Kenzie-Hall in 1941, Paignton, Devon.

I had a motorcycle, I was made a despatch rider and promoted to corporal. We then became 'Home Guard' and gave up our arm bands for battledress and broomsticks for rifles. I can't bear to think what would have happened had there been an invasion.

A False Emergency

One late afternoon I was contacted to say that there was an emergency and I was to contact all members of the Platoon and tell them to report in full kit with rifle (we had all been issued with five rounds of ammunition). I jumped on my motorcycle which was an old Levis [Editor's note: Birmingham-made, possibly a 1932 OHV Model A 350cc) and on my first call broke down at the crossroads out of Paignton. However, there was an AA man with his motorcycle combination parked nearby. So, wearing my battledress blouse, riding breeches and boots with a .45 revolver in a highly polished holster, I commandeered his machine with some difficulty. I had never ridden with a side-car attached and in my haste to make up time I rounded the corner too fast. The side-car rose like a balloon and I went one way and the motorcycle combination another, turning turtle as it did so. Thankfully I was out of sight of the AA man but returned the machine eventually in a sorry state claiming 'war damage'. Of course there was no Nazi invasion but I was not popular in general and very bruised in several places.

During this period, to earn some more money, I took a job as an assistant in an electrical shop in Torquay which had just changed hands and changed its name from Greys to Stones. The manager was ill-tempered, extremely fat and ran the shop to suit himself, not for the owner or the customers. His lunch time sessions at the pub left him quite incapable in the afternoons, which he spent asleep in the office behind a pile of papers and account books. I was left to serve customers and learn prices and components without help. I was also sent out to collect and return accumulators from customers' houses where electricity for radios was not available. I remember one call on a family who lived in two rooms in a wretched neighbourhood. The only furniture they had was an old radiogram in the centre of a room, which they used as a table for eating from, with four chairs and a mattress on the floor for their three children. I could not help noticing that the walls were black with mildew, while condensation caused rivulets of water down the walls next to fragmented electrical wiring. The smell was quite foul and, of course, the only window was tight shut.

Joining the RAF in June 1941.

I suffered this job for a wage of 12 shillings a week until just after my 18th birthday in June 1941, when I was called to RAF Reception Centre at St. John's Wood in London to begin kitting out. This was followed by the long trail through the Initial Training Wing (ITW) in South Devon and subsequent posting to Elementary Flying Training School (EFTS) at Carlisle in Cumberland where, at long last, I saw my first training aircraft.

Visit to Sir Charles Allom at Westbury Court.

Just prior to my joining the RAF my Mother was invited, together with my Sister and myself, to visit a cousin in Gloucestershire in the little village of Westbury on Severn. Our cousin, Sir Charles Allom (1865–1947), met us at Gloucester railway station and drove us back to Westbury Court, which was situated with its magnificent lawns and water gardens running down to the river Severn. Sir Charles Allom was the grandson of the architect Thomas Allom (1804–1872). George Hay Edwards I had married Martha Allom (Thomas Allom's sister). A few years ago I was sent extracts from a diary by my great-grandfather George Hay Edwards II, who lived a very long and fulfilling life (1815–1912), and was successively a barrister, civil engineer, a good watercolour artist and who had worked briefly with his uncle Thomas Allom. His son was my grandfather, George Hay Edwards III, who went out to Australia as a railway engineer in the late 1860s. A cast-iron bridge over the Murray River at Echuca on the New South Wales–Victoria border, which my grandfather built in 1879, still stands.

Sir Charles Allom in his own right had become a very successful architect, decorator and yacht designer, and his history is well documented. His firm White Allom & Company did extensive works at Buckingham Palace in 1907 on the ballroom, supper room, east gallery, and bow drawing-room for Edward VII and later for George V and Queen Mary including the centre room (the room leading to the famous balcony overlooking the Mall). He refurbished Leeds Castle in Kent and also shipped period rooms from English country houses to rich clients in America (including the Frick in New York) during the 1920s and 1930s. He also designed the first 'Marconi' all-steel tubular mast which he fitted to his yacht, the *White Heather*, and he frequently beat King George V in quite a number of not-so-friendly races during Cowes Week.

A footman greeted us at the entrance to Westbury Court and my suitcase was carried up to a bedroom which overlooked the garden and canals and over the lawns to the gazebo. The bedroom was three or four times the size of any I had been in before, and it was somewhat awe-inspiring with its period furniture and decoration. My small and rather shabby suitcase held only the bare necessities with a single change of clothing, and it looked pitiful on the mahogany stand beside the canopied bed. Imagine my feelings of shame and embarrassment when the under-butler entered and proceeded to unpack for me. He said 'I will just put these away, Sir, before you change for dinner'. I believe he spoke before he looked for I distinctly remember his slight 'ugh' and cough as he hung up a pair of flannels and a much worn sports jacket in the wardrobe that was large enough to take a dozen suits and a dinner jacket, which I did not have!

Apart from my not-dressing-for-dinner and being somewhat confused on which silver to be used for each course, the meal went relatively well, as did

With the Allom family and my sister Joanna (right) at Westbury Court, Gloucestershire, 1941.

the rest of the weekend. Sir Charles and Lady Allom were very charming and understanding hosts in the circumstances but I suffered a last embarrassment when we left as I had only a ten-shilling note for the butler, which he accepted with very good grace. Little did he know (though he probably guessed) that that represented almost a week's pay for me. I made a mental note that it was not always a good idea to visit well-to-do relatives.

ITW Paignton, Devon

I now return to the real world and the beginning of my career in the Royal Air Force. After some three weeks of 'square bashing', lectures, drawing more kit, medical examinations, inoculations (four at the same time, with many in the queue fainting before reaching the needle), aptitude tests and what I can only describe as indoctrination in service law, I was posted to ITW, Paignton in Devon. I wore a white flash in the side cap indicating that I was now an aircrew cadet for pilot training on a pay of two shillings a day.

The Initial Training Wing was situated on the seafront in Paignton and we were billeted in one of the many small hotels that had been taken over for the duration of the war.

My fellow cadets were a motley group who neither had much idea of discipline, technical knowledge nor knew the meaning of *esprit de corps*. We were taken in hand very quickly and very firmly. We were in the charge of a horrible little corporal whose only wish was to make our lives miserable. He would awaken us in the morning at 6.00 am by beating his baton on a refuse bin and then letting it roll down the stairs in a series of crashing rebounds with the last up having to recover it, clean it and bring it back for next morning. After breakfast we were taken under the wing of a drill sergeant for some hours on the drill square before attending lectures. After lunch more lectures interspersed with a period of double marching, dressed in full gas capes and masks, or learning Morse code and Aldis lamp signalling. There were lectures in aircraft recognition, mathematics, simple science, air force law, personal hygiene, living under canvas and many other subjects which to ignorant cadets seemed to have nothing to do with learning to fly.

As officer cadets we were upgraded to LAC (leading aircraftsmen) with an increase of pay up to two shillings and sixpence per day. I cannot remember how we could afford to go out in the evenings but go out we did. The attraction of pubs, girls, cinemas and other relaxations overcame our relative poverty and our uniforms generally attracted hospitality. This training period was really intense and mentally fatiguing, but when one knew that others were fighting in worse conditions and being killed we were really living in clover until our turn would come to join the real war. I think we were a little ashamed at our temporary non-combatant status but excused ourselves with the knowledge that we would in due course be in the thick of it.

The front door of our hotel was locked at 10.00 pm every evening and we were instructed, at our own peril, to be in before this. There was no back door entrance, since this was also locked, although there were plenty of ground floor windows that would in various ways be left open or could be helped to open. Unfortunately there was a broad band of gravel chippings fronting the whole length of the back garden and this had to be crossed for access.

There was no shortage of after-ten-o'clock arrivals every night; some sober, some not, but all aware of our horrible little Corporal Lawson who was on watch most nights, armed with a very bright torch. Much of the time we ran the gauntlet successfully, since he could not keep a 24-hour watch. I was apprehended with others quite a few times over the gravel with his parrot cry of "Stand still lads, I've got you". He would then take our names and instruct us to report to the admin office in the morning for punishment. How we hated him and vowed vengeance in the most extreme ways if we ever met him later. I did. On my way back from America as a Flight Lieutenant I met him at a reception centre in London. He had been promoted to Flight Sergeant and was one of the nicest and most efficient NCOs I came in to contact with during the war.

Two Friends

I made two friends during this period at ITW. The first was Leslie Knott who had joined from the London Metropolitan Police. He possessed a truly magnificent bass baritone voice and one of our favourite pubs, The Drum at Cockington in Devon, always filled up to capacity when he was persuaded to perform. My favourite was *Ma Curly Headed Baba* and I always thought of Paul Robeson in *Sanders of the River* when this deep, fruity tone almost brought us all to tears. We completed the initial training together but I went on to pilot training while he became a navigator. I was devastated to hear that he had been killed on his first mission over Germany.

My second friend was a fairly small, intense character on a parallel but different course to mine. We met fairly frequently in a little cafe in the late afternoon after our work. This was situated on the Paignton harbour and was called the Green Dragon. It was quiet and ideal to do our homework and test each other on questions to be expected in forthcoming exams. I cannot now recall his surname, if I ever knew it, but his Christian name was Richard. He spent more time studying film scripts than air force law or aerodynamics and one day mentioned that he had to go to London to take part in a wartime film. I never saw him again but is it my imagination, whenever I see any early wartime film, that I am recognising a very young and intense actor called Attenborough who left the air force in late 1941, just as I finished ITW?

Stress and Loss of Hair

I must admit that, in my intense desire to fly, I had overlooked the academic requirements. I found it a great disadvantage that I had missed in my many changes of schools the early introduction into subjects which were now necessary.

The continued pressure and mental stress led to my contracting *Alopecia areata*. This resulted in a complete loss of hair initially and, later, a complete head of white hair, which gradually turned brown and then made a permanent retreat. Although practically bald from about the age of 19, I was thankfully saved from being called a 'Brylcreem Boy'. Some of my ultraviolet light treatment, however, interrupted my training and I frequently had to borrow notes to catch up on lectures missed.

RAF Heroes

This ailment did me one favour, however, since I had to go to Torquay for treatment. This was at the Palace Hotel, which had been taken over as a hospital for Air Force rehabilitation purposes, for serious cases of aircrew casualties. I have vivid memories of limbless, burnt, deformed and mentally impaired young pilots. Some were still there from the early air battle in France, others from the Battle of Britain onwards. Later in my life I knew Douglas Bader very well but at that time I could not imagine his problems in flying when so disabled or the courage that brought him back time after time.

I thought myself greatly honoured on these visits if any of these young heroes spoke to me. It all made a great impression and I was staggered at the amount of pain and suffering they must have endured. Youth was on my side however, and made me even more determined to qualify as a fighter pilot. I was pleased to complete ITW successfully on April 2nd 1942.

No.15 EFTS, Kingstown, Carlisle, 1942

I was immediately posted to No. 15 Elementary Flying Training School (EFTS) at Kingstown, Carlisle, on a three-and-a-half-week training course to reach solo standard on the Miles Magister aircraft. This was the standard trainer that, to a large extent, had replaced the Tiger Moth. The airfield at Kingstown was a grass one and the surface was slightly dome shaped. This meant that an aircraft landing on one edge of the airfield was momentarily lost from view from the other side until it came back in to view on the top of the rise. I mention this because of the only three pilot incidents in my whole flying career the first happened here on the momentous day of my first solo flight.

My instructor was a Sgt. Gaskell and he had from 13 April to 8 May 1942 to patiently teach me the controls of the aircraft and the rudiments of taking off, controlling flight and landing. After just over 12 hours of instruction I took off on the morning of 8 May for dual instruction on further powered approaches and landings. After two or three of these he told me to taxi to the side of the field and then asked me if I wished to go solo. I hesitated between the feeling of exuberance and the shock of thinking that, while he had confidence in me, I was not sure I had any in myself. Of course I said yes, whereupon he jumped out and said that after a quick test with the flight commander I could have the aircraft to myself. Pilot Officer Phipps then came over and climbed in. I carried out a couple of take-offs, approaches and a fairly good landing and taxied to dispersal, where Sgt Gaskell was waiting. He said to me "Off you go. Make one circuit and landing and come back here. I shall be watching your every action. Good luck."

It is difficult to explain how I felt at that moment; a little bit of terror overcome by a determination to do well and a feeling of exhilaration that, at long last, after all this training, I was about to fly by myself. Little did I think that it would be a long time before I could call myself a pilot, and a successful one. In later years Winston Churchill commented to me on this long-held aspiration in a few very choice words (see Chapter Five: Biggin Hill, 1949).

My initial nervousness faded away as I taxied out for take-off and concentrated on keeping straight as I operated the throttle and the aircraft gathered speed. As I eased the stick back and the wheels left the ground I expected to hear the voice of the instructor saying "Now level out, keep the nose down". All I heard was the wind being out-voiced by my suddenly relaxing and singing at the top of my voice. I completed the circuit pattern and turned on the approach feeling quite confident for the landing. I had judged the distance to touch down just over the perimeter fence quite well and touched down with a three point landing. As I congratulated myself on the best landing of the day I relaxed a little. A little was just enough for the aircraft to start yawing to the left and although I applied immediate right rudder, it had no effect. The aircraft did a waltz on one wheel with one wing rising above the other, which was almost touching the grass. The aircraft proceeded through a rapid 360^0 turn that left me dumbfounded and quite terrified. As we came back into wind the wheel came down to the ground again and we sublimely took a straight course to the top of the rising ground and taxied back to my instructor at dispersal. I expected him to say "Stop the engine, get out, you will never make a pilot" – instead he touched my shoulder as he climbed in and shouted "Don't stop the engine, let's go up and do a few more like that. It was a very good first solo, congratulations". I was too shocked to argue and I realised that because of the airfield hump he had not, and apparently neither had anybody else, witnessed my landing and

The Arnold Scheme

In the early years of the Second World War there was an acute need to train pilots for the Royal Air Force. The United Kingdom was considered largely unsuitable due to a combination of enemy action, high operational traffic at airfields, unpredictable weather and a shortage of training instructors.

The Arnold Scheme was established to train British RAF pilots in the United States of America. Its name derived from US General Henry H. Arnold, Chief of the United States Army Air Forces, the instigator of the scheme, which ran from June 1941 to March 1943.

Lieutenant-General Henry H. Arnold, Commanding General, US Army Air Force.

ground loop on the other side of the hump. The aircraft was quite undamaged and I never mentioned the incident then, or since, but I certainly learned the lesson that flight is never over until the aircraft is stationary and the engine is switched off.

Having completed the course I joined an aircrew holding unit at Heaton Park, Manchester, to await transportation by sea to America, for further training under the Arnold Scheme. I had previously been told during my ITW training that, since I was an Australian citizen, my aircrew training had to be completed either in Rhodesia or America and that Rhodesian courses were already over-subscribed. The RAF holding station at Heaton Park was loosely run, badly administered and a cause of constant frustration to all cadets sent there. Apart from occasional roll-calls there were no specific duties, training or organised recreational facilities and I, for one, used to disappear for days on end, either into the surrounding countryside or down to London, until a timely tip-off brought me back to camp in the hope of movement. There were many false alarms about embarkation, probably due to the shipping losses and the hazards of the Atlantic crossing.

In June 1942 we gathered together to draw tropical kit and spent many days in speculation that we were going to Rhodesia after all. This equipment was then required to be handed back and we drew heavy winter equipment, which included every piece of webbing and strapping for holding on water bottles, pistols, bayonets, ammunition, gas masks, gas capes, packsacks, food tins, first aid packs, rations etc. Several days later, dressed in serge uniforms under greatcoats, covered with this paraphernalia of equipment and carrying two kit bags apiece, we were paraded in the rain for some two hours, inspected and dismissed. The next day we began to hand it all back in to stores again due to another change of plan. Again I escaped to London for the best part of a week before being warned of a short-notice movement pending for two days time. I arrived back in camp just in time to pack my kit bag with a minimum issue of everyday items before joining a column marching for the railway station. Of course it was raining and, with sodden greatcoats, we waited for some hours until, at about 10.00 pm, we boarded a train heading north. Rumour had it that we would sail from Glasgow via Greenock and this had been calculated, by those who knew, as a journey of some 300 miles, making an arrival at about dawn. Other speculation based on the experience of friends who had passed this way before said Liverpool for sure and that by dawn we would be sailing down the Mersey River out of Runcorn or Bootle. Dawn saw us in a railway siding where we remained for the rest of the day without getting off the train. We ate a disgusting concoction of various emergency rations and drank nothing but NAAFI-brewed tea until late in the evening, when we backtracked on our previous journey for some hours before again heading north. Of course the only lights allowed were the tiny dark blue 'black-out' bulbs usual in all wartime railway carriages, supplemented by the glowing cigarette tips and irregular but constant use of lighters and matches. The soggy smell of wet uniforms and men in close proximity was bad enough but a journey down a packed corridor, littered with kit, to the over-used, clogged and urine-swirling toilets was disgusting. Before the sickly purple-orange haze of our environment gave way to another dawn, a thoroughly disillusioned group of young men arrived to board an ex-cattle boat lying alongside the quay at Greenock. Our immediate discomfort seemed to be over for, after having left the train, we were given breakfast and prepared in batches to embark.

Most of those in my group had never been on board a ship before, let alone sailed on one. It was only natural, in fact almost a relief, for me to hold forth as an expert on the types of cabins, the various decks, the best side of the ship and the worst end to be berthed – i.e. over the propellers. After all, I had travelled several times to Australia and India with my parents and had often voyaged on my own during school holidays, between Australia and Singapore aboard those wonderful old Somerset Maugham-ish Blue Funnel cargo boats. Reality was therefore more of a shock to me than to most of my companions when, having ascended the gangway, we descended in to the holds.

Metal stanchions, about eight feet apart, had been fixed in rows from deck floor to deck head and in between each alternate row were two foot wide wooden tables with close-fitting immovable wooden benches. Between each stanchion hung a loosely drooping hammock and to most of us came the new and unstable experience of tying up, getting in and staying in. There were several hundred of us packed like sardines in row after row and nowhere to stow kit except the deck beneath. Two days were spent in harbour, and we had no option but to accept the conditions below deck. Most of us, once we had claimed our territory, passed our time (except for meals) on deck in the restricted areas allowed to us.

Chapter Three

America

Slipping away from Greenock and sailing down the Firth of Clyde, past the Isle of Bute and the Isle of Arran before turning north of Ireland into the Atlantic, still has dream-like memories of pleasurable anticipation of the future and the excitement of a break from the dreary greyness of war-time Britain. How short-lived that was! Air-sickness had obviously been overcome by most of the cadets, but sea-sickness was something entirely different.

Ship routine was now in force and being in submarine-infested waters in a fairly slow moving convoy meant endless restrictions. No lights, battened-down hatches at night. Nothing was to be thrown overboard. There was no access to deck space except at specific times for short periods. Meals were arranged on a roster but, with so many in such cramped quarters, the timings were never adhered to and some ate and some did not for many different reasons. Food came in buckets, like pigswill, and was ladled out into each person's mess tin. The constant smell of stale food, unwashed bodies, regurgitated food and spilled food rotting pervaded each hold and was only partly relieved by periods when, if weather permitted, the hatches were opened for a short time. Hammocks were slung so tightly together that the constant contact because of ship movement was unavoidable and the effect of turning over by one body could bring forth a torrent of abuse from a whole row. Many of us abandoned our hammocks for the tops of the tables or odd corners on the decking where (being wedged in without fear of being trodden on) one could get a measure of comfortable sleep. Some people even found sleep more comfortable on the lifebelt racks after having disposed the contents into their hammocks.

The sick bay, and its comfortably spaced bunks, was of course overflowing from the first day at sea but I was too green to realise the advantage of claiming illness as soon as the anchor was weighed. While much of the day was taken up attending to the basic necessities of life by queuing, trying to wash, or simply finding somewhere to sit, the constant activity of boat drills, parades, orderly duties and night watches greatly assisted the nightmare crossing. The occasional incident also helped us to forget our mundane grumbles and think of our skins. This was particularly so one night when someone turned on all the ship's external lights; for a short time before the switches could be found pandemonium broke out as orders and counter-orders came from crew and passengers completely taken by surprise. Everyone started to smash the lights nearest them and some bright individual began shooting at those out of reach, which caused even more panic. I cannot remember a culprit being found but I do recall our already irksome restrictions on fresh air being tightened still further.

Two enemy submarine alerts passed uneventfully and, although I spent many hours on the lookout for something round protruding just above the surface of the sea showing a creamy wake, I invariably ended up with bleary eyes and a headache.

Sometime during the first week at sea we seemed to lose the convoy when we ran into heavy weather, and we found ourselves alone in the Atlantic. It was rumoured that we had been diverted down toward the Azores and were now heading for some port on the American East Coast. By about the tenth day conditions on board had become unbearable, illness, particularly diarrhoea, was spreading rapidly and not helped by inadequate toilets. The seas seemed to be getting rougher when, suddenly, we entered the shelter of Nova Scotia, shortly afterwards we passed Cape Sambro and rounded into Terence Bay, then sailing on to Halifax and calm water.

We anchored just after dusk and towards us drifted the warm, musky smell of pine forests. We also caught an occasional glimpse of lights from harboured ships or hillside homes. It is doubtful whether anybody remained below decks that night since the exhilaration of our arrival and the change in conditions brought about a sudden recovery of spirits and health that only youth can manage.

The water surrounding us was limpid calm and, as the evening darkened, the half-mile to shore became streaked and dappled with the reflections of the red, blue, green, orange, white and other coloured lights that appeared and which seemed to festoon and hang over every building in the town. Drifting snatches of music, broken by the usual muted mechanical noises from other working ships, carried us in our imagination across the warm evening air to the streets of this 'Christmas-tree' lit town, where there were shops, pubs, restaurants, cinemas, dance halls and friendly people who were all out enjoying themselves. Most of us fell asleep alongside the rails in an exhaustion of over-reaction to our journey and the happy expectation of early disembarkation into the land of plenty.

Our euphoria had carried us so high that, when we did wake up, we found our paradise town consisted of rusting oil storage tanks, metal pylons, railway sidings and a few neglected wooden buildings. Our immediate reaction was one of hilarity. Humour in the face of the unknown turned out to be a useful prerequisite in the months to come.

There was little delay in disembarkation and a short railway journey took us to Moncton, New Brunswick, which was to be our holding unit before dispersal to various training schools in Canada and the USA.

In Transit: RAF Depot, Moncton, New Brunswick, Canada

During our two weeks' stay in the huge camp, just outside Moncton, we had the time of our lives. I am sure that all inhabitants of the town had committed themselves to supply non-stop entertainment to every cadet they could lay their hands on. This was not difficult since there was practically no routine or duties and we were free to come and go as we pleased.

I met up with a family who owned a jewellery business in Moncton and during my stay I fear their profits must have slumped as we were out every day; picnics in the forests, canoeing on still lakes and turbulent rivers, parties in the evening and barbecues all night long. The journey from England faded quickly and for a short time the war seemed irrelevant whilst we unashamedly immersed ourselves in the Utopian climate of midsummer and limitless hospitality.

We were eventually called together to be divided into groups. My group was posted to a reception camp in the USA where we were to undergo an acclimatisation course. Although most of us were eager to get on with our flying training it was sad to make our final excursions into Moncton to say "goodbye" to the many friends we had made and thank them for so much unselfish hospitality. Despite good intentions, the type and intensity of our work over the next few months left no time for keeping in touch and, in my case, the departure by train for the long journey to Georgia was a complete and final break from an idyllic first visit to Canada.

The British contingent found boarding trains up steps from rail level a great novelty. The size of the carriages and their layout, the peculiar bell-tolling engine, the swiftly-passed audible rail crossings and the stops for meals were all new experiences for us and retained our interest for most of the journey. Although I had been on similar trains in Australia and the Far East I was nonetheless carried along by the excitement of the others, and I experienced, for the first time, air-conditioning of a somewhat primitive type.

Unlike on Australian trains, there was plenty of space to move around in and a constant supply of iced drinking water.

It is difficult now to remember how many days we were on the train, three or four I think, or details of the scenery we passed through. Memories come floating back of hours spent looking out at prairie-type terrain, broken by areas of cultivated homesteads. I can, though, still recall seeing few mountains and no cities whatsoever. If there were any on our track we must have passed through them at night. I have vivid recollections of daily stops at small towns. We pulled slowly in with a bell clanging to find our arrival already signalled ahead and what appeared to be the entire town's population lining the tracks, handing out supplies of fresh fruit, hot and cold drinks and other goodies. Their effusive hospitality and goodwill seemed pleasantly genuine and their curiosity about these airmen from England never, apparently, waned.

Few of us were bored on this journey and I believe that it enabled us to begin the absorption of a new way of life without difficulty. One or two of our contingent must have been over-enthusiastic at their reception for on a couple of occasions we restarted our journey less the full complement and, to my knowledge, the missing airmen never joined us again.

Our destination was Georgia, where General Arnold of the Army Air Corps had established the base camp for the training of aircrew. This was appropriately called 'The Arnold Scheme' and under 'lease-lend' arrangements it took selected British students to undergo the full training for qualification as either fighter or bomber pilots at various training establishments in the Southern States.

Turner Field, Georgia, USA.

We finally arrived at Turner Army Airfield, Georgia and de-trained into buses for the hot, dry and sandy Reception Centre. We had gradually become acclimatised to the increasing heat on the way down, but to begin with a sun-blistering parade of some two hours duration burnt up a little of our enthusiastic feelings on arrival. We were lectured and praised, harangued and insulted and finally allocated to four-man tents that were too hot to enter. It was hard for us to realise that whatever our nationality, education or previous training, we were now to be treated as new recruits and were on a survival course quaintly called 'pre-flight training'.

We proceeded to be tested by weeks of dawn callisthenics (athletics), drilling, firing range exercises and academic studies which, once again, appeared to have nothing to do with aviation. Not only were we presented with an enormous number of diverse and apparently illogical subjects as a syllabus for study but we were also required to conform to many procedures very alien to most of us.

Each course of cadets commenced their training as 'under' classmen and rose to 'upper' classmen at the halfway stage. The American aviation cadet spent nine weeks learning this type of military discipline but, due to morale problems with the British cadets, this period had been shortened considerably. However, we still had to suffer a system very similar to the English public school practice of 'fagging', in that an 'under' classman was at the constant call of 'upper' classmen for duties such as cleaning shoes, blancoing belts, running messages, reciting poems while standing at attention and so on. This petty tyranny was described by the term 'hazing'. I remember one occasion very clearly when, feeling more than somewhat irate, I was instructed to stand to attention in the middle of the mess table and recite some pieces of melodramatic propaganda on the war effort, all for the misdemeanour of incorrectly addressing an 'upper' classman at mealtime.

Meals of course were timed and, if it had not been for friends filling their pockets with bread rolls and fruit, I would on that occasion have missed the main meal of the day. Trivial as the incident was I mention it to illustrate the problems that existed initially between already-disciplined servicemen and those immature American students just entering from various colleges or civilian occupations. Unfortunately, due to the fact that all classes followed each other throughout their pilot training, the process was repeated afresh at each new training airfield where, on reversion to 'under' classman, it was not unusual to find the same individual waiting to pick up his aggressive sense of power where he had left off.

I believe the outstanding memory for me of this stage was the impact made in the mess hall by the long wooden tables almost collapsing under the weight of fresh fruit, jugs of milk, fresh bread, butter and mouth-watering food of all descriptions. Although our time for eating was short, the amount put away was adequate. Memories of England under rationing, with foods such as butter, meat and cheese in short supply, soon faded or were conveniently brushed to one side, as were the initial feelings of guilt at the availability of such a glut of food.

This was the first opportunity we had had to meet our American allies and fellow cadets and a period of adjustment took place on both sides. Despite our very differing backgrounds, many incidents drew us together as comrades and broke the ice. For instance, we were certainly all of one mind during an invasion of rats in our tents and I was forgiven for hitting one sleeping American over the head with a wooden tent peg, in an effort to kill the rat about to crawl over his face. Another common interest was, of course, 'girls', but contact with them was infrequent on base and at this period of our training we were not allowed outside the gates.

A 1942 Boeing PT-17 Stearman. My first American flights were in this primary trainer.

Primary Flying School: 51st AAFFTD
Alabama Institute of Aeronautics, Tuscaloosa, Alabama, 1942.

By the beginning of August 1942 those of us who had survived, and that meant the majority, were considered sufficiently indoctrinated and acclimatised to move on to our primary flying schools. We were again divided into groups and I joined 63 Englishmen and 51 Americans who composed the new 'lower' class of 43B at the 51st Army Air Forces Primary Flying School at Tuscaloosa, Alabama.

There were no tents this time but dormitories with polished wooden floors and furnished with tubular metal double-stacked beds, metal cabinets for possessions and wooden tables and chairs between each bed. In addition to the American cadets we also had a number of Americans who had volunteered to rejoin their own Air Force after service with the RCAF.

We were all introduced to our Commanding Officer, Major Kinney, and to Mr S. F. G. Gammon, who was Director of Ground School. Our Chief Instructor was Mr Greavis Nelson. The administration was carried out by some eleven American Army Air Force Officers and one British Air Force Officer, Pilot Officer Manning, who was an Engineering Officer. Our day started at 5.45 am and the last meal of the day was at 6.00 pm. We had night study for five nights of the week from 7.00 pm to 8.00 pm and 'lights out' was at 9.45 pm.

All flying instructors and most of the ground maintenance staff were civilian and on 10 August 1942, I first became airborne in a PT-17 Stearman with a Mr E. L. Raynor as my instructor. By looking at my log books, after I had become a flying instructor, I can still recall every one of my pupils going

LAC J. E. M'Kenzie-Hall No. 1339664 1942 Aircrew Training, Tuscaloosa Course 43B. "Straddled by two American aviation cadets – I had just arrived at Maxwell Field in 1942."

Maxwell Field, Montgomery, Alabama was Southeast Air Corps' training centre for flying training as part of 51st AAFFTD Alabama Institute of Aeronautics, Tuscaloosa, Alabama. Motto: 'Prepare for Combat'.

back some 40 years and I am sure that somewhere Mr Raynor (I never knew his Christian name), if alive, would recall my name and my total ineptitude to carry out even the simplest manoeuvre under his tuition. I am sure he was an excellent pilot but as an instructor his pupil relationship left much to be desired. Temperamentally we just could not come to terms. In the first place I could hardly interpret his dialect, while he did not take to fools easily, especially to this damned cross between an Australian and an Englishman who thought he could fly, when he had left England with 12 hours 35 minutes dual and 10 minutes solo. He would work himself up by shouting down the intercom tube and then throttle back to make the point again by bellowing and finally jerk the stick or rudder pedals violently in the position and direction I should already have adopted. Many times I was heartily glad to have been strapped in securely, as a sudden and repeated pushing forward of the stick which indicated that the nose of the aircraft had once again come too high over the horizon, would have thrown me up and out of the cockpit like a well pressed pea from its pod. After a total instruction of 3 hours 45 minutes of unadulterated hell for both of us, he threw in the towel. If he had not given up I would have, but I was desperately afraid that if I made the first move it would be seen as lack of moral fibre and provide an excuse for possible elimination from pilot training. Even so, I hung around the PX from August 17th to August 21st in a state of misery while my fate was discussed and decided. However, on a gloriously blue morning with fair weather cumulus bouncing around above our heads, I was taken up to start again by a Mr Henry.

Looking back now, to that period in 1942, it is quite clear that although there was an organised general system of training, little emphasis had been given to the co-ordination of instructional technique by civilian flying instructors. On the whole they were left to 'do their own thing' within the guidelines of the set syllabus of flying exercises. Mr Henry, unlike Mr Raynor, not only believed in ground briefing before a flight but also in the simple method of building up confidence through gentle in-flight demonstrations of the aircraft's attitudes and controls and a clear-cut, in-flight explanation of the manoeuvres required. Unlike so many cadets on the Arnold Scheme, I was lucky to have found an instructor with the kind of temperament and technique that matched my ability to absorb.

The Stearman (PT-17) was ideal as a primary trainer. It had all the stability of a biplane but was tougher and less kind than its British opposite, the Tiger Moth, in that it let you know in a positive manner the result of unbalanced or unstable control. It did, however, have a steerable tail wheel instead of a skid and this required a further period of control on touchdown, instead of a rapid stop. After the Miles Magister it seemed huge and enveloping but I grew to be very fond of it.

Strobel home, September 1942, Tuscaloosa, Alabama, where I spent many relaxing hours.

We covered a total of 23 exercises before first solo. This took an average of about seven–eight hours, generally in flight periods of approximately 30–40 minutes. Curiously I note from my logbook that I recorded times to the nearest minute during primary training, whereas from basic onwards all times were rounded up to the nearest five minutes. Whether this was a requirement to instil accuracy or just ignorance on my part I cannot remember. The exercises I can record from my logbook however were:

Effect of controls
Straight and level flight
Turns
Co-ordination exercises
Climbs and climbing turns
Glides and gliding turns
'S' turns across straight land lines, i.e. roads
Rectangular courses
Stalls
Taxiing
Take-offs
Landing
Spinnings
Spirals
Forced landings
Steep turns

Elementary figures of 8
Lazy '8's
Chandelles
Progress checks
Judgement checks
Orientation
Cockpit drill and first solo

Between 10 August 1942, and 7 October 1942, I flew a total of 60 hours and five minutes, and I successfully completed both the academic and flying requirements to allow advancement to the 'Basic' stage.

During the eight weeks at Tuscaloosa I can remember leaving camp on 'open post', as we called leave, on very few occasions. Tuscaloosa was a small, dusty, sleepy town with mainly wooden buildings where, in the hot mid-afternoon sun, we sought refuge in the only drugstore, to cool down with chocolate malted milk and ice cream. I visited Bessemer and saw the steel works and went in to Birmingham to see the nightlife, which at this time we could not afford. I met an extremely nice farming family called Strobel and spent very relaxing hours at their small wood-built home.

Our camp activities never ceased and once again the 'upper' classmen descended upon us 'lower' men in no uncertain manner. The British contingent stood the indignities for a week or so, and then rebelled against the system by confining themselves to the dormitory and refusing as a whole to undertake further training until 'hazing' stopped. Two days later successful RAF liaison took place and from then onwards I cannot remember further clashes between senior or junior classes, be they American or British aviation cadets.

Much of the initial ground school instruction at this early stage went over my head, but I cannot now remember whether this was because of poor teaching techniques, which I doubt, or the relationship between the subjects in the classroom and the far more stringent needs of the practical side of flying. Link trainer practice was certainly encouraged and I can recall very sound basic knowledge being imparted to me by a Sgt. Gibson, in many 30-minute sessions. Much of my success, firstly as a night-fighter pilot, then an instrument examiner and finally a transport pilot, stemmed from this early interest in the psychological approach to instrument flying. The tenseness brought about by an inability to concentrate brings sweating and physical discomfort. This is aggravated by small mistakes which multiply into large control errors, which further increases tension and aircraft control is lost. The quiet, confident voice of the instructor gave me an early opportunity to learn self-control over the mental conflicts between instrumental visual images and physical sensations of the body's balance mechanism. I have since come across many pilots with thousands of hours flying who are still unhappy and tense when flying in full instrument conditions.

At this stage the students were very reliant on each others' company during between-work periods, since we were virtually cut off from the outside world. My particular group of friends, though varying widely in backgrounds and temperamentally dissimilar, were attracted together by a wartime situation in an alien country and a youthful zest to live dangerously. Juan Alberto Adams-Langley (1917–1944) from Chile was excitable, highly temperamental and explosive, but brought a mature character to our group since he was older than most of us and had previous flying experience. John D. Ditchburn was quiet, sometimes moody but had a presence which reflected a Middle Eastern background, from a diplomatic family of some pre-war eminence. Hugh Owen Robinson, an electric character of infinite charm from Jamaica. His father trained racehorses and Hugh was just as frisky and unreliable as some of them must have been. Marvellous to own one but do not put your shirt on it! Lastly, there was Michael Gordon Welch (1921–2020) from Argentina who was quiet, intensely religious, reliable, very determined and a staunch friend. We remained in America after graduation to instruct at American schools, but I lost touch with Michael after his posting to No. 3 BFTS at Miami, Oklahoma. (Editor's note: Flying Officer Adams-Langley was killed in action on 8 July 1944, aged 26. He is listed as being the air gunner in Avro Lancaster III no.PB144, markings ZN-P of 106 Squadron which took off from RAF Metheringham, Lincolnshire at 22H30 on 7 July 1944 to attack a flying bomb storage site in northern France. The aircraft was hit by flak and crashed 01h30 on 8 July 1944 bursting into flames some 500 metres west of Sainte Genevieve with the loss of the seven crew. He is buried at the Sainte Genevieve Cemetery, Oise, Picardy in military plot no. 1, located eight km north east of Meru and 18 km south-south-east of Beauvais).

Juan Alberto Adams-Langley.

Michael Gordon Welch, from Argentina.

Although we were an amalgamated British and American course, I cannot recall a great deal of social mixing except at meal times and at such communal gathering places as the PX or the post cinema. Having just looked through their names

A US Air Force Vultee Valiant BT-13A in flight. The BT-13 served almost exclusively as the basic trainer for all aircrews trained in the US during World War II. By 1945, the aircraft was being replaced with other advanced models and after the war the aircraft was retired.

I am unable to remember any particular individual, and wonder whether there might have been an intentional separation of accommodation at this stage of training.

Basic Training: Gunter Field, Alabama, October 1942

I finished Primary Training on 7 October 1942, after 30 hours dual and 30 hours solo, and started Basic Training at Gunter Field, Alabama, on 12 October 1942. By this time I had become acclimatised both to the country and to the methods of teaching, and I experienced no difficulties in adapting to the BT-13 (Vultee Valiant, with fixed wheels).

Several changes took place, during this period, which stand out in my memory. For the first time since leaving the United Kingdom, I had a British flying instructor, a Pilot Officer D. W. Fields. I am ashamed to say that I cannot recall his face or remember him except through my logbook. However, the entries indicate that he was very thorough and led me progressively in to the more advanced techniques of instrument flying, night flying, formation and cross-country navigation. We also carried out a number of exercises called 'chandelles' and 'lazy eights' but I can only trace two 30-minute sessions of dual aerobatics, towards the end of the course, spelt in my logbook as 'acrobatics!'. With a fixed undercarriage and the low power weight ratio of the BT-13 I am not sure that my spelling was so inaccurate!

This course also introduced, for the first time, student pair flying and I

*Excerpts from
the Gunter Field
introductory
literature, 1942.*

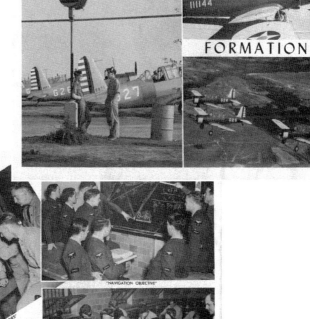

appear to have carried out a number of hours instrument flying with an American student called Theiler. Again, I cannot recall the gentleman, or anyone else who flew with me at that time, except for a Captain J. Garrett, who gave me a 40-hour check and sent me on to the Advanced Course with an above average rating and a strong sense of confidence. On this course I carried out 26 hours dual and 37 hours solo up to 16 December 1942.

I have no recollection whatsoever of any social life during these two months at Gunter Field and I do not think I left the airfield. Quite a few bodies disappeared off the course for one reason or another and I seem to recall that a greater percentage of American cadets were eliminated than British at this stage. This was probably quite logical because the American intake was greater than the British at all stages of training.

The USAAF system of flight training was, in my opinion, highly wasteful of potential pilots. If a student, for any number of minor reasons, was not up to scratch in his exercises or fell behind in the accumulated hours required, he was given a check ride. This was enough to unsettle any student who knew that if he made a mistake or fell out with the instructor it was a 'wash out' for him. On one course in early 1943 there was a 'wash out' rate of 107 out of 175 students. There was therefore a continuous dark shadow hanging over all students from Primary to Advanced and this threat was magnified by rumours and added to by an automatic elimination if a percentage of 70% was not obtained, as an overall average, in the compulsory ten examination subjects.

Although by this time the British cadets were largely left alone, the 'upper' and 'lower' class system was still in full swing and by this time the 'upper' class had learned by experience to be more sadistic and bullying than at primary. Staff bureaucracy in discipline and punishment, however, was also at its height and we were rigorously introduced to the system of receiving punishment 'gigs', for which the result of collecting too many produced a number of hours 'walking tours' wearing white gloves and backpacks. 'Gigs' would be awarded for almost anything that displeased the inspecting officer or offended against the long list of requirements. A few examples that come to mind are:

1. The turnover of the sheet measured from the base of the pillow to the edge of the 'X' inches exactly, and a ruler was used.
2. Footwear of various types had to be arranged in a specific order and laces tied in the prescribed manner.
3. No dust to be found anywhere, including underneath the bedsprings.
4. Locker doors open to show a correct angle, measured by the inspecting officer with a set square, and all contents to be shown in order and only as listed on a card to be displayed.

5. The bed to be laid out with items of uniform and kit exactly in the order and to the measurements laid down.

6. Window blinds to be lowered in all windows to the exact length laid down.

Woe betide any aviation cadet who offended and no excuses were entertained. However necessary this might have been for disciplinary or character-building reasons, this type of imposition was bitterly resented by the British contingent. However, most of us had come to realise by this time that no good would come to our future progress by fighting the system, and we therefore became resigned to the childish indignities and persevered with an intense period of ground school and pre-flight study.

I carried out a further 15 hours of link training (air simulation) and progressed on to beam systems, bracketing and let downs, as well as continuing the usual sequence of climbing and descending turns and timed exercises. I was now, of course, also carrying out these exercises in the air. I found that, although instrument flying was as physically demanding as aerobatics and mentally far more exhausting, it was becoming easier and more enjoyable. What I would not have done in those days for a modern instrument panel and servo controls. With the artificial horizon always liable to topple, the needle and ball's being the only secondary instrument and the gyro compass frequently spinning, one had a tiring task in maintaining accurate flying attitudes over long exercise periods. By 15 December 1942 I had flown 26 hours dual and 36 hours solo on the BT-13, making a flying hours total of 145 hours.

There were a number of eliminations during the Basic Training course but the remaining members of Class 43B left Gunter Field on 17 December 1942 for Craig Field, Selma, Alabama.

Advanced Flying School at Craig Field, Selma, Alabama.

By 20 December I had been allocated 1st Lieut. G. B. Hillman as my instructor on the AT6A (Harvard). On 30 December I had mastered retractable undercarriage and flaps, and I had gone solo. Although from time to time we returned to the more mundane exercise for flying accuracy, we spent most of the next 80 hours in formation, instrument and cross-country flying. We were also introduced to high altitude use of oxygen and ground and air-to-air gunnery. I do not know whether my concentration on instrument flying had produced certain smoothness in control, but I found co-ordination in gunnery extremely easy. From the beginning of the course I returned high scores and on one occasion, to the amazement of my instructor, I recorded a maximum of 100 hits on the drogue with 100 rounds in three passes.

Apart from the unnoticed ground loop on my first solo at Carlisle in

England, I had never come close to having an accident and this, together with my feeling of confidence in my new-found ability, led to my one and only accident, through pilot error, in 25 years of flying. On 13 February 1943 I carried out a cross-country night flight from Craig Field to Maxwell to Dothan and returned via Maxwell to Craig. This was a 3-hour, 15-minute flight, partly following light lines, partly DR navigation and partly radio beam interception. On rejoining at Craig I was given clear to land and made what I thought was a perfect approach and touchdown. However, I stopped very quickly without the use of brakes and never veered from the centre line of the runway. The tower called to clear the runway immediately as another aircraft was on the approach. My logbook is annotated forever with the cryptic note signed by a very irate Captain A. S. Cresswell; 'Student landed wheels-up due to neglecting to lower the landing gear while making a night landing'. I do not remember the undercarriage warning horn blowing as I throttled back on the final approach. I do not remember the absence of the undercarriage green lights indicating wheels down and locked. I do not remember failing to carry out down-wind checks and final approach checks on the undercarriage. I do, however, remember that sickening, sliding,

*Graduating Class of 43B,
following Wings Presentation,
18 February 1943,
Advanced Flying School at
Craig Field, Selma, Alabama.*

*Award of Wings: "None means
quite as much to me as those first
silver wings pinned on a khaki shirt
under a blazing Alabama sun."*

metallic noise as propeller grinds in to tarmac and flaps crumple in to the trailing edge of the wing. Then, with a sudden and complete silence under a beautiful canopy of bright stars, one can step from the wing directly on to the ground to await the arrival of fire engines, jeeps, crash wagons, ambulance and the prospect of making two footslogging circuits of the airfield next day, with an aircraft tyre around one's neck, as a punishment. All this, to my shame, was just five days before graduation and the coveted award of silver wings. I am happy to say that so little damage was done to the plane that, with a change of flaps and a new prop, it was flying again in a couple of days.

Awarded American Army Air Force Wings.

I was awarded the American Army Air Force wings on 18th February 1943, with an above average assessment and recommendation as

1. Instructor
2. Single Day Fighter
3. Single Night Fighter   Total hours: 233 hours, 40 minutes.

Along with this came the news that I had been awarded a commission as Pilot Officer and the marks of the tyre around my neck began to wear off, but the lesson did not.

The period at Craig Field had not been all work however. For the first time I had been able to get off the field and see something of the area and those who lived around the airfield. Apart from the occasions when I was confined to camp to walk 'tours', I enjoyed freedom of access to town in off duty time. A dusty bus journey would take us to Selma, where the hospitality of the local inhabitants had to be experienced to be believed. If we wanted to sample a bigger-city life we would go to Montgomery. We young strangers were an experience to most Americans in Alabama it seemed, with our very Britishness and, above all, how we spoke 'most peculiar'. I was always being asked to say "grass" and similar words with a distinctive English pronunciation and these Anglo-American exchanges would almost inevitably bring the next round of drinks, probably an invitation to visit and, on many occasions, an introduction to a very pretty young daughter. Though we were young, most of us caught on very quickly than an English husband was a sought-after commodity and, in such an endeavour succeeding, a prelude to absolute disaster. The very mention of such an idea to Administration led to withdrawal from training and re-posting to Canada or Britain. I only came to know one girl during this period and that was quite enough, as it turned out. Many an evening I spent off camp limits having succumbed to her suggestion that exit and entry was easier in the boot of her car than by joining the queue who exited by forcing the perimeter fence. I began my further education in the American way of life at this time and, being very young and immature, was fortunate in these lessons, which gave me a thorough preparation for the months ahead.

In summarising my American flying training period, after some 25 years in world-wide aviation, I feel that the teaching of technical ground school subjects was very intensive but not to the same standard and technique as in the United Kingdom training establishments. However, I believe it was sufficient at that time, apart from an artificially high pass mark, to support the flying training of those who managed to avoid an excessively stringent elimination rate.

The flying training was of a very high standard and instilled an accuracy of pilot control and an awareness of procedures that I do not believe could have been better matched anywhere in 1942. I feel, however, that it is no criticism to say that the whole training programme was more geared to peacetime flying training than the wartime equivalent in Britain or Rhodesia. At this time America had only entered the war shortly before, and the essential contribution by those living and fighting in the front line could not be fully appreciated, nor could this be expected.

Flying instruction was not co-ordinated in theory or practice through a central instructors' school and, consequently, with so many part-military, part-civilian establishments operating, variations in the end-product of pilot proficiency was bound to occur.

However, I can say with sincerity that, in spite of these reservations regarding some aspects of training techniques and attitudes towards discipline, the whole experience was extremely rewarding and has stood me in good stead over the years. Although I have also gained Royal Air Force and Royal Navy Fleet Air Arm wings, and many civilian qualifications in a number of countries, none means quite as much to me as those first silver wings pinned on to a khaki shirt under a blazing Alabama sun on 18 February 1943.

Randolph Field, San Antonio, Texas:
46th Fighter Squadron Class 43C.

In March 1943 the US Army Air Force opened America's first Central Instructors' School at Randolph Field, San Antonio, Texas. I joined the first course on 15 March 1943 as the only Australian pilot. Our class was named as 46th Fighter Squadron Class 43C and was made up of 61 USAAF officer pilots and 10 RAF

Administration block, Randolph Field, Texas.

Randolph Field Instructors course: lineup of aircraft.

officer pilots. Colonel Walter Cornelius "Whoppy" White (1896–1969) was the Commanding Officer. On April 2nd, well after the course had started, he gathered the full course of 1,000 students together and told them that their job was 100 times as big as any previous work undertaken. He concluded in a rather melodramatic way with the words, "When you graduate from here you are going to be the first contingent of shock troops in the nation's drive to produce

Randolph Field night flight.

Harvard trainer on ground, Randolph Field.

Men Training at Randolph's Central Instructors' School Told Their Job Is 100 Times as Big as Previous One of Field

ABOUT 1,000 MEN WHO ARE TRAINING TO INSTRUCT FLYERS HEAR THEIR COMMANDING OFFICER tell them of the "100 times as big a job as the one the field has just discontinued" which they are tackling at Randolph Field's newly inaugurated Central Instructors' School. Previously, the field served for 12 years as the backbone of the Nation's Army aviation cadet training program. Although instructor training began at the field about three weeks ago, the new school was formally inaugurated Wednesday with an address by Col. Walter C. White, commanding officer of the school.

If Pvt. Joe Smith, mechanic at Randolph Field, were asked about the lone school for Army flying instructors, he would probably continue tinkering with his plane and say, "So that's what they were doing?"

Joe and hundreds of other Joes continued their duties as Col. Walter C. White, commanding officer of the Central Instructors' School, formally inaugurated the field in an address before about 1,000 work-garbed student-officers.

Even during his dedication address Col. White wasted no words, nor sentiment.

"Today Randolph Field is tackling a job just about 100 times as the one we've just discontinued," he said.

The officer group was told by their commanding officer that "no airplane that ever left the ground is a damned bit better than the man who sits at the controls."

For the past 12 years the field had been the backbone of the Nation's Army aviation cadet training program. The last class of cadets was graduated from the field March 18, and a huge class for the new curriculum received.

The mass khakied group, speckled with the blue of British, Mexican, South American and Australian uniforms, were warned that:

"You are expected to turn out the best pilots in the world. To do that you've got to be the best instructors who ever climbed into a cockpit."

Col. White continued, "When you graduate from here you are going to be the first contingent of shock troops in this Nation's drive to produce the biggest and best trained armada of air fighters that ever blasted an enemy to hell."

Then, as Col. White concluded his address with the warning "not to discount the enemy," the student officers were dismissed to the flight lines, where they took off in training planes for a mass aerial demonstration before an audience of the field's various commanders.

Col. Edward H. Underhill is director of the school. The school is divided into eight departments, one for each general phase of flying, including instruments, tactical flying, and the like.

Each instructor will specialize to teach one particular type of flying—primary, basic, advanced, twin-engine and tactical flying.

Courses for flying officers will last four weeks; for civilians and ground school instructors, eight weeks and for tactical officers, three weeks.

"I was the only Australian to attend this inaugural course and I was wearing American uniform."

Randolph Field, Texas: 46th Fighter Squadron, Class 43C Instructors Course, 1943.

the biggest and best-trained armada of air fighters that ever blasted an enemy to hell." We spent the rest of the day carrying out a mass aerial low-level fly-past in which I was wedged in the middle of an 18-aircraft formation team.

My flying instructor on this course was 1st Lt. Howard Emery Ahrns (1920–1978) and with him I carried out some 37 hours of instructional techniques over the range of exercise requirements for primary and advanced flying. This took four weeks and in many ways we were feeling our way with various new methods of teaching and co-ordinating ground syllabus with practical air demonstration. Despite this, it served to provide me with the polish and fluency in both the demonstration and explanation that I required. We were accommodated in great luxury in bachelors officers' quarters. I took an early opportunity to visit San Antonio and, in my suddenly acquired freedom, painted the town red on many occasions in the company of new found friends, amongst the American officer students.

In between graduating from Craig Field and arriving at Randolph Field I took a quick trip to Toronto in Canada and equipped myself with a British Air Force Officer's uniform. For practically the whole of my time on American bases, though, I conformed with United States Army Air Force dress and wings, except for the peaked RAF cap and British-type rank braid on shoulder epaulettes.

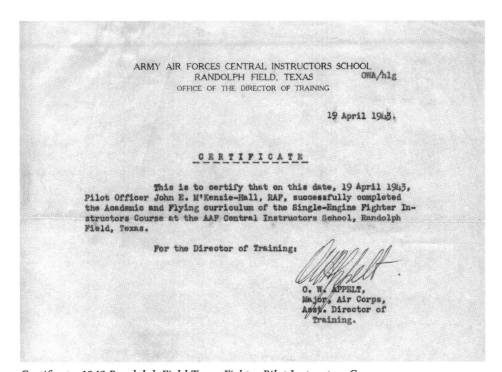

Certificate, 1943 Randolph Field Texas Fighter Pilot Instructors Course.

Apart from Michael Welch, the only other British officers on the course whom I can remember were Pilot Officers Machon, Massey and Mann. My logbook shows I also flew with Capt. Kevin G. Rafferty [Editor's note: after instructing at Randolph Field, Rafferty went to Europe in August 1944 as a pursuit pilot of P-51s with the Eighth Air Force. On 11 September 1944, during his fifth or sixth combat mission, he was shot down and killed in the vicinity of Marburg, Germany] and Capt. Donald Pierce for progress checks but I cannot remember either of them.

Although these four weeks were spent flying, every weekday they allowed us frequent evening and weekend visits to San Antonio and the surrounding countryside. The freedom to come and go as one pleased after a period of almost complete incarceration for pilot training made an immense impression. Total strangers would stop one in the street and exclaim "Gee! Are you British?" and on receipt of an affirmative there would be a display of pleasure and hospitality that I have never encountered elsewhere. It was either "come home for a meal" or "stay the weekend". There was of course often a daughter in tow. On one occasion I not only spent a weekend of total luxury but also enjoyed the daughter's company and her father's car, with all expenses paid, from Friday to Monday. Apart from getting to know the night life of San Antonio very well in a short time, particularly a little night spot called 'The Plantations', I also got to know the town and the people and returned later on a number of occasions to look up families and, in particular, one young lady who subsequently followed me to Dallas.

In retrospect I believe this short period at San Antonio was a particularly important one in my personal, as well as my professional, development. I felt, at 20 years old, suddenly and for the first time, a whole person who was able both to take responsibility for my actions and also to enjoy the pleasures that beckoned from every side. It was easy to shrug off a war in Europe and join in with everyone else who, at this time, gave few outward indications of knowing that World War Two had been on for just over three years.

We completed the course with another mass formation flight and two cross-country flights; one by day to Ellington Field, New Orleans, and one by night to Pawnee, Yoakum and San Marcus. On 17 April 1943 I received an above-average grade as Flying Instructor and was posted to the Advanced Flying School at Eagle Pass, Texas. This was on the Mexican border, opposite Piedras Negras.

Eagle Pass, Texas: Advanced Flying School, April, 1943.

At Eagle Pass I was welcomed as the 'doggoned' Britisher. I soon settled in, and found no differentiation between their treatment of me and all the other American-born instructors posted in. On 24 April I was allocated my first four

A pupil at Eagle Pass.

pupils, J. J. Hotz, D. J. Hovingh, V. F. Howlett and R. K. Isham. I commenced a practice at this stage, which I have continued ever since. While the other scheduled training flights hurriedly got airborne, I extended the ground briefing into a 'getting to know' session and did not take my first pupil, Hotz, into the air until the morning of 25 April. By this time I had discovered many little characteristics of my four. I now understood each one's motivation and in one of them a latent fear which I was able to cure over the period of instruction. I was distressed at their poor absorption of ground-school subjects, and I realised that much time would have to be spent in linking their academic lessons to the practical side of flying and explaining why. All four could fly reasonably well but mechanically rather than naturally, as if each manoeuvre was to be carried out by numbers in isolation to any continuity. I frequently found that they were tensely awaiting the next exercise number to be 'bawled out'.

As instructors we were all in a difficult position since time was at a premium. Our briefing was clear; turn out pilots in the time allocated – eliminate those whose progress cannot be maintained, within the hours available – only in exceptional circumstances give a pupil a second chance. The aviation cadets also knew the thin line they were treading and that others were queuing up to take their place. All this resulted in many unfair cases of elimination, because pupils do have good and bad periods which they are unable to control. Over-enthusiasm can bring on flying inaccuracies and, without doubt, poor communication and lack of clear understanding between pupil and instructor can lead to a relationship tense to the point of open hostility. The whole question of the 'elimination complex' was exacerbated, later during my stay, when the practice of grading pupils by coloured card was extended to include a percentage of 'sudden death' pink cards. As a result of an over-productive training programme, too many pilots were being fed in to a system that could not utilise them and a slowing down process was required as a temporary measure. I could think of many ways of doing this but our orders were to eliminate at least one of our pupils, no matter how good or how bad he was. The decision to drop a perfectly good pupil's pink card through the flight commander's letterbox caused me, and many other conscientious instructors, a great deal of heart-searching.

The main aim of the course was to concentrate on the more advanced stages of flying exercises and appropriate techniques. After an initial orientation flight with each pupil we began straight away on instrument precision and beam flying. Since I had never been airborne at Eagle Pass previously, I suspect those first few flights were as much for my benefit as my pupils. We then proceeded to cover aerobatics, formation flying, gunnery (air-to-air and air-to-ground), night flying, aerial combat and, of course, navigational cross-country flights. Courses lasted approximately five weeks and a great deal of this time was concentrated on gunnery exercises. For air-to-ground these were carried out at an auxiliary field, called in my log book 'Municipal', and from an airstrip on Matagorda Island in the Gulf of Mexico.

'Municipal' was just a hard dirt, and very stony, strip of land close to Eagle Pass. Just off to one side were mounted six large canvas ground targets. There were no services, no fire appliances or personnel and the only identification, apart from the targets, was a very dilapidated windsock. My procedure was as follows; after briefing my pupils at Eagle Pass I departed and, having arrived in one piece on the strip, I positioned my aircraft as far away from the approach to the targets as possible and then acted as fire control. With several missions to fly for re-arming and re-fuelling, my pupils came and went while I spent most of the day in a cockpit hot enough to fry an egg on, praying that (a) my radio would keep working, (b) I could prevent them becoming hypnotised by the target and flying into the ground and (c) eventually I could get my own aircraft started and get out in one piece. I seem to remember that the strip was so short that full flap was required for a short landing technique, and the use of maximum brake for a sliding stop before entering the cactus bushes. Take-off was always a matter of full power and a prayer.

Matagorda Island was a different proposition. Here we had a tarmacadam runway and all ground services, although accommodation was something in the order of a camping holiday. There were several hazards, however, and not least among these was the deep soft sand on each side of the runway and woe betide any pupil, or instructor, who veered off on landing or who suffered the famous AT6C ground loop. In addition we were in the hurricane belt here, and on one side of the hangarage was a tall wooden structure with a siren on top. When this sounded, whatever you were doing, you stopped. Every pilot ran to the nearest aircraft and got airborne. Where you went depended on the fuel state of the aircraft but, generally, as far north as possible to avoid the impending hurricane. It goes without saying that most of us were fully prepared for such an eventuality, and we had even agreed the hotel we would all meet up in to celebrate an unscheduled exercise when it occurred. And it did!

I have already mentioned the danger of pilots flying into their ground targets during a gunnery exercise, and I was witness to such an occurrence on two occasions. Air-to-ground firing was carried out by several groups of pupils flying solo. At Matagorda Island, in addition to a permanent ground target control operation, most instructors would accompany one of their pupils. They would follow through the various target runs as a demonstration to control, as far as possible, the conduct and timing of their pupils. On one such exercise I was flying with a pupil and diving from about 1000ft to the ground target. On my left, and parallel in the dive, I could see a solo pupil slightly in front. I was keeping an eye on our own position but suddenly realised that the other aircraft was passing the safe point of pull out. We were all on a common radio frequency and I just had time to shout out "Pull out, pull out", when he hit the ground just above the target and exploded with the most horrendous fireball. My pupil had of course mistaken my shout as an order to him and pulled out early without

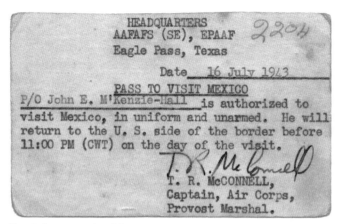

HEADQUARTERS
AAFAFS (SE), EPAAF   2204
Eagle Pass, Texas

Date___16 July 1943___
PASS TO VISIT MEXICO
P/O John E. M'Kenzie-Hall   is authorized to
visit Mexico, in uniform and unarmed. He will
return to the U. S. side of the border before
11:00 PM (CWT) on the day of the visit.

T. R. McCONNELL,
Captain, Air Corps,
Provost Marshal.

Special pass to visit Mexico.

realising what was happening. This was the first time I had witnessed instant death and it was a new experience, but at what price? Despite our immediate warnings against hypnotic 'locking on', a similar tragedy occurred shortly afterwards to another pupil.

Air-to-air gunnery also had its dangers, since the drogue is not positioned very far behind the towing aircraft. Many an instructor had his tail shot through by a pupil practising a 'curve of pursuit' and pulling the trigger with too great a lead on the target drogue. There were also several incidents where the attacking aircraft misjudged his approach and collided with the drogue and cable.

Apart from my instructional duties, which added to my own experiences from day to day, I also led a very full life in other directions. Although Eagle Pass was an isolated airfield, there was no lack of activity both on and off duty. Our nearest town, over the border, was the tiny Mexican one of Piedras Negras. There was nothing much to see, but it was useful for a change of food. In order to cross the border we were issued with special passes by the Provost Marshal, which stipulated that "… F/O John E M'Kenzie-Hall is authorised to visit Mexico, in uniform and unarmed. He will return to the U.S. side of the border before 11:00 pm (CWT) on the day of the visit". An additional note advised all personnel to remain on the paved and lighted streets of any Mexican town they visited.

Stories of knifings and robberies after dark had their effect on most personnel and, as a result, arrangements had been made for an officers' stag party to be held once a fortnight at base, with imported Mexican female entertainers. The early shows were reasonably conducted affairs but, prior to my departure, several had got right out of hand and ended up as drunken and messy sex orgies.

The subject of sex was always very close to the thoughts and conversations of most of the male population of the dispersed and isolated airfields and more so towards the weekends, when the American services' hospitality knew no bounds. The provision was DIY style, in that you had to choose your particular place of entertainment, but the USAAF would provide the means of getting there and back. There were only two mandatory requirements; you had to be qualified on the type of aircraft available and you had to be back at base by midnight on Sunday. No restrictions as to distance or area within the United States were placed in our way and, in consequence, I was able to visit such diverse places as Denver, Colorado and Miami, Florida, which in ordinary circumstances I would never have had the time to reach. I emphasise the service hospitality aspect, since in addition to providing the aircraft it invariably turned out that on arrival at one's destination a USAAF staff car would take you to a hotel, which a little planning had arranged. At no time on my many trips was I asked to pay for the room or any other service provided by the USAAF.

The freedom of travel opened up extensive opportunities to meet a variety of people and to undergo some interesting and never-to-be-forgotten experiences, some pleasant and some highly dangerous, but this is another story! In order to be fully independent, the use of self-drive hire cars was essential and for this it was necessary to hold a driving licence. To this end I had spent, while based at Randolph Field, one very difficult and sweaty weekend in San Antonio persuading officialdom to give me one on the basis of a British provisional licence and a driving test that intimidated not only my examiner but also everyone else on the right-hand side of the road.

Petrol or gas rationing was of course very severe at this time and particularly so in Southern Texas. Mexico had no rationing however and we organised an unofficial intelligence network to advise us of US deliveries of gas across the border. Small teams of us would then lie in wait just off the highway, follow the delivery tanker across to Piedras Negras and fill our tanks and cans to capacity at a lower price, surprisingly, than rationed gas in Texas.

Apart from the AT6 (Harvard) and other training aircraft, I qualified on as many types as possible including the L-4, P-36 (Warhawk), P-40 (Tomahawk), P-39 (Airacobra) and P-51 (Mustang). I never thought at the time that these pleasure flights were giving me good training for the future when I was to be catapulted in to the Royal Navy and join the first Hellcat nightfighter squadron.

Of course many, if not most, incidents that happen to one add to total experience and, one in particular, at Eagle Pass taught me the value of maintaining rapid reactions at a very high level of automatic response. Our training exercises included a great deal of formation flying, not only with pupils but also amongst instructors, to keep both in practice as wingmen and for demonstration purposes. One very hot morning I was acting as no. 2 wingman in a flight formation of six AT6C's, although we were taking off in two sections of three. We were in a steady close position as we crossed the end of the runway at about 150 feet, keeping fairly low to gain speed. The undercarriage had just clunked in to its bay when I flew through a hot-air vortex that literally turned me upside down. The incident happened so quickly that it was only an instinctive reaction that made me open the throttle and continue the roll through 360° back in to the upright position and still within close formation. Only later did I realise that, had I tried any other corrective manoeuvre, it would have resulted in an immediate loss of height and almost certain ground impact within seconds. The formation leader had not noticed the incident but my opposite wingman at first thought that I had done a 'snap roll' on purpose and came over the radio with "You silly bastard!" At below 200 feet and as a deliberate act, he would have understated my origins.

One weekend I decided to fly to Denver, Colorado. I had heard stories of the magnificent countryside and, in particular, a mountain called 'Pikes Peak'. An accounts officer at Eagle Pass heard I was going, and asked if he could come along as a passenger, since he lived there. We set off very early on Saturday morning, in a Harvard, and arrived well before lunchtime. My passenger disappeared with a promise to be back in time for a Sunday afternoon take-off. A staff car took me to a pre-booked hotel where, having changed and rung up for a hire car, I went in to Denver to enjoy myself for the evening.

It was not long before I met a very charming young lady who was a school teacher and we danced the evening away. She was very willing to show me the countryside so next morning I picked her up from her duplex, in my very super Lincoln convertible. It was a lovely sunny day but threatened rain as we sped out towards the mountains and Pikes Peak. As we climbed the mountain passes and descended in to deep, shadow-filled valleys, I thought how lovely it would be to come back and live here after the war. My girlfriend, Celia, looking lovely in a blue and white silk dress which matched her beautifully coiffured blonde hair, encouraged me in my thoughts and painted a very rosy picture of married life. Just as I sensed a possible entrapment looming up we rounded a corner and there was Pikes Peak towering above us and crested in clouds. As we climbed further it began to drizzle so I pulled the knob on the dashboard that said 'Hood'. Nothing happened and although I nearly pulled it out of its socket the hood refused to come up. I stopped the car, as it really began to rain harder, and physically tried to raise the hood. Both Celia and I were, by this time, soaked. Shelter was not to be seen and the car was beginning to feel like a swimming pool. Laughter gave way to tears as Celia's streaky makeup was covered by collapsed blonde hair and was made worse by her now soaked silk dress.

What an end to a beautiful youthful encounter! I dropped her off at her apartment and returned the car to the hirer. He was less than impressed when he heard my complaint. He leaned in to the sodden car and pushed the lever marked 'Hood'. The hood rose cleanly and tucked itself into waterproof slots. He muttered something about 'stupid limey' before he charged me for a complete dry out of car and upholstery. How could I complain?!

However, this was only the beginning of my troubled weekend. By 4.00 pm the rain had stopped and I made my way to the airport to meet my passenger and file a flight plan back to Eagle Pass. When I got to the flight-planning section I found three other crews there that had also come from Eagle Pass for the weekend and were all heading back at the same time. We all agreed it would be a good idea to fly back together in loose formation and filed our flight plan accordingly. Shortly after this the meteorological office rang to say that an unexpected weather front had shown up and, since it was expected to be severe but short, we would be advised to delay our departure for a few hours until it had cleared out of the way. We all adjourned to the airport lounge where the other officers ordered liqueurs. Being unaware of this American habit and considering that such a small drink could not affect me much I joined in.

A couple of hours later a phone call came through to the effect that the front had passed through and the weather was now clear for us to depart for our destination. We all departed to our particular aircraft and, with my passenger securely aboard, we took off about an hour after dark in a loose formation. The lead aircraft was flying in a rather scattered layer of cloud at about 7,000 feet and, trusting him to navigate, we all closed up in order not to lose him. I had not been badly affected by the small amount of alcohol I had consumed, but began to feel drowsy as I concentrated on keeping his wing light in view. I was suddenly brought to my senses by a brilliant red flash and instinctively broke away to my left to avoid whatever it was. The formation had flown into a patch of thick cloud and the leading aircraft had his wing lights on bright for us to see him. The sudden glare of this light in thick cloud had taken me by surprise and resulted in my taking unnecessary evasive action. Since I had not been navigating, I was now lost as the formation was ahead and out of sight. I called the leader to tell him I was proceeding independently but did not tell him my quandary. I was still at 7,000 feet, but had no idea where I was. In those days there were no homing bearings to call up and, at night, trying to pinpoint one's position on the ground was well nigh impossible. America did, however, have a series of light lines on the ground and, by knowing the colours and codes, it was possible to read one's way if you could see them. I could see from my dimly illuminated map that there was no high ground in the general direction of my flight, and I descended until I could see the lights clearly and identify which one to follow and at which intersection to change over to the next.

All this was going very well until I caught up with the weather front that we had previously avoided. Low cloud forced me to climb, and I lost the light lines and was now flying on instruments alone and only in the general direction of my airfield. Fortunately each airfield had a localised radio beam system that gives off a series of dots and dashes along very narrow channels. If you tune in to their frequency and interpret the signals you can track accurately to the centre of the airfield. At this point you enter a silence cone, and from there you rejoin the beam again and undertake an approach procedure for descent to the runway for a landing.

I tuned in to what we termed 'the coffee grinder' and found I could just pick up the signal for the airfield at Eagle Pass. I commenced the laborious procedure of beam flying and came over the centre of the airfield at least an hour after my contemporaries had landed. As I broke cloud on my descent I saw that the airfield, although identifiable, had no runway lights on and this meant I could not see sufficiently to land. I buzzed the airfield a couple of times at low altitude and the light suddenly came on, and I landed with a sigh of relief. Waiting for me at dispersal was a jeep with a very irate commanding officer who had been called from his bed to authorise the airfield to open up for this 'god-damned Englishman'. My passenger had slept through the whole flight and only woke up when we touched down. I survived the wrath of the commanding officer and learned two lessons; do not ever have even the smallest amount of alcohol before a flight, and practise instrument flying procedures until any airborne incident merely leads to a change of procedure, but never to a panic reaction.

By August 1943 I had instructed 31 pupil aviation cadets through the Advanced Flying School syllabus and added some 350 hours to my own total. I was itching to return to England and join an RAF fighter squadron, for two very good reasons. The first was to justify my training with service in action but the second was to extricate myself from the designs of a young lady whom I had met in San Antonio and who, for some time, had been trying to persuade me into a more permanent form of lease-lend.

No.1 British Flying Training School, Terrell, Texas, September 1943

My pleas to the RAF Delegation in Washington were ignored, however, and I found myself posted to No. 1 BFTS, Terrell, Texas, as the Gunnery Instructor, to replace a Flying Officer Chedlow who was returning to England for operational flying. I arrived in Dallas on 2 September 1943 and, having paid several previous visits to the city, spent a few days renewing acquaintances, until reporting to the commanding officer of No. 1 BFTS Terrell, Wing Commander Moxham, AFC.

My feelings on rejoining my compatriots were rather mixed. On the one hand there were the satisfying new responsibilities of organising and running a department and of being a member of the senior staff. On the other hand there was my re-introduction to RAF service discipline and etiquette, which came as a bit of a climax. Up until now I had been wearing a very unorthodox type of American tropical uniform and my only dress connection with the RAF had been my rank epaulettes and my peaked cap. Due to the fact that I had been wearing it continually during my instructional flying, over-clamped with a radio headset and in tropical conditions, this piece of headgear had

Flying Officer
J. E. M'KENZIE-HALL
Gunnery Officer

Taken from photo in No.1 BFTS album when John M'Kenzie-Hall was Gunnery Officer at Terrell Texas.

become a limp object of despair to the more conventional of my acquaintances and a pride of joy to me. It was almost as good, I persuaded myself, as walking around Britain with the top button of my tunic undone. However, I was now not only back in blue but also subject to the routine of the service, based largely on wartime Britain. It was very apparent that at this period in 1943, much of the American system of flying training was still continuing to a peacetime standard. This was, of course, very high, and similar to that adopted by the pre-war Royal Air Force College at Cranwell. However, there was in the USAAF, in general, a slower pace and a more relaxed attitude off duty. Having become accustomed to this, my first impression of the British officers at Terrell was that they seemed imbued with an almost overbearing stuffiness and formality.

Having greeted me with an order to get a new peaked cap and find some accommodation in the local town, Wing Commander Moxham passed me on to a Flight Lieutenant M. W. Palmer who was the RAF Administrative Officer. This officer conscientiously tried to take me under his wing and introduced me to a local housewife by the name of Mrs Bass, who offered to find me somewhere to stay. I believe this good lady did excellent work among many homesick cadets but, having tasted freedom, I had no intention of being drawn in to homely circles of local town activities when the bright lights of Dallas were literally just over the horizon. Palmer and I did not have much in common but we kept in contact occasionally over the years. He rose to a very senior rank in the Judge Advocate General's office and died in harness at Grays Inn, London, in about 1980.

I took a duplex apartment in Dallas, bought a car and drove to Terrell each day for work.

No. 1 BFTS, apart from the RAF staff, was operated by a civilian contracting company called Terrell Aviation Limited, and a Director by the name of Luckey. Under his control there were eight Ground School Instructors, about 20 office staff and countless maintenance staff, under the Chief of Maintenance, Jimmy Hadden. Civilian flying instructors exceeded 100, in addition to seven or eight Link instructors. USAAF staff for ambulance and post-technical inspection work numbered about 14, while five AAP officers and five NCOs made up the American complement. The British staff consisted of W/Cdr. F. W. Moxham, AFC, shortly to be replaced by W/Cdr. Tomkins, Commanding Officer; S/Ldr. A. Beveridge, Ground Supervisor; F/Lt. M. W. Palmer, Administrative Officer; F/Lt. G. I. Hutchinson, Assistant CFI; F/Lt. E. J. L. Robb, Station Navigation Officer; F/O J. L. Cornish, Navigation Officer and F/O J. E. M'Kenzie-Hall, Gunnery Officer. A typical complement of students would be approximately 200 British cadets and approximately 53 American cadets. These were divided amongst the flying instructors into 12 flights of which four flights were primary training and eight flights were advanced training. The primary section had a civilian supervisor, Mr. C. W. Roderick and six civilian flight commanders, while the advanced section had a civilian supervisor, Mr. E. Van Lloyd, an assistant supervisor and eight civilian flight commanders.

I never fail to be amazed that such a hotchpotch of civilian and service personnel, with all their different requirements and loyalties, could work so well together in turning out a constant flow of very-adequately-trained aircrew.

I took up my new post with enthusiasm and a determination to turn every cadet in to a potential fighter pilot who could hit the enemy at any time, from any angle. I was almost immediately disillusioned however, for two reasons. The first being simply that some cadets, although being good pilots, could not grasp, or were not mentally programmed for grasping, the idea of using an aeroplane as a moving platform. The second was because the training aids, both on the ground and in the air, were inadequate for good instruction. It was also unfair on the pupils to push them back to Britain with only half an idea of how to look after themselves.

Mirror designed by John M'Kenzie-Hall for gunnery training to see what a pupil is looking at.

Gunsight innovation in cockpit.

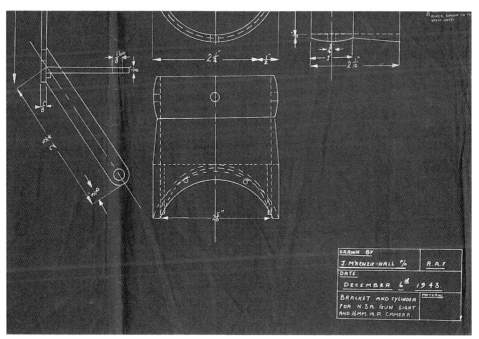

Detail from Blueprint of N3A gunsight designed by John M'Kenzie-Hall at No.1 BFTS, Terrell, Texas.

W/Cdr. Tomkins was, by this time, installed as commanding officer. After listening to my feelings on the subject, he gave me *carte blanche* to set up a special room for illustrated lectures on gunnery techniques and to change the syllabus to incorporate more time for technical explanations and ground demonstrations. At one point I even had a link trainer rigged up with a compressed-air gun firing ball bearings at a moving target on a miniature rail system, to illustrate the curve of pursuit and closing angles of attack.

It was in the air, however, that I became baulked in teaching small corrections in aiming and sighting that make all the difference between a lucky hit and successful target coverage. Since the instructor sat in the rear seat, tandem fashion, and the gun sight was directly in front of the pupil pilot, it was impossible to tell whether the illuminated graticule of the gunsight was held with sufficient lead, or in line with the flight path of the target, unless you asked the pupil to move his head. Directly he did this, apart from losing concentration and probably the target, the indication of exactly where he had been aiming became inaccurate to assess and to explain before a breakaway procedure was necessary.

With the help of the station workshop, I was able to design and mount on a gunnery aircraft a type of periscopic mirror that imposed the image seen by the pupil onto a second mirror mounted in line with the gunsight, directly in front of the instructor. Thus both occupants of the attacking aircraft saw the same images and the instructor had time to complete corrections for a smooth and co-ordinated sighting line and attack, with either film or live ammunition, on the appropriate target.

Another problem was encountered with the N3A gunsight, used for training exercises, and the difficulty in obtaining replacement parts. The aiming circle and central point was produced by light reflected through a scribed glass mirror on to a glass screen (graticule) in front of the pilot. The heat generated inside the gunsight compartment by the bulb, after a period of use, caused the mirror plating, through which the circle was scribed, to peel or shred. This resulted in a jagged circle presentation and in some cases just a series of blobs of light, which was impossible to use for accurate marksmanship. I was very keen on photography at this time and, with the help of a colleague from the Ground School section, Marvin Krieger (1914–2013), I sandwiched a negative with a finely inscribed circle of the exact dimensions between two sheets of glass and was able to obtain a more finely detailed presentation which did not deteriorate with constant use.

I received a letter of commendation from Washington on my work and was asked to prepare blueprints on all my ideas for passing on to the other BFTSs.

These attempts to improve the equipment for teaching gunnery involved me to such an extent that I moved into a hotel in Terrell and never returned to live in Dallas again. I had, however, made a number of friends, both among the

Four Freedoms Warbond Show, Dallas, Texas (John M'Kenzie-Hall is under loudspeaker).

civilian instructors who lived in Dallas and others of the community busy doing their utmost for the war effort. Many of the names now escape me but amongst the people with whom I became involved in fundraising were an AAF General Donovan; Mrs. Clarke, the wife of General Mark Clark; and many prominent businessmen in Dallas who helped me to raise money by promoting rallies such as the 'Four Freedoms War Bond Show', sponsored by the US Treasury Department and the Saturday Evening Post. I still retain, amongst my papers, correspondence from J. Edward Shugrue of the Treasury and Scott Faron of the Post thanking me for my efforts, together with photographs showing the results of weeks of committee planning. Through the good offices of a Mr E. Campbell Russell the board of directors of the Dallas Athletics Club gave me an indefinite extension of the courtesies of the club. I wonder what would happen if I turned up after all these years?

I was very friendly with Jimmy Barr, a civilian instructor at Terrell, and I found visiting his home in Dallas and meeting his family a pleasant and relaxing way of escaping from an increasing involvement in the very active social life of the city. Jimmy and I planned to set up a feeder line service in the southern states after the war and this would have come about had it not been for the three-year waiting restriction imposed on intending Australian immigrants at the end of hostilities. Three incidents from this time stand out in my memory as underlining the absolute difference between the American and British ways of life.

Jimmy and I were sitting quietly enjoying an evening drink at his home in Cole Avenue, Dallas, when the doorbell rang. Jimmy opened the door to a next-door neighbour who was holding a massive handgun and appeared highly agitated. "There's a fellow in my garden with his throat cut and a negro hiding in the bushes in your garden – call the police!" Jimmy phoned police and ambulance and, with a gun, which everyone seemed to keep in their houses, he joined his neighbour in keeping a watch of any movement in the garden. I was standing by the gate when the police car screamed up. A very tall, rangy policeman and a very short, fat one got out. The tall character was obviously in charge and, just as he was being put in the picture, there was a shout from Jim's neighbour, "There he goes!" and over the wall, running in to the dark and down an adjacent narrow lane, I caught a glimpse of a huge black man.

Shots were fired by the two policemen, with the tall one leading his perspiring and rotund companion into a useless chase for several minutes. By this time we had discovered that the victim, an elderly white man, had not had his throat cut but had been hit over the head with a bottle and was generously splattered with blood. He was just beginning to regain consciousness. At the same time as the policemen returned from their abortive pursuit, the ambulance arrived and the casualty was removed with great speed and all became calm again. I was, however, astounded at the parting remark of the police. The little fat policeman turned to Jim and said, "We lost him over the rail tracks. If anything like this happens again, shoot the bastard and then call us to take the body away".

The second incident occurred when I exceeded the speed limit between Terrell and White Rock Airport, Dallas. Two traffic policemen, on huge white Harley Davidson motorcycles, roared past me with lights flashing and, having signalled me in to the side of the road, swaggered back with thumbs in belt, holster flaps undone and mirrored sunglasses glinting, leaving little to the imagination. "Say, do you know what you were clocking back there?" Why is it that, however innocent one is, the immediate response to the law is always an apology? "I am so sorry, officer, I did not realise I was exceeding the speed limit". As I said this I put my service cap on and got out, expecting a ticket or a fine or both. "Are you British?" one of them asked. On my affirmative, the sunglasses came off, a beaming smile replaced the "I've got you now" look and my hand was gripped in friendship. "Say, I have a cousin in England, Lennie Price, have you ever come across him?" I didn't want to say 'no' but, since I could not truthfully say 'yes', I asked some questions about this particular gentleman and found he had settled in Ireland some 20 years previously. After it was agreed to be a sure thing that I would probably meet up with Mr Price on my return to the UK, I could do no wrong. My over-speeding was a thing of the past and my new friend Hank said, "There's a fair by the road a couple of miles further on and a bit of a hold-up. Follow us and we'll see you through." So preceded by two holster-flapping policemen on two enormous white and chrome machines

RAF STAFF

Contemporary cartoon (1943) of RAF staff at No. 1 British Flying Training School at Terrell, Texas; John M'Kenzie-Hall, Gunnery Officer, is depicted top left.

coupled together as a battering ram, I went through that small town and fair site with my foot flat on the accelerator. Then, to a waving twin salute, I proceeded at well over the limit for the rest of my journey.

The third incident was unpleasant and the result hearsay, but nonetheless I learnt from it. With a few friends I was returning to Terrell very late one night after an evening in Dallas and we stopped at a Pigstand [Editor's note: 'Pigstand' was a pioneering drive-in fast-food chain.] for a sandwich and coffee. Entering a long, narrow room with stalls on each side and a serving bar at one end, we ordered our food and settled ourselves at a table nearest the door. Apart from our party of four, there was a naval rating and his girlfriend sitting quietly in a stall halfway up the room and a 'local', complete with boots, belt and stetson, playing 'craps' with the barman. The Texan had been drinking heavily and, at a point when the barman had gone to attend to something in the back, he staggered over to the sailor's table and asked him to join him in a game. I do not know what the sailor said in reply but the Texan suddenly swept all the crockery off the table and grabbed the sailor by the front of his tunic. The sailor reacted naturally and hit the Texan, who recoiled back and fell over a table. Events then sped up. The sailor's girlfriend made a rapid exit past us, but only just. As British officers we would have been foolish to become embroiled in a local skirmish which did not concern us so we also beat a hasty retreat to our car and drove on to Terrell. I found out later, from a friend, what took place immediately after our departure. The sailor, a local boy on leave, backed up before the now steamed-up Texan reached the bar. He found his arms gripped from behind by the barman who, on his return to the bar, assumed that his friend the Texan was being attacked by the sailor. The Texan then drew out a knife and stabbed the sailor in the shoulders just before the arrival of the police, who had been summoned by the girl. The police arrested all three of them and they were taken before the 'all night' justice. As they were leaving the 'drive-in' the Texan let fly at the girl and knocked her down. The penalties awarded show an interesting bias within the flexibility of instant justice. The barman was let off with a warning. The Texan was fined five dollars and jailed for the night, but was immediately released because it was daylight by then. The sailor and his girlfriend were fined 100 dollars each for disturbing the peace – whose peace?!

I have recounted these incidents at some length because they illustrate, more clearly than anything else I encountered, the wide differences that existed at that time between life, as I knew it, in Europe and America.

My girlfriend had, by now, turned up in Dallas and, having got herself a job, was pressing her case again for a more permanent relationship with tearful entreaties. Her arrival coincided with an additional duty I found myself landed with. A number of British cadets had become involved with girlfriends to the extent that Mums and Dads and other relatives were pressing their daughters' interests for marriage. It was common for evidence to be produced of pregnancy accompanied by heart-rending stories of disgraced families unless there was a marriage. Some of the stories might have been true but the first case I examined showed that the cadet in question had not even arrived in America at the time the young lady had conceived. Other instances were not so clear-cut but a number of rapid postings back to the United Kingdom usually resulted from inquiries where evidence appeared to have been falsified but where this could not be proved. I was only 21 years old myself at this time and the revelations behind the seemingly intense desire, at any cost, for a British husband, caused me to lecture, with great severity, those amorous cadets seeking advice and also to carry out a short series of 'breakaway' tactics myself.

These cases of 'broken heart' affairs were of course not widespread when placed in the context of the tremendous friendship and hospitality shown to the very large number of British personnel passing through the various states and schools of training. Cadets were adopted by families and shown the very best that the American way of life had to offer. This applied right across the whole spectrum of American society, from the affluent who could afford to impress, to the low-wage earners who earnestly endeavoured to play their part in saying "Welcome, come again".

I began to find that my gunnery instruction was showing improving results, however, my social and war effort work in Dallas and district was becoming too much and began to intrude on my flying duties, which were my main priority. To counter this I started to assist with some general flying instruction, as well as gunnery, and joined in progress-check flights, formation and cross-country exercises etc. It was at this time also, that I discovered a new exercise in which I became increasingly absorbed. I had previously only experienced night aerobatics under instruction but I now took every opportunity to sneak away and practise on my own and became something of a night owl, right up to my departure from America.

From time to time, senior RAF officers visited No. 1 BFTS from Washington, either formally for inspections or informally, as I suspect, to justify their existence in an 'out of theatre' posting. We had one such visitor fairly frequently who would fly in, in a P-40 (Tomahawk) and taxi past the assembled parade with canopy open, hat on and displaying 'scrambled eggs' looking for the salute. This was a Group Captain Donaldson, one of the famous wartime brothers – I cannot remember which one of them came to see me to discuss gunnery tactics but I recall being much impressed by his wartime experience. One of these brothers was later killed, I believe, in North Africa, while the other settled in as Air Correspondent to the Daily Telegraph, until his death in the 1970s.

By May 1944 I had been promoted to Flight Lieutenant and my
request for a return to the UK was
finally granted. I handed over to my
successor, a Flt. Lt. Barkell who was
a highly decorated, ex-operational
fighter pilot and was, in my opinion, as
mad as a hatter, totally irresponsible
but extremely likeable. I never heard
of him again but I doubt whether his
stay at Terrell lasted very long before
explosions occurred. [Editor's note:
a letter of recommendation dated 10
May 1944 from the RAF delegation in
Washington DC states "McKenzie-
Hall has done an excellent job in my
opinion and is now flat out to get to
grips with the 'Hun' and loathes the
thought of Training Command"].

*F/Lt. Barkell. Took over from me as Gunnery
Officer No. 1 BFTS during May 1944.*

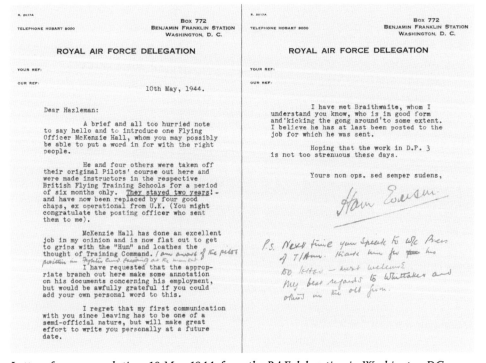

Letter of recommendation, 10 May 1944, from the RAF delegation in Washington DC.

Chapter Four

England (Part II)
and Fleet Air Arm

I returned from America by sea, in a convoy of supply ships. We sailed slowly, mostly in fog and long sea swells, back to the United Kingdom, arriving in June 1944. Unlike my outward-bound trip I travelled in comfort, with a cabin to myself and the refinement of dining-room service. I was laden down with cosmetics, silk stockings, cigarettes, chocolates and numerous small gifts for mother, sister and hopefully girlfriends. What a different place England was in 1944 to when I left nearly three years before. Morale appeared high but there seemed a greyness of attitude in most people, but cemented together by a strong feeling of unity of purpose. There was also a discipline apparent in the way all grades of society pulled together towards the common goal of victory.

After a couple of weeks disembarkation leave, I was posted to a little grass airfield called Clyffe Pypard in Wiltshire, where for a further two weeks I joined a refresher course on Tiger Moths. This was to re-orientate me on navigation in England, to re-learn ground procedures and wait for a posting to an operational squadron.

This proved an enjoyable period, making new friends and flying the DH 82A (Tiger Moth), with the wind whistling once again through an open cockpit. One incident spoiled this pleasure and underlined the old saying that 'a foolish pilot doesn't live long'. A group of us were sitting around the dispersal site on a lovely August day when a fighter aircraft flew over us very fast and low, carrying out slow rolls as he climbed away for another pass. This, we found out later, was an Australian pilot flying the newly operational 'Typhoon' and showing off its paces to a friend at our airfield (Editor's note: an email from Duncan Curtis informs me the crash happened on Friday 25 August 1944 and the aircraft was a Typhoon MN207 from 165 squadron piloted by Flight Sergeant Colin Cameron). We next saw him diving very steeply and very fast towards us. He pulled up too late to clear the ground and hit just outside the perimeter of the airfield in one colossal explosion. We all rushed over to view the crater and what been a first class aircraft and a third rate pilot. I kept a souvenir from the fuselage for some years to remind me forcibly of the danger of being over confident and the stupidity of showing off.

During the course I had mulled over what operational aircraft I wished to fly and had decided that PRU Mosquitoes was the right choice. This was a mixture of low flying, photography and intruder operation. I had already flown twin-engined aircraft in the States and considered my temperament suitable for this highly specialised work. Having put my name down for this choice I went on leave for three weeks. I was recalled to a holding unit and then sent on leave again. 'Holding units' were quite inaptly named since one was not held. Provided you were seen to be available once a week, your time was your own and this was fully used by all concerned. By this time I was a little bored with what seemed like endless delays. We were hardly given time to think in America, where time off was valued highly. Here, no one seemed to know what was going on or seemed to care. I decided to go to Bournemouth to see the sea and booked in to a hotel recommended as the one where all the BOAC flying boat aircrew stayed between their trips to America via Lisbon. It was at this time that I went totally against my better instincts and did a very foolish thing. I had become very pally at the bar with one of the BOAC air-stewards (no stewardesses in those days) and was fascinated with his stories of neutral Lisbon and the intrigue carried out there by many nations. To cut a long story short I became, for the period between an outgoing and return flight, an unauthorised supernumerary steward of BOAC. I began to feel slightly fearful before I reached Lisbon but with the assurance of my friend that in the routine of aircraft staff passing through no one would know. I arrived at a hotel with no trouble and spent the period with short visits out and much time in my room. I dared not use the bar in case I drank too much and gave myself away and in any case I felt every eye was on me. I decided there and then that I was not the material for a spy and was almighty grateful when my friend picked me up on his return trip. I shudder to think what would have happened had he been taken ill or suddenly taken off the return flight.

On my return to Bournemouth I found I had been posted, at long last, to a twin-engined conversion course at Kidlington in Oxfordshire. I was a little shocked when I learned the course would take five months and felt that with my previous experience, both in instructing and twin-engined flying, this could have been curtailed by several weeks. Right at the beginning it nearly was. I had gone solo in the twin-engined Oxford in three hours and the next few hours were spent flying locally and getting used to the aircraft. Each flying period was about an hour and I had been performing various manoeuvres for about half an hour when I urgently wanted to spend a penny. No relief tube had been

Airspeed Oxford twin-engined trainer.

fitted but the Verry pistol tube between the pilot and co-pilot seats seemed to provide the ideal solution. I removed the pistol, undid my harness, slipped out of the parachute and climbed over to a position to use the tube while keeping the aircraft in steady flight. I can confirm that when flying solo it is impossible. My urgency made me think of another alternative. However I realised this was impractical, stupid and probably would not work anyway. In any case it was too late and I slid back in to a rather soggy and uncomfortable seat.

When I eventually landed I saw the next pupil, with his instructor, waiting for me to emerge. In my haste to leave the aircraft I pulled the jettison door handle by mistake and went flying out, still holding the door, on to the wing and then rolled off it on to the ground, coming to rest at the feet of the instructor. I was embarrassed at being told off, in no uncertain terms, that I was stupid and responsible for a cancelled period of instruction for his pupil. On top of all this, he ended up by letting me know how 'wet' I was. He was right in both respects.

Another incident occurred a little later on when, once again, I had to kill time. On this occasion it was two hours and I decided to have a look at London from the air, for the first time. It was a lovely, sunny, late afternoon with blue sky and a scattering of fair weather cumulus clouds. As I reached the outskirts of London, flying at almost 2,000ft, I suddenly spotted, just a little way ahead and above me, several large sausage shaped objects. As I realised they were barrage balloons I pulled the aircraft in a steep turn to starboard, back the way I had come, hoping fervently that I had seen them in time and there was no wire cable waiting to cut me in half. Having failed in my attempt to see London I headed back to Kidlington. I found myself flying into the full glare of a low setting sun which was so blinding that I could not see the ground to map read. There was also a low haze and to avoid getting lost I decided to follow the line of the Thames which, in reflecting the sun, shone like a silver snake twisting its way to Oxford.

There were no radio navigation aids on this aircraft and the radio only produced static. I began to realise that I was taking rather a long time to reach the small grass airfield. I suddenly saw a large airfield with runways and decided it would be safer to land there before it got too dark. I therefore flew low over the airfield before entering the circuit pattern and landing. It was RAF Benson, a very busy operational airfield. I was greeted with a questioning response when I rang Kidlington to tell them I was staying the night and would return in the morning. This was understandable when it was pointed out to me that I was only about six or seven minutes away. However, I was accommodated in the officers' mess overnight and spent the evening of my first visit to an operation unit in the bar. This bar was a Nissen hut, built onto the side of the officers' mess. As I walked in I felt almost ashamed that I was still not operationally baptised. I probably had more flying hours than most people in the room yet I was still 'wet' behind the ears as regards combat experience. There were two RAF Officers and an American sitting at the bar and at first I did not recognise who the American was. While talking to another Officer it came out that I had just finished a tour of instructing in America. My new friend immediately said, "You must meet Jimmy, he's our new tame 'Yank'". I was steered to meet Col. James Stewart. He told me they were just discussing the differences between American and British fighter tactics and asked whether I could join him because he was outnumbered. We kept in contact for some time, but went our own ways when the war ended and he went back to films. The five months came to an end eventually without my being very impressed with twin-engine flying in such a low-powered, unmanoeuvrable aircraft as the Oxford.

During the course, rumours had been passed around that there was a requirement for glider pilots and that some of us could be recruited, if our requested postings did not come through. The thought horrified me and the reality became even more possible when I heard that postings onto Mosquitoes were few and far between.

One morning I read that the Royal Naval Fleet Air Arm was asking for pilots to volunteer to join the first carrier-borne night-fighter squadron. They were looking to the RAF for night-fighter flying experience and offering a straight swap from one service to the other. When further enquiries seemed to point towards gliders I volunteered to become a naval officer. Almost before I had signed the application I was called to the Admiralty in London, Royal Naval Volunteer Reserve (Fleet Air Arm), and told to go and get myself kitted out and report to *HMS Macaw* at Bootle in a week's time. I now entered an Alice-in-

Colonel James Stewart, film actor, B-24 Liberator pilot and instructor, shown here receiving the Croix de Guerre. John M'Kenzie-Hall met him at RAF Benson in 1944 and they stayed in contact for some time.

Wonderland world where the right hand had not a clue what the left hand was doing and both sides blamed the other for what happened next.

I was recommended to a tailor in Sackville Street called Jones, Chalk and Dawson and, in my ignorance, went there. Since I had purchased my RAF uniform in Canada I knew little of English tailors and no one pointed me towards Gieves or Austin Reed etc, where prices for junior officers met their pockets. "Yes, they could produce me a uniform in a week but, of course, two would be better, plus the etceteras". The bill for two doeskin uniforms and the gold braid was so high that I could not afford the greatcoat, but managed to pick one up second-hand. At this point a great stroke of luck came my way in the shape of a charming old couple who had known my mother before the war. They offered me the use of their Vauxhall car, which had been laid up on blocks in their garage since the beginning of the war. It started first time, with a recharged battery and a tank full of petrol, which I was able to get with a month's supply of coupons. So, looking like a very smart naval officer and acting and feeling like a very mixed up RAF officer, I set off for Liverpool. I booked in to a Naval Club that evening and the next morning I drove down to the dockyards at Bootle. At the gates the conversation went something like this, "Lt. M'Kenzie-Hall for HMS Macaw". "What ship Sir?" "HMS Macaw". "Just a minute Sir, I'll call the harbour master". The gate remained firmly locked. "May I help you Sir? I am the harbour master".

"My name is Lt. M'Kenzie-Hall, I have come to join *HMS Macaw*". "I am sorry Sir, *HMS Macaw* is still in the Pacific and is not due to be paid off for a month yet. Could I see your identity card please?" I must have appeared most suspect! Having explained how new I was and that somehow a mistake had been made, I turned back to London and to the Admiralty where I was greeted as a complete idiot. They explained that *HMS Macaw* was a 'stone frigate' (shore based unit), situated at Bootle in Cumberland. If I had read my papers more carefully I would have seen that the word Cumberland was clearly printed under Bootle. Macaw was a shore station where newly commissioned officers were sent for a knife and fork course on naval etiquette and procedure. Now they tell me! Having scrounged more petrol coupons, I set off on the long drive to Cumberland and found *HMS Macaw* to be a series of huts on a windswept hillside and wired around like a prison, with absolutely nothing else in sight.

When I stopped at the guardroom, the sentry looked in the car, stood back, saluted and waved me in. As I parked outside what looked like the administrative block a lieutenant came out to greet me. "Welcome aboard. What can I do for you?" This time, not to be caught out, I presented my papers and said, "Lt. M'Kenzie-Hall, I have come to join the course". The lieutenant gave me a horrified look and then asked me my seniority. As I had been a flight lieutenant for some time I had carried two years seniority in to my naval rank. I therefore outranked my commanding officer by over a year. He thought I had come to undertake a surprise inspection and was totally taken aback. He finally said, "I can't accept you here. All my pupils are on a two-week course for midshipman and temporary sub-lieutenants on first entry in to the navy. Most have to be taught how to use a knife and fork". I went in for a cup of tea, was given a pass certificate and piped ashore at the end of a course that must have lasted all of fifteen minutes. My departure must have saved us both days of embarrassment.

So, once again, I set off for London to see what else they had in store for me. I was driving south somewhere east of Liverpool and thinking what a 'Fred Karno' outfit the Navy seemed to be when I passed a naval officer carrying a small bag. In those days everyone gave lifts, if at all possible, and the thought of undesirables was remote. I stopped, he climbed in very gratefully, told me his name was Murray (George), that his ship had just been paid off (decommissioned) and he was trying to get to London as quickly as possible. It seemed there was some hold up with the trains, which was not surprising with V1s and V2s landing all over the place.

George, as he asked me to call him, chatted about various minor matters and was amused to hear that I had just transferred in to the Navy. He suddenly asked me if I had had lunch and, when I said "no", he suggested we stop at an army camp just a little way ahead where he had a friend.

I was only too pleased to agree and we duly pulled into the guardroom of what looked like an army supply depot. George got out and when he put his cap on I saw the peak had 'scrambled eggs' on it [Editor's note: "scrambled eggs' refers to the leaf-shaped braid clusters that distinguish higher-rank officers – in the case of the Royal Navy, commander and above.]. I had not noticed this when I picked him up. When he returned from a chat with the guard and we were driving towards the officer's mess I explained that I had not realised his rank and began calling him 'Sir'. "Don't bother with formality, we are not on duty now, I am still George". When he took his mac off there, for all to see, were gold bands seemingly running from wrist to elbow and a chest full of ribbons. I dropped him off at the mess and while I parked the car he went inside. When I joined him a few minutes later he was at the bar talking to the colonel in command with great gusto. I joined them for a drink and, bedazzled by such illustrious company, hardly uttered a word. During a splendid lunch George suddenly asked me what the petrol stakes were like and when I said I had just about enough to get me to London he asked the CO whether we could fill up before we moved on. After lunch, while George was saying goodbye to his old friend the colonel, I filled my tank with pink petrol, which was for service use only and was totally prohibited for private vehicles.

We arrived in London early evening on a Friday and, on leaving me, he thanked me profusely and suggested in return for the lift could I join him the next day for a drink. I cannot remember the name of the pub now but it was somewhere in the Chelsea area. His last words to me were, "I can get you some more petrol tomorrow if you like, meet you at 12 o'clock".

'Petrol, like pearls, does not grow on trees', so, on the stroke of 12 I was in the saloon lounge on Saturday morning sampling a pink gin and looking forward to another full tank. I waited until 1.30 pm, and then gave up because he had obviously been delayed or had forgotten. As I was leaving George suddenly appeared, apologising profusely for keeping me waiting, and explained why. He had been trying to cash a cheque but the banks were shut and he could not contact any of his friends since they were all away for the weekend. I knew exactly what it was like to run out of cash and how embarrassing it must be for such a senior officer. I did not hesitate, "Oh, I can lend you some George. How much would you like?" I had drawn quite a lot out before my journey to Cumberland and also had brought extra for petrol. "Could you make it £10?" he suggested tentatively. "Of course," I replied, "will that be enough?" "Well if you could spare £25 I could give you a cheque". He took the money with great gratitude and then over another drink, which I paid for, he said he had left his chequebook in his room but that he would change the bank on my cheque if I had my chequebook with me. You might think that by now I would have begun to suspect that something was not quite right. I had not. I was still overawed by his rank, his manner, his acquaintances and I had had a few gins whilst waiting for him. He altered and signed my cheque, had another drink and then we went out to get the petrol he promised. A short distance away he knocked on two double doors leading in to a courtyard and, getting no reply, said, "They have obviously gone to lunch but they will be open later this afternoon. I'll see you back here at 2.30 pm". No warning bells rang. I actually thanked him! The last I saw of him, with my £25, was his back as he jauntily turned a corner. I pounded on the door at 2.30 pm but, not surprisingly, no one came.

On Monday the bank (his so-called bank), told me that the cheque was worthless since no one of that name held an account there. My feelings towards the navy and its so-called senior officers took another dive downwards. The police, when I called on them, thought it a huge joke. "You've been had by 'General Jack'. We have been chasing him for months. He changes service and rank regularly and pops up all over England picking off service personnel. You were lucky, the last case we heard of he had got away with over £100". It turned out that he did not know the colonel where we had stopped for lunch. It was another case of rank and bluff. I was fed up with being conned and agonised for some time over the pink staining in my petrol tank. However, more immediate matters soon took my attention.

I was posted, with immediate effect, to the Naval College at Greenwich where I became the Senior Course Officer. On the first morning we assembled outside for 'divisions' (what we called 'parade' in the RAF) and I found myself in charge of the flag-hoisting ceremony. As an orderly officer in the RAF I had raised and lowered the flag many times but naval procedure was quite different and completely beyond me. After a long pause the captain sent a petty officer to ask me what the delay was. Embarrassing as it was, I told the PO to stand behind me and tell me what to say. The flag safely hoisted, I was called before the captain to explain my actions. When he learned that I had been in the navy such a short time and had never been indoctrinated with naval routine and command, I was released from all ceremonial duties but remained course leader for classroom studies.

I ate in the Painted Hall, walked the marble-columned halls and learned a little of naval traditions and customs. Towards the end of the course I was called before the captain again for nearly running down a sailing barge on the Thames. I admit there was temporary panic on the bridge of which I was technically in command but I didn't hit it!

At the end of the course we learned that two new naval squadrons were to be formed; 891 Squadron to fly Hellcats and 892 Squadron to fly Corsairs. These were the first two night-fighter squadrons in the Fleet Air Arm and we were to

891 Squadron, Fleet Air Arm; a night-fighter squadron flying Grumman Hellcats.

start life in Northern Ireland at RNAS Eglinton. I was posted to 891 Squadron to serve under the Commanding Officer, Lt. Com. Perrett.

I had a couple of days leave before leaving for Ireland and decided to spend it in London enjoying myself. I spent the evening in a very pleasant little club not far from Curzon Street and the next morning I went for a walk in Hyde Park, to clear some of the mists from the night before. As I approached the top of Park Lane, near to Marble Arch, I noticed two people in front of me walking towards what I think must have been a wooden building, possibly a canteen. I only remember an enormous roar. I woke up lying on my back, some distance from where I had been, dirty but completely unscathed. The hut and two people had vanished but a ragged crater and pieces of trees were scattered far and wide. It was my first near miss with a V2 and a most unpleasant experience. This may have been my initial experience of the dangers of being in London in wartime but not my last. Next day I had taken the tube to Gloucester Road to pick up my things for the journey to Ireland and was leaving the tube station when it all happened again. A V2 landed just outside the entrance and the blast came all the way along the passageway and blew us all off our feet. The sound of splintering wood and flying glass didn't help. As far as I know no one was killed but, after a clean-up and a stiff drink, I left London as fast as I could for the

Grumman Hellcats, 891 Squadron, Fleet Air Arm, based in Northern Ireland.

peace of an operational fighter squadron in Northern Ireland.

The Hellcat was a delightful aircraft. It weighed 5,200 kg and was powered by a Pratt and Whitney R-2800 radial engine of 2,000 hp. At this time, together with my civilian flying hours in the USA, I had well over 1,000 hours flying experience. The other members of the squadron were, in the main, young naval officers having recently completed their training and having very few flying hours. As a result, I became the Senior Pilot under the command of Lieutenant Commander Perrett. Another of the pilots was a Sub Lieutenant Sear (Slim). He had been a Sergeant Pilot on Spitfires prior to transferring to the Fleet Air Arm with me and we had formed a friendship during the Greenwich course. He was an excellent pilot and finished up in the 1970s as Chief Helicopter Test Pilot to the Westland Aircraft Company. Cdr. Perrett on the other hand was, in my opinion, a disaster both as a person and as a Commanding Officer. He was a large, red-headed New Zealander with a bullying manner who did not take kindly to ex RAF personnel with more experience and more hours than he had. I found his flying, as formation leader, erratic and his manner to his juniors unbearable. For some three months I flew 60 hours in dummy deck landings, air firing, formation, carrier range, night flying and lastly, as Germany surrendered, accompanying their German submarines from the North Sea in

891 Squadron, with Hellcat. The only wartime photo of John M'Kenzie-Hall with plane.

to Eglinton Harbour. During all this time tension built between us. Eventually two incidents brought our dislike of each other to a head. Firstly, I objected to his continued comments on Slim Sear as "a Cockney without the manners of an officer" and secondly, his continuous driving of some of the junior pilots beyond their abilities in certain training exercises which, I was sure, would end

Hellcat at RNAS Eglinton.

891 Squadron escorted in a number of German U Boats (shown here in harbour at Londonderry) following Germany's surrender.

in tragedy. After 'working up' the squadron we were due to join a carrier at sea for final exercises, before travelling out to the Far East to combine with Force 136 for the invasion of Malaya. After completing this exercise we returned to Eglinton.

One morning Perrett let fly with one of his caustic remarks and I had had enough. I told him exactly what I thought of him and his Navy and accused him of being worse than Captain Bligh and a New Zealander to boot. One of us had to go and, since I could not put him adrift, I packed my bags. After a rather difficult half-hour with the commanding officer of RNAS Eglinton, I was sent on indefinite leave pending re-posting.

I believe that others must have shared some of my misgivings over Perrett since I heard no more of the matter and in fact, after a period of leave, I was told to put up a half ring (promoted to Acting Temporary Lieutenant Commander) and report to Heston. This airfield has now been swallowed up by Heathrow but, before being part of London airport, it was used extensively for test flying and receiving VIPs to England. I stayed there until I was given the opportunity to leave the Fleet Air Arm on demobilisation, following the surrender of the Japanese.

It was at Heston that I first met test pilots Alex Hensaw, the first pilot to fly the Spitfire, and Geoffrey De Havilland. The task was test flying, for acceptance by the Navy, for a new version of the Seafire with contra rotating propellers. It also involved the experimental use of rockets fixed to the trailing edge of the wing which, when fired during the take-off run, shot the aircraft in to the air with dramatic effect. I remember quite a few happy, if rather alcoholic, lunches with Alex and Geoffrey at the 'Comet' on the Great North Road. This period was the only one in which I enjoyed being a naval officer but I was glad to leave, even though the future held little joy. I was not to know this at the time, however, and I drove down to Torquay for my demobilisation leave and spent most of my gratuity on one enormous party at the Queen's Hotel. After a couple of weeks I thought I had better find employment of some kind. I was still wearing uniform, since I had not drawn my civilian entitlement and could not afford to kit myself out. Had I had the sense to sit down and think out the future, I might have:

1. Asked for a permanent commission in the Navy. I was at the time acting temporary 'war time' Lt. Commander.

2. Taken a university course offered by the services and finished my architectural training.

3. Taken any number of courses to fit me for civilian life and been paid for doing it.

Unfortunately I was only 22 years old and too young and eager for the freedom that post war Britain seemed to offer. When it came to flying I was experienced, I had good judgement, I could command and I had learned to be disciplined towards achieving an objective. If I had a failing it was that I sometimes became impatient with incidents that I thought unfair or foolish and took actions to show my feelings. Why did I not apply these attributes in carrying out a new career?

Without money my party times came to an end and a girlfriend (one of many) suggested I get a job. She was more interested in my pocket than my uniform. Since this had already occurred to me I decided to act immediately. I went to the local labour exchange in Torquay with high hopes. They looked at me aghast, "We haven't anything that would suit you Sir". I was a little taken aback but told them I was not proud and that I would take anything they had to offer. This brought forth a tentative offer of the only job they had available that day of a filing clerk with a firm called British Celanese, which had been evacuated to Torquay. I took it.

The offices of British Celanese, in Torquay, were up a flight of stairs off the main street and next door to a Kardomah coffee shop. I parked the car opposite and climbed the stairs to enter an enormously large room. At one end, sitting in a chair on a wooden dais, about one and a half feet above the floor, was a shabby 'Victorian looking' little man in a suit and starched wing collar. He had a table in front of him on which stood a number of papers, an inkwell and a bell. Spreading away from him for about 40 feet were four rows of desks, uniformly placed with avenues running between them. At these desks were what seemed to me to be dozens of miserable looking 'Cratchits'. They were all wearing dark suits, wing collars and each seemed hunched over a portfolio of some sort, most were scratching away with steel nibs. I had never seen anything like it before but my amazement was interrupted by the man on the platform standing up respectfully and looking at me with an invitation to join him. As I approached he indicated a chair on the platform in which, after shaking hands, I duly sat. "What may I do for you Sir?" he said as he also sat down. I handed him my scrap of paper from the labour exchange. While he looked at it, I looked at him. There was a sudden downturn of the mouth, raised eyebrows and I swear his face and neck turned a hue towards red. "You're applying for this job?" he said, this time less cordially. I said, "Yes", and explained I was ready to start anywhere as a beginning. He paused, looked at me, at my uniform, "You should have seen my chief clerk on this matter, I am the manager. You will only approach me again if I call for you. Mr. Hills is over there, he'll see you". I approached a meek and mild Mr. Hills who stuttered his way through my duties. "You're writing is copper plate I hope", he asked at the end. It was not but I did not want to make him more uncomfortable than he was so I just nodded half-heartedly.

I was now a file clerk and, instead of spending my days as an idle senior officer in the navy, I was to engage myself by sitting at a little table at the opposite end of the room to the manager writing, in my so called 'copper plate' hand, names and accounts in pounds, shillings and pence on share certificates of various types. If called, by any of the many elderly clerks, I was to down pen and either take their file or bring them one from a huge rack of well-worn and indexed file boxes. It was anything but hard work, it was not strenuous but very irritating. Just as I picked up my pen to commence writing in my best hand I would receive a call and this was repeated all morning. At 11.00 am the manager rang his little bell and everyone put their pen down. After looking around the room the manager raised his hand and everyone stood up and filed down the stairs to Kardomah for coffee. A room had been set aside at the back and coffee already poured. Fifteen minutes was allowed before, with everyone seated at their desks once more, the bell rang to commence work. Just like a chapter out of Charles Dickens.

I stood two tedious days of the torture until the third day I arrived by car and, while parking, nearly collided with a cyclist who turned out to be the manager. He was already on his platform when I entered with all the other clerks waiting at attention for the bell. I was summarily summoned to the great man's table to be told, I thought, to be more careful in future. However, to my surprise, in full voice for all to hear he said, "in future you will either walk or ride a bicycle to work and don't appear in that uniform again. In addition you are far too slow in writing up the share certificates, I expect much improvement". This silly upstart of a man suddenly infuriated me. I looked around at the rows of beaten-down little men and thought 'God help you all to put up with this way of life for 25 shillings a week'. I turned back to the table and, without malice aforethought, gripped both sides and tipped it, the chair and the weasel of a manager off his dais in to a heap in the corner. I walked out in dead silence, except for the little bell that was still rolling around. I was now jobless and had just enough cash to drive to London and return the car, which I could no longer afford to keep running.

I should skip the next few weeks, for they do me little credit, but at least I was to experience life on the down side and, in later years, this was to prove useful. Having very little gratuity left I drew my civilian clothes and sold my uniform. All during the war I had arranged to make an allowance to my mother, since my father was a prisoner of war in Changi, Malaya. In order to safeguard this I had little left for bed and breakfast, I therefore decided to sleep rough in order to have enough to eat. For two miserable nights and days I slept on a bench in Hyde Park. On the third day, however, my luck seemed to change. I ran in to an old friend from the Air Force who, having been demobbed, had bought a hotel with his gratuity and savings. He offered me a job and asked me to come to the hotel that afternoon. It was a small, family type building in Kensington and I envisaged acting as manager. He was terribly sorry but he could only offer me work as a porter, of course only until things took off. I carried the suitcases, I cleaned the common parts and I cleaned shoes outside doors at 5.30 am. I think the good Lord considered my apprenticeship should finish because I ran in to a lady I had met while serving in the Royal Air Force. Through my cousin, Viscountess Torrington, I had been introduced to a charming lady at a party and we had spent much of the evening together. She was now married to Air Vice Marshal Bowen-Buscarlett (1893–1967) and lived just off the Cromwell Road. When she offered to put me up I jumped at the chance to get away from the hotel slavery and resigned forthwith. It was not long before my plight came out and, as it was put to me, 'just in time to be of great help to several ladies'. Now you should not jump to hasty conclusions! My hostess was some 30 years my senior and, before the war, she and three lady friends had started a business called McKenzie Traders. During the war two of them married. There was a Mrs Wylie, the wife of a scientist of some repute, a Miss Atkinson, the daughter of a General, and a Mrs Powell, who was always beautifully turned out and I never learned to whom she was married.

In 1937, before the 'decline and fall of the British Empire', McKenzie Traders was flourishing, when they sought the custom of colonial families returning to

England on leave, or going abroad for the first time. They would buy, on behalf of customers, all items required to be shipped such as crockery, china, glass materials, furniture etc, pack it and deliver it to whichever ship was sailing.

Now that the war was over the three ladies had decided that they would re-open the old firm. I was, so they said, just the perfect person to open it for them as Company Secretary. I do not know to this day whether it was a decision for them through nostalgia or an idea by Mrs. Wylie to save a young man from a bleak future. Since they were all wealthy in their own right I must suspect the latter. A suitable shop was rented from Lewis's in James Street, just off Wigmore Street. It was to be run on different lines to the original business, since colonial life had not returned to any great extent and shipping was still on a wartime basis. McKenzie Traders was re-opened as a sales room for antique furniture and fabrics of high quality, plus bric-a-brac for the discernible. I opened up a set of books and made myself comfortable in a small office.

Since I was now an earning employee, I moved from Mrs Bowen-Buscarlett's house to a bed-sit at number 14, Gledhow Gardens, Kensington and began a working day from 8.30 am to 4.30 pm. I have to admit that it was not long before I became a little bored and on some days a 'clock watcher'. Mrs Wylie came in occasionally, Mrs Powell never and Miss Atkinson nearly all the time. Business, to begin with, was slow but it gradually built up until both Miss Atkinson and I were buying and selling on a fairly regular basis. I had one famous customer who broke the monotony for a brief period. A fairly elderly and portly gentleman breezed in one day and looked at materials. I had no idea who he was, but he wanted to furnish his yacht and decided on some very expensive cotton weave upholstery fabric. We got on very well and when I learned who he was, having just read his book *English Journey*, I was glad to have the opportunity of meeting J. B. Priestley. I was invited down to his yacht, moored on the Isle of Wight, to view the finished curtains and coverings.

On another occasion, I was just about to close up shop on a wet and drizzly afternoon when in came a very shabby man whom I didn't like the look of. We were close to St Christopher's Market and many shady characters hung about the area. I followed him closely around the shop as he looked at various antiques and their prices. Since I suspected he had no money and was using the time to keep warm and dry, I eventually edged him out and shut the door. At that moment Miss Atkinson came in very excitedly, "What did he buy?" she asked. When I told her that he hadn't bought anything, hadn't stolen anything and was finally seen off, she was anything but amused. "You have just got rid of Sir John Ellerman, the millionaire shipping magnate. He always wanders about like that but when something takes his fancy no cost is too high". I swear she sulked for the next few days.

MCKENZIE TRADERS, LTD.

DIRECTORS:
J. ATKINSON.
M. WILLIAMSON.
M. K. LAWS.
M. WYETH.

39 JAMES STREET, WIGMORE STREET

LONDON, W.1.

TELEPHONE:
WELBECK 0394.

November 25th. 1946.

To Whom It May Concern.

Mr M'Kenzie-Hall has been Secretary to this
Company for the past five months. He had the

difficult task of restarting a business which
had been dormant during the war years and showed
great resourcefullness and initiative in the
undertaking.

We can confidently recommend him for any
post where integrity and unfailing courtesy are
essential.

If at any time we could answer any personal
enquiry we should be happy to do so.

McKenzie Traders Limited.

Directors.

My reference from McKenzie Traders.

While I had been in the Fleet Air Arm, I had spent quite a lot of leave in London and I had met a Bill Humphreys at a small drinking club. We became friends and as he lived in Hendon Central we used to meet in North London, frequenting Hampstead and Hampstead Heath areas, running from Swiss Cottage to Golders Green. 'Jack Straw's Castle' or 'The Spaniards' were two pubs where we were always able to meet taxi drivers and buy petrol coupons from them. Bill was a rough diamond and I always had the feeling that he trod a very narrow path in his business, which included motorcars. One day he turned up in an old, open-touring, fabric-covered Bentley. I fell in love with it and immediately asked him to sell it to me. I had an old Riley which I had picked up cheaply while at McKenzie Traders and Bill took this and £150 for, if I remember correctly, a four-litre Blue Label 1926 or 1927 Bentley tourer. I had a terrible time learning to change gear and double-declutch but the deep roar of the engine and the feel of the car was magnificent. Unfortunately bits kept falling off, my bills mounted and very reluctantly, after a short time, I sold it back to Bill.

There was one occasion, which I have felt deeply ashamed about ever since it happened. During my initial flying tour in Carlisle in 1942, I met a girl and wrote to her the whole time I was in America. I kept up with her when I returned to England but could not make up my mind whether to advance the relationship or end it. We eventually arranged that she should come down to London. I realised when I saw her that there was no future for us together. On that same day Bill arrived in another Bentley which he thought I might like and I hurriedly pushed her on the train to Carlisle with some stupid excuse of urgent business. I never saw or heard from her again. I know I must have hurt her terribly and the guilt remains with me. I liked the Bentley but I could not afford it.

It was not long after this episode that tragedy occurred. At 4.00 am, on a wintry morning, I was fast asleep at my bed-sit when there was a banging on the front door and a policeman asking whether I was the key holder to McKenzie Traders. When told, "Yes", he said, "You had better get down there, the shop is on fire and the fire brigade is trying to prevent it from catching the shop next door". I walked from Gledhow Gardens in Kensington to James Street without seeing a taxi, only to find the fire was out and the whole shop black, sodden and dripping in to a flooded cellar with all our stock destroyed or ruined.

The fire officer told me that some idiot had left the electric fire on and it had caught the curtains hanging close by. Since one of my tasks on re-opening the business had been to take out adequate fire insurance the lady directors were saddened by the incident but quite pleased by the outcome. They told me that they had been thinking for a little while that their enthusiasm for starting it up again was tending to wane since their lives were so different. The fire solved this problem and they decided not to continue. Although I was obviously to blame for the fire they never questioned that it was an oversight on closing up and backed up their decision by giving me six months' salary and their thanks for setting up the business.

After all the setbacks I had encountered since leaving the Navy, I began to see post-war England in a rather sour light. All my happy times, apart from Australia, had been abroad and there now seemed good reason for me to go overseas again.

Chapter Five

East Africa 1946–1948
and back to England

After the demise of McKenzie Traders and with the money I had been given by the Directors, I booked a passage to Mombasa with the hope that something would turn up and that, at least, I would see my parents again. The ship was the *HMT Georgic* and was still fitted out for carrying troops. It had seen extensive service in the Far East during the war and still bore wounds of close encounters. In particular it was very noticeable that the hull, although watertight, had considerable buckling on the starboard side.

The fare was a flat £80 from London to Mombasa, which I considered quite reasonable, although it ate in to my savings. I soon realised it was relatively expensive when I went aboard. The accommodation was not as bad as my wartime journey to America but one could hardly call it luxurious. Passengers were berthed in the holds in makeshift cabins of eight or ten, in tiers or bunks. Meals were taken by rota and of course there was complete separation of sexes, including families. There was no special accommodation for VIPs and the wartime feeling of togetherness still held. The journey was long, boring and uneventful except for one incident which unnerved some and amused others. One day in the Mediterranean the Captain announced a change of course. He was taking the ship to America to see his brother–in–law!! After a period of confused shock another announcement came to the effect that the Captain had been taken sick, that the First Officer had assumed command and that our next stop would be Port Said. The Captain, in the advanced stages of the DTs, was duly removed and the passengers resumed their daily tedium of guessing the days travel in knots or playing bingo. In the open sea, travelling at a reasonable speed, the wind had a cooling effect but moving at a snail's pace through the Suez Canal was truly stifling. This period, plus the Red Sea, did however acclimatize us for Africa. At last we arrived! Sailing past the entrance to Mombasa in the cool of early morning, after days of empty water, the sight of brilliant green foliage and bright golden sand with coconut palms was invigorating. All this to be capped with splashes of frangipani, oleanders, hibiscus, bougainvillea and many other bright flowers brought expectation, heightened by relief, that we were at our journeys end.

Once the ship had berthed, Customs and Immigration Officers came on board and one by one we attended for interview. In most cases it was a question of having your passport stamped, showing correct vaccination and assuring immigration of your status and destination before departing ashore. In my case it was not so easy. At that period in my life I travelled on an Australian passport. After some muttering this was stamped and then I was asked what my job was. I told them I had not arranged a job but hoped to find work as soon as possible. They were very dubious at this and asked how much money I had. When I told them truthfully that I had about £200 they closed their book and mine saying, "Without a job and without sufficient funds to maintain yourself we cannot allow you to enter Kenya". This meant a return journey to the United Kingdom when the ship turned around. I was devastated, and returned to my bunk in the depths of despair.

The passenger on the bunk above me asked what the trouble was. I had hardly spoken to him on the voyage, but I now poured out my troubles. He said he thought he may be able to help and went up on deck. A short time later he came back and said if I was to go up to Immigration again and they might prove more amenable. He was right! The same officer very kindly advised me to get a job as soon as possible and let them know when I had. When I returned to the cabin to collect my luggage my newly acquired friend had gone. I did not know his name or what he did and it saddened me that I could not thank him or ask him how he had persuaded the official.

During my first week in Mombasa I met a man called Stubbs in the bar of a hotel. During our conversation he told me he was the manager of The Old East Africa Trading Company. This firm dealt in general produce including hides and timber. When he learned I was looking for a job he enquired as to my experience. He did not think flying was appropriate to commercial work but my administrative and sales period in London showed enterprise. I may have exaggerated the importance of McKenzie Traders but he offered me a job as 'Godown' assistant. This job amounted to supervision of a very large warehouse for the receipt and despatch of various produce. What he did not tell me about were the working conditions. All the staff was either Indian or African. I spoke no Swahili and had difficulty in understanding the Indians' pronunciation of English. My second-in-command was an elderly Indian from Ceylon who ran the day-to-day routine very expertly. I was at a loss to understand why I had been employed, since my complete ignorance of the work made me almost redundant.

The heat and smell of the Godown was indescribably horrible. The incessant noise and chattering of the workers was tiring and my lack of knowledge was overwhelmingly clear to those earning a fraction of my salary. I decided to learn, from the bottom up, all aspects of the trading routine. I purchased books on drying skins, grading of timber, curing and storing of coffee, grading of ivory, packing and shipping of agricultural produce, purchase and sale of agricultural machinery and chemicals etc. My early days of intense study, when learning the various subjects required as a pilot, returned. Any time off was spent learning Swahili and studying the areas of Kenya and Tanganyika from where all the produce came [Editor's note: place names are left as they were in 1946]. Against the European accepted form of behaviour, I got my hands dirty. I helped in shade drying skins, holding down my nausea. I moved and graded timber. I weighed and packed papain (dried pawpaw milk), and sweated outside in the sun at the loading bays.

I have always tried to avoid any discussions regarding racial issues and this is not the place to begin. However, it was very obvious to me that Europeans, coming out to Africa after World War II, had very little knowledge of the Africans or their culture. They appeared to relish their feeling of racial superiority and frequently failed to appreciate the workers' view. This led to countless misunderstandings and eventually mistakes for which they were reluctant to accept blame.

By joining in with the workforce my Swahili quickly became proficient and when Stubbs suggested a period up country I jumped at the chance. My knowledge of timber had now reached the stage when I could name and identify over 30 types of tree timbers and I could grade them according to their use for, say railway sleepers, building lumber and joinery work amongst others. I also felt fairly competent in spotting diseased wood, insect attacked and flawed wood for rejection before shipment to the coast.

Whilst in Mombasa I had visited local areas of interest; Voi on the railway line to Nairobi, Kilifi and Kipiri on the coast north of Mombasa. I had not yet experienced the hugeness of East Africa and the excitement of finding new places, undergoing new experiences where only a limited number of others had been before me. It was only about 40 years since the first railways were built between Kenya and Tanganyika and not much longer than 75 years since Livingstone and Stanley had made their journeys and met in 1871.

Burton and Speke had arrived in Zanzibar in 1856 from Bombay where they were serving as army officers. They crossed over to the mainland at Bagamoga and left the following year to walk to Tabora then on to Lake Tanganyika (13 February 1858). However, they found that the water flowed into the lake and it could not, therefore, be the source of the Nile. They then returned to Tabora and, as Burton was ill, Speke set off for Mwanza (Tanganyika) on the shores of Lake Victoria, one of the largest lakes in the world. This was the source of the Nile. Much later on I travelled much of the same route and, standing at Thomson's Falls in Kenya (in 1883 Joseph Thomson, a Scottish geologist was the first European to walk from Mombasa to Lake Victoria), I marvelled at the courage and tenacity of these 19th-century explorers.

I had now served my apprenticeship in yet another field and was eager to progress in agricultural management. My new position up country was as a timber grader on the slopes of Mount Kilimanjaro. To this day this is the nearest point to heaven I shall ever get, on foot! I now had money in the bank and the opportunity to see Africa.

Tanganyika: Moshi and Arusha

I took the train from Mombasa through Voi to Moshi in Tanganyika. This territory was ruled under mandate by Britain, having previously been ruled by Germany. Moshi was a small trading town, about 2,600 feet above sea level, and it is the nearest approach to Kilimanjaro (Kibo). Strange as it may seem, this was the headquarters for my father who, as the Custodian of Enemy Property, assessed and dispersed ex-German properties throughout the area, to new settlers.

There were one or two hotels to choose from and, to begin with, having picked up my new car I took a room at the Lion Club Hotel, some two miles out of town, with a direct and magnificent view of the mountains. Having met my parents again I spent a little time travelling around the area before settling in to the routine of grading timber from the slopes of Kilimanjaro. I had much contact with the Chagga Tribe, who lived on the slopes and cultivated coffee and bananas. I now had a Chevrolet pickup, but I had no time to explore since my work kept me very busy. I saw little of my parents until I took a holiday and stayed in their bungalow. They told me that Arusha was a very pleasant town to visit, cooler than Moshi and at the foot of another mountain called Meru. I took the first opportunity to go there and, once again, sowed the seeds for another change in my life.

Travelling was either undertaken by car or on foot, since railways were almost non-existent inland. Living costs were low and time was the period between working and sleeping, when haste paid no dividends and patience led to longer life. I paid 40 shillings a month for my cook, 35 shillings for my houseboy and 25 shillings for my gardener/driver. Bread was 45 cents a pound, milk 40 cents per pint, butter two shillings and 50 cents per pound, petrol two shillings a gallon. Whisky and brandy was in the region of 20 shillings a bottle. I thought I paid rather a lot for an Electrolux refrigerator at the English

Kilimanjaro from Serengeti Plain, 1948.

equivalent of 1,000 shillings, the equivalent of £50.

Although I believe that now, well over 70 years later, there is a railway between Moshi and Arusha, during my time one either walked or drove the 52 miles between. This was over an unmade road and across a dry, dusty plain called Sanya. I have walked it in the rainy season when no vehicle could get through and I have driven across it many times during the years I was there. Huge herds of tommy gazelles and zebra, many giraffe, ostrich, some lion and leopard could be encountered, together with numerous bird life and uncomfortable insects. Arusha was a charming town and being at a higher altitude was cooler and greener than Moshi. It was here, while staying at the New Arusha Hotel, that I met Jorgen Larsen. Jorgen was Danish and had been appointed to Arusha as Director of Bovill Matheson and Company. This firm mainly dealt in agricultural produce and operated in England through R. C. Treatt and Company, at Plantation House. Fairly soon after we met he suggested that I should consider joining him as an assistant, as he was away a great deal of time, in Kenya and Uganda, and needed office continuity and local contact with farmers. I put the offer on one side at the time since I was extremely busy with timber but then, one day, I fell out with Stubbs in Mombasa and resigned. I was grateful to Stubbs for giving me the job but became increasingly upset by his dictatorial manner and bullying treatment of his Eurasian staff. It reminded me of Perrett's lack of leadership qualities. The one thing in life I have never

Bovill Matheson office, Arusha, 1948.

been able to stand is rudeness to those under one, and I have never been afraid to say so when it continues over a period of time. I left Mombasa for a week or so holiday in Nairobi and while there renewed my pilot's licence. During my stay at the Norfolk Hotel I was approached by someone whose name I no longer remember, to enquire whether I was interested in carrying out some Tsetse fly spraying for a firm called Airwork. This was to be a temporary measure to fill in while one of their pilots was sick. I agreed to fly an Anson and made several trips. I disliked it so much that after a short time I pulled out and returned to Arusha. I never heard from Airwork, and again I was never paid.

I was pleased to take up Larsen's offer as assistant and took over an office in Bovill Matheson's building in the centre of town. For the first time in a civilian job I began to enjoy the busy routine of office administration, mixed with regular visits to farmers and to various Estates under the management of the firm.

There were several other trading companies in Arusha and one in particular, Exporters' Syndicate, was in intense competition with us in the buying-in of papain. Prices varied from week to week depending on demand from America and a number of European buyers. We also traded in crops of vegetables, flower seed, pyrethrum, sisal and other commodities for shipment to Europe, in particular Hamburg, with all our orders stemming from London.

In order to maintain market prices secret we used Bentleys second phrase code for our weekly schedules and I enjoyed this side of the work. I also took over the booking agency of the Union Castle Line, which in 1946 was extremely busy. With the supervision of incoming crops and the responsibility for shipping documents, I had little time to spare for the first few months. Larsen was away a lot to begin with but eventually, with him in the office and our accountant able to relieve me of some of the work, I was able to get out and about with visits to the various farmers in the area. This is where the fun really began. Many, in fact the majority, of the farmers at the time were Greek. They averaged between 50 and 200 acres per farm and grew a variety of crops such as pyrethrum, seed beans and peas, flower seed, pawpaw, coffee or any cash crop where we could deliver them the seed and a guaranteed price for the resultant product. The Greeks were great gamblers and once money had been lost they would use anything they owned as surety for a bet. I have called on many who had lost their cars, their machinery and, in some cases, their farms. I can remember several examples where even the wives changed partners, at a price, and later returned to the farm if it still belonged to her husband. I will give one example of a typical visit. Departing Arusha early in the morning and driving some 30 miles to a farm owned by Mr Koukopulous, if in fact it was still his. It was and he met me with great civility and ushered me in to the bungalow. It was customary to accept the offer of a coffee which came, black as pitch, half filled with bitter grounds and accompanied by a dessert such as Baklava soaked in

Arusha: geographical hub of East Africa. Note the Recital of Music sign lists both Ruth Lany and Margaret Cordell as soloists – both love interests of John M'Kenzie-Hall.

syrup. When this was finished we talked business. I began by asking, "How many acres could he offer me and what condition were they in?" and "How many labourers did he have?" This was necessary because African labour was very unreliable and, depending on the tribe, sometimes worked and sometimes did not. I then offered him the seed or plants and we discussed yields and timing and contracts. This finished, there was more coffee and more Baklava to seal the deal before he either brought his wife out to meet me or showed me around his farm and labour area. One could not offend him by refusing yet another coffee and sweetmeat before driving off. A mile or so down the road I stopped the car, took out a dessertspoon, kept especially for the purpose of pushing it down my throat to dispense, in a rather sickening way, the morning's intake. However distasteful it was I had gained a contract for the current year's crop and that was business. Without a lie I underwent this procedure many times and, in one case, three times in one day.

One farm I enjoyed visiting was owned by an Englishman called Anderson. He had built himself a replica of an English cottage, complete with thatched roof. The cool interior was most welcome during the heat of the day. He grew acres of beautiful roses for their essential oils and the air around the estate was heavy with perfume.

Almost everyone in East Africa belonged to a club in their town. These were generally known as gymkhana clubs and sported tennis courts, golf courses and, in many cases, swimming pools. Of course they also offered food and drink and most days, from 4.00 pm onwards, there was a goodly company gathered to relax from the heat and work of the day. It was here in Arusha that I met my 'nemesis'. There were three members whom I will never forget. Judah Bloom, a farmer working a large farm of about 1,000 acres. A large man, bull-necked, deeply-tanned through years in the sun and one would take him, at first meeting, to be a 'thickie'. He was the opposite, softly spoken, intelligent and with enormous knowledge of bush craft and animal husbandry. He was a copious drinker. Then there was Milsom Rees, the son of a surgeon to the royal family (Sir John Milsom Rees 1866–1952). He farmed, I think, somewhat as a hobby but seemed very proficient in producing large returns. He was a copious drinker. Then there was Richard Dearden. He was also farming in a rather small way. Much of his produce was amalgamated with that from Milsom's farm at Leganaga. He was an excellent shot and spent much time in the bush. He was a copious drinker.

These three had a reputation as being tough in the 'shooting, hunting and fishing field'. I was only 23 but, in my youth, I admired this trio as well experienced and well-worn champions. It was not long before the trio became a quartet and I think they let me join them after the story of my first experience of the African Bush. I had been asked by a group of farmers, mainly South African, to join them in a guinea fowl shoot. I eagerly accepted, borrowed a shotgun, and joined them on the edge of the Serengeti Plain just before dawn. About 12 of us lined up, about 25 yards apart, and walked slowly in to the scrub bush looking for birds. Guinea fowl are no fools and when they see one coming they slowly retreat just out of range for some time before something causes them to take flight. Just in front of me I could make out about six or eight of them just keeping out of range. They stopped when I stopped and moved on in front of me when I continued. I must have quietly walked for some 200 yards when my birds vanished in to a large bush. I picked up a stone and threw it in to the foliage and was prepared to shoot as they flew out. I hardly expected the result. In the half-light I saw an enormous lion bound out of the bush straight for me. In that instant I was paralysed with fear. I never even raised the gun as it charged, swerved around me and was gone. My heart was thumping, my legs were weak and no way was I going to continue chasing those stupid birds. I returned to the road and sat in my car until the others returned with their bag. I had more or less recovered by this time and told my story with slight exaggeration as to the size of the lion. It was somewhat of a humiliation to be laughed at and told how green I was. The lion was not a lion, it was a hyena and those either side of me had witnessed the scene. They asked me why I had thrown a stone in to the bush. When I said it was to make the guinea fowl fly before I shot them they were amazed. They were not interested in the sporting instincts. The birds were for eating, why make it more difficult when you can shoot a close bunch on the ground. I can still visualise that large head, vicious teeth and harsh breathing as the poor, frightened animal rushed straight at me in his terrified state.

Following that incident I was determined to learn the rudiments of bush craft to give me the confidence needed in Africa. My three new friends, over a period, and between many 'boozy' weekend parties, took me on Safari to the middle of the Serengeti, the Masai Mara, Ngorongoro, Lake Manyara and many other areas. We hunted lion, leopard, elephant, buffalo, rhino and even hippo. In the small game field we supplied ourselves with meat from herds of Grant's or Thomson's gazelles or sometimes impala or the lesser kudu. We shot zebra for their skins and nearly killed ourselves on several occasions stalking buffalo. I also learned how to make biltong. One cut strips of meat from the rump area a couple of inches thick, peppered it and squeezed it in water and soaked it for almost an hour. One then repeated the process in warm salted water. When dried it was again treated to copious quantities of salt, well rubbed in and then hung to dry and after a couple of days it was ready to eat or kept as an emergency ration.

Scenes from the Serengeti:
Photos taken by John M'Kenzie-Hall.

As a child in Malaya I had been brought up to respect the crocodile, since our garden bordered a river in which there were a great many. Judah told me he knew of a crossing on the Pangani River, just south of Moshi, where there were quite a few and, one weekend, we motored out to see them. The water was fairly low and the mud banks seemed empty. We walked along looking for a little while and just when we were giving up we saw an enormous crocodile, half hidden by a tussock of grass. We were in direct line for his return to the river and Judah suddenly pointed down the way we had come where, solidly plodding towards us, was a rather dry and dusty rhino. Our escape route lay up a very loose earth bank but we made so much noise getting up that we disturbed the crocodile which then came crashing down the path towards the rhino who, not knowing what was going on, did the only thing he knew. He charged. We watched, fascinated, as both animals missed each other by what seemed like inches. Both disappeared, the rhino up the bank past us and the crocodile, with a splash, in to the water. We did not see another crocodile all day, but the experience was not one to have missed.

At a later date I went on safari to the Mara River where I witnessed the amazing sight of the crocodiles choosing and attacking many of the thousands of wildebeest, as they crossed the river to their grazing grounds in the Serengeti. I can now see it on television but nothing can compare with being on the spot with the smells, the heat, the noise and the cool killing that takes place amidst the pandemonium and panic of those few minutes of crossing the water.

As time went on I acquired a selection of guns. My first was a .318 Westley Richards Express, excellent for most game. I also bought a German short-barrelled .375 Mannlicher for close bush work and finally exhausted all my savings on a .375 double-barrelled Holland and Holland Magnum, powerful enough to drop any animal on four legs. After my episode with the guinea fowl I never used a shotgun again, but I did carry an ex-service Webley 45 revolver at all times, except in the towns.

It would take too long to go into my explorations but I visited Kondoa, Tabora, Dodoma, Iringa, Mwanga and Morogoro and many other towns in a country hardly yet discovered. There were a few main roads which were dirt, no electricity, little water and very occasionally, in small towns, a few Indian shops. Everywhere it was hot, dusty and smelly. If a car broke down you walked for the nearest help. This could be an hour, a day or even two days and you had to know how to survive. You were bitten by mosquitoes, ants, leeches, ticks, tsetse fly and got quite used to swarms of flies descending on the sweaty brow or neck. It was a hate-love relationship. Hate at the moment of discomfort or pain but overwhelmed by love of a country which gave so much joy and pleasure in an entirely unsophisticated and uncivilised way.

In between the network of small towns there were vast areas where various tribes, making up over five million people, scraped a living. This population was made up of over 125 different tribes, all with their own language, but most of them understanding Swahili. By this time I was fairly fluent in the language but knew little of the many tribal customs. One weekend I had gone out with a friend to the Serengeti to seek a pride of lion that had been causing some trouble to the local Masai. After walking all day and seeing nothing we returned to the Masai boma to tell them we would come again at a later date.

As we entered the village I leant my rifle against the side of a rondavel and squatted down for a rest. Out came a Masai Moran (warrior) and greeted me with enthusiasm. He then went back inside and returned with a very old and wrinkled woman. She was dressed in skins and wore multicoloured beads and bangles, and she had two acid bottle corks inserted through her earlobes. Her smell was abhorrent and, since the rondavel had no chimney, the smoke from the fire in the middle of the floor clung to her in a sort of misty haze. She was one of the wives of my host who, having seen me rest my rifle (or spear) against his hut, was honour bound to offer me one of his wives to sleep with. She had hardly any teeth and one breast was a tattered shred of skin hanging down to her waist. I was dumbfounded but knew that to refuse would be considered a tremendous slur and demeanour not only on the husband but also on the tribe. My companion hurriedly stepped in to explain that I was completely exhausted and that, although I deeply appreciated the honour, on this occasion I could not accept. I learned that this was the only excuse acceptable and never again to indicate my preference for a bed by leaning my gun against a Masai rondavel.

Of course life was not all play and entertainment. The serious part was my work and in this I did not shirk. I moved up to General Manager and started a procedure of regular reports to London on the crop position and condition of farms and reports to farmers on available remedies for many of the diseases affecting their crops. In this I liaised with the Lyamungo Research Station just outside Moshi. We also had a branch in Uganda and when Larsen could not go I happily drove in to Kenya and on to Kampala for an inspection visit. Incidentally, it was here I visited the source of the Nile at Thomson's Falls. The firm had supplied me with a Nash motorcar, which was very solid. Since there were no tarmac roads, all driving was done over corrugated earth roads at a speed sufficient for the springs to take up the shuddering of the chassis. This was between 50 and 60 miles per hour for maximum comfort. On each side of the road there would be deep monsoon ditches to take the water through the rainy seasons and for flash floods, that were a regular hazard.

After much travelling I was offered a new car. A Hudson was ready

The Masai:
Photos taken by John M'Kenzie-Hall.

The Hudson car which hit a donkey on the road from Nairobi back to the Tanganyika border.

for collection in Nairobi and I went up over a weekend to collect it. On the Monday I found the new car almost ready but it was afternoon before I started off for Arusha, a journey of some 170 miles. I thought five hours should be enough, and I had about four hours of daylight left. The tarmac road out of Nairobi finished after a short distance and I was back to the red and dusty earth. After about two hours of steady driving I was rounding a long curve when I saw, some way ahead, a Masai with a spear leaning on his shoulder holding a donkey by the head. As I approached nearer, at about 50 miles an hour, I saw the spear fall away from his shoulder. He let go of the donkey to pick it up and the donkey turned sideways across the road. There was little time to react but I had three choices. The first was to brake but, at that speed on earth, I would skid probably in to the monsoon ditches on either side of the road which were 8–10 feet deep. Secondly, I could try to drive around the donkey and almost certainly end up in the ditch, or my third choice was to hit the donkey. I put my foot fully down on the accelerator and hit the donkey square on at almost 60 miles per hour. There was an enormous bang as the poor animal exploded and the windscreen was covered in blood, fur, bone and everything contained within. I managed to stop in a straight line and, on getting out, was surprised to see the Masai footing it at a fast pace in to the distance. This was unusual as they prized their livestock above everything. I believe the event must have shocked and panicked him more than it did me. I was just furious with him and the donkey. A new car now a very much battered, second-hand wreck in the front. On survey I found both headlamps gone, bumpers gone, the radiator pushed back in to the cooling fan, water dribbling from the radiator and the beautiful Hudson radiator ornament bent backwards and spearing what looked like a rump steak. I cleaned up the mess as best I could and then considered my position. By levering the radiator away from the fan I could possibly get the engine started but, with no lights, how far would I get before dark? Apart from a first-aid kit, two bottles of orangeade, a packet of cigarettes and a revolver, I had little to help me. I decided that if the car would start and answer to the steering I had better get on as far as I could before dark. It started and steered fairly straight but at the speed I could muster I was being shaken to pieces. The radiator started boiling so, having stopped to apply Elastoplasts in layers to the leak and filled the radiator with orange juice, I proceeded for some time in a steamy orange haze. It then became too dark to see properly so I stopped again and by means of a little wire removal (somewhat violently) from the courtesy light and taping it to the split in the battered bumper, I was able to proceed at a snail's pace. This then fell off and I was left totally in the dark.

The Tanganyika border was about 10 miles ahead at a place called Namanga and, just before this, there was a rhino camp with accommodation for those wishing to observe or photograph these animals. I hoped someone would come along, since it was impossible to see to walk along the road. After several hours and the end of my cigarettes the moon started to rise above the scrub trees and I began to see the outline of the road ahead. I decided to walk, since there was very little chance of anyone coming along for hours, even days and I was stiff, hungry and a little overconfident in my new found knowledge of Africa. After about half an hour of my estimated three-hour walk I could see quite well and hear even better. Suddenly I heard a typical rusty snort of rhino and I thought I saw a shadow or two a little way ahead of me, in the centre of the road. My immediate reaction was to slide down in to the monsoon ditch on my right where I thought they would never go. I was right in that assumption since there was so much debris in the bottom that I could hardly move, so I climbed up the other side, believing myself safe with a gulf between us. I was wrong of course. They were not in the road at all but some 20 yards on my right but, very fortunately, had not scented, sighted or heard me. Since I did not know where any others might be I played safe and headed for the nearest tree. This happened to be an acacia thorn tree which was rather nasty, but it had a branch that enabled me to lodge about 10 feet above the ground. I spent about two hours taking out thorns and being stung by savage safari ants before the risen moon and clear sky showed me that the rhino family had moved on and I was able to do the same. I arrived at

Kibo, a peak of Kilimanjaro at 5,895 metres/19,341 feet.

the camp some time before dawn to find no one about and the only available furniture on which to collapse was a slightly worn and forlorn wicker chair with three legs. Later that morning I persuaded an Indian lorry driver to take me back to the car which, by then, showed that copious dung had been used by a herd of elephant to play 'ring-a-rosy, let's plop down'.

To my amazement and joy, the insurance company in Nairobi accepted my claim, collected the car and in a couple of weeks I flew up to collect and enjoy an uneventful drive back to Arusha.

By now I was a fully accepted member of the 'quartet' but found that my capacity for alcohol was far short of the others who, through experience, could down large quantities and still appear normal and capable. This was brought home to me in no uncertain manner. One night, having left the party to drive home, I woke up in the car some way off the main road with engine running, headlights full on and the car's nose in a bush. On sobering up I felt it was time to take my leave and turn the 'quartet' back in to a 'trio'. There was no ill feeling from the others and we remained friends for the rest of my time in Tanganyika. It was also a time to change from hunting to something equally testing and this turned out to be Mount Kilimanjaro.

Climbing Mount Kilimanjaro

The highest mountain in Africa at 19,341 feet and joined by a saddle to the smaller, rough peak of Mawenzi. This is not a mountainous climb. It is a steady climb up and back of five or six days. I joined the Mountain Club of East Africa for information and advice.

There are five huts stationed at intervals up the mountain. 'Johannes' and 'Bismarck' at 9,000 feet, 'Peters' (two huts) at about 12,000 feet and 'Kibo' at 17,000 feet. There are two routes one can take to begin the ascent. One can start from Old Moshi and walk through the rain forest for some four hours to reach 'Johannes' hut. The night is then spent here, and it is needed since it is a very steep climb, although more direct than the alternative.

The second route starts at Moshi and a drive of some 30 miles to the lower slopes of the mountain, past the farm of Major Russell and on to the Marangu Guest House or the Kibo Hotel. On my many climbs I always used the Marangu Guest House. I had a special purpose for doing this and for good reason. The Hotel was owned by the Lany Family and I fell madly in love with their daughter Ruth. It never came to anything as I will describe later, but to this day I look at her photograph and regret my loss. From Marangu one walks through the rain forest for some few hours before reaching 'Bismarck Hut'. Another four hours to 'Peters Hut'. After a day of acclimatisation one climbs for about five hours to 'Kibo Hut'.

On the way to the first two huts, through the rain forest, one is aware of all the sounds of invisible animals and birds. Sometimes one hears the calls of elephant and regularly that of monkeys and birds. The crashing of undergrowth as something rushes away can be quite unnerving at first, until one realises that, whatever it was, it was more frightened than you. When one breaks out of the forest in to the beginning of coarse moorland, where the soggy ground and humps of marsh grass vie with flowers and exotic plants, one has a view for the first time of the mountain and over the plains far below.

Between the first and second huts, the walk to 'Kibo Hut' is strenuous – more soggy moorland and the beginning of loose scree, lack of vegetation and much panting up to the saddle. One night there and then the final climb to the peak, over deeper scree and up a steeper slope. Breathing is harder and harder for the four hours it takes to reach Johannes Notch. This is the crater edge and you have reached the top, or almost. The actual summit is a little further on at Kaiser Wilhelm Spitze. One can keep walking around the rim to several other points with magnificent views and some have local histories, like the frozen leopard in a block of ice. After having looked down in to the crater, seen Ratzel Glacier, it is time to return to Peters Hut for the last night. After having paid off the guides and porters it remains to drive home with 'Kibo' shimmering

The Boma: administrative headquarters, court, police station and prison.

behind one. I forgot to mention that the snow begins first above the saddle and can vary considerably in quantity and cloud can bring the temperature down considerably, together with visibility. Of the five times I have climbed 'Kibo', only once have I been treated to bad weather, and then I sheltered for a while in some caves called Hans Meyer Caves, which had been used by climbers for many years when Germany occupied Tanganyika.

Although I was now considered capable of managing a branch of Bovill Matheson I had little, if any, experience of the day-to-day running of any of the estates that came under our general management. One of these was at Nduruma and comprised a fairly large acreage of coffee. The manager was taken very ill, just as the crop was ready for picking. This is one of the busiest times of the year, and it involves a large labour force. Larsen asked me to take temporary charge until a replacement could be found. The East African Groundnut Scheme had recently started and I shall describe this in some detail later. I found on my first day at the estate that there seemed very little labour at muster time. Word had spread about that the 'ground-nutters' (as we called them), had offered twice as much as we paid and half my labour force had gone over to them. This was a calamity as I had very limited time to get the crop in. In desperation I gathered all the muscle men I could find, loaded them into lorries. With little ceremony, I drove around all the villages in the area conscripting men and women (plus a bribe or two) for the period of time it took to harvest the coffee. Of course I ran into a little trouble with the District Officer and was called to the 'Boma' (area headquarters) to explain my actions.

The Boma was a whitewashed fort-like building that served as the administrative headquarters, court, police station and prison. It happened to be particularly interesting since it was here that the Germans surrendered to General

Smuts in 1916. The British had divided Tanganyika into eight provinces run by Provisional Commissioners (PCs) reporting to the Governor and into 56 districts under District Commissioners (DCs). The day I arrived there was intense activity with everyone in their best uniforms and whitewash being splashed about on walls and stones and anything else that looked as if it needed to stand to attention. It seemed the arrival of the Provincial Commissioner was due at any minute. The District Officer was tied up with the District Commissioner and everyone was too busy to attend to me. I was asked to wait in a small room until 'God' had gone on his inspection tour. I was standing in the doorway, trying to keep cool, when the big man arrived to survey his domain. As he entered the main archway of the fort he saw me and I saw him clearly. He ignored the others and came straight over to me. It was my co-passenger on the *Georgic*, who had obviously pulled rank and authorised my entry in to Kenya. His name was Tim Revington and he was delighted to hear of my position with Bovill Matheson. He thought Larsen had made a good choice. When I mentioned my purpose of visiting the District Office he admitted that the ground-nutters were wreaking havoc in all their operating areas and complimented (or almost) me on my initiative, but cautioned me not to use such methods too frequently. I never heard another word from the District Officer. However, from then on I was always treated with the greatest respect by all the Boma, and I met Tim from time to time.

One day when I was in Nairobi on business I met a Colonel Grogan in the Torrs Hotel and we got talking about big-game hunting techniques. Despite

Torrs Hotel, Nairobi, where I met Colonel Grogan.

an age difference – I was 24 years old while he must have been well over 70 – he enthralled me with his knowledge of Africa and he was interested to hear of my roaming the Serengeti and Masai. This meeting resulted in an invitation to one of his farms at Taveta, where he was building a new house. This site was on an ancient steam jet or, to be more accurate, a miniature extinct volcano that had erupted millions of years ago and then given up the ghost. It sat in the middle of a plain and towered to about 100 feet. A road which had been made to encircle it to the top had been cut off to make a base for foundations. A fairly modern concrete structure had been built with a tower rising above the walls. Enormous wrought iron gates of intricate design had been made in Italy and shipped out. As they swung open, above a flight of steps, the layout of an indoor expanse of garden could be seen. The building divided in to two circular blocks studded with wide and high 'D-shaped' windows. The windows of one wing had glass, the other a series of round ceramic cylinders that shaded the sunlight but were otherwise wide open to the elements. This was Colonel Grogan's wing and, according to his spartan tastes, his bed was a flat block rather like a mortuary slab. On entering the building from the garden one was taken aback by a highly polished, dark wood floor covered in a number of beautiful and priceless Persian rugs. Equally rich, carved doors opened into various rooms until the main door into the drawing room was reached. The size of the room, which was under the tower, could be judged by the high ceiling, which had been supported by beams that had been the main spars for the wings of a Sunderland Flying Boat. These supports all came together in a central column that in its turn, just above the floor, was surrounded by a highly polished table that had been a sisal corona wheel in one of his factories.

From all windows and the towers, game could be spotted through the conveniently placed telescopes. The guest wing had all the necessary amenities, including a comfortable bar, but the dining room was spectacular, if laughable. In the centre was a circular dining table which, in size, was a giant compared to the one in the drawing room. Its diameter was all of 12–14 feet and every inch was inlaid with a thick veneer of all the various African woods. I gave up after identifying 30 of them. The table was highly polished to a glass-like finish. There was, however, one fault. The various cruets, in silver and wood, were set in the centre. If a guest asked for the salt it was impossible either to reach for it in the centre or pass it on except round the table from hand to hand, if there were sufficient guests. The problem was solved, however, by a number of servants who seemed to read one's mind and appeared with the correct ingredient. I suggested a rotating centre or even a miniature railway but I do not believe the Colonel had ever dined in the room

The extravagant mansion built by
Colonel Grogan on his farm at Taveta.

Mt Meru.

with his guests, as he preferred to remain in his own quarters. I was able to photograph almost every aspect of this remarkable house and enjoyed many chats while he walked me off my feet. I felt privileged to have met and talked to such a legend of a man and, in addition, to secure some of his business.

In later years I learned more of this legendary figure through a book by Edward Paice, called *Lost Lion of Empire* (published 2001). Grogan had become famous in 1898 by walking from Cape to Cairo. During the incredible trek he had bought some swamp land in Kenya and this was eventually to become Nairobi. His development of a number of agricultural estates, including sisal and coffee, made him several fortunes and he was deeply involved in the political build up and future of Nairobi.

There was a much smaller mountain than Kilimanjaro just outside Arusha called Meru and on its slopes there was a farm called Olkokola Syndicate. This belonged to a Mrs Rydon and she contacted me with her idea of planting pyrethrum. It was ideal for the purpose and in time it was producing well. Gladys Rydon (or as she was generally known, Margot), had a lovely house surrounded by verandas on the edge of one of the blow-out sides of Meru's crater. Her house looked straight down on to the extinct volcanic crater lake called Duluti. I have swum there many times and stories have it that it is almost bottomless. It is deep and icy cold. From a boat one day I dropped a leaded weight the extent of many rolls of hemp rope and it never touched the bottom.

View from Gladys Rydon's terrace overlooking Lake Duluti.

Gladys was old enough to be my mother but we became great friends and I was a constant visitor. She was a marvellous hostess and internationally known for her hospitality towards VIPs visiting Africa. She used to use me to take her guests on safaris and watch game, or explore the fauna and flora around Meru, or visit Lake Manyara to see the flamingos, or look at the hot springs at Moji Moto. One of the guests I found interesting, but with a rather strange habit, was Ferguson, the tractor king. He asked innumerable questions and was never without a notebook in which he seemed to write down every word said. I kept fairly quiet about tractors, since I was using and selling his rivals Massey Harris. Another guest was Sir Geoffrey De Havilland. We got on very well, especially when I told him I knew his son while I was at Heston (now part of Heathrow) and had had many lunches with him and Alex Henshaw at the Comet on the Great North Road. He was a keen photographer, better than an amateur, and I enjoyed taking him to a rhino hide. He took some excellent photographs and we got the scare of our lives when one of the rhinos came too close, decided to charge and then changed its mind and lost interest in us.

When Elspeth Huxley (1907–1997) paid a visit to Margot I showed her around Lake Manyara, on to Mbulu and up to Oldeani. I have since read all her books on Africa, which are so wonderfully detailed on the flora and fauna. No one can better describe the life and adversities of the white man in Kenya. I very nearly met her wonderful mother, Eleanor/Nellie, who continued farming in

Lake Manyara.

Kenya until a great age and then proceeded to start again in Portugal. Mr. Bovill was coming to Nairobi on business, and he wanted me to deliver a package, which was either bulbs or eggs, to Elspeth's mother. Unfortunately I was unable to get away, and I missed the chance of meeting her.

My favourite hunting ground had been around Lake Manyara, towards the Rift. I never saw anybody else there and game was prolific. Like so many pursuits one can over do it and lose interest. To a certain extent this happened to me and I began to do little shooting but much stalking and photography. I wish I had had my camera with me one day when I visited Olkokola Syndicate. The Manager, an ex guardsman named Hamilton, asked me to stay the night and it turned out to be very exciting in two respects. In the afternoon we were walking around an area of pyrethrum, which bordered on the rain forest, and we heard this peculiar plomping, slithering sound with soft elephant trumpeting. We quietly approached a steep slope and, peering through the branches, we saw a small herd of elephants on a mudslide. They were like small children climbing up on one side, sitting down on their back legs and sliding with great joy down to the bottom. We watched for some time when, like children, they tired of the sport and wandered off. I have never seen this again but I believe it had been observed by others. The next incident occurred that evening. It gets very cold at night on the mountain and we were sitting before a roaring log fire with a bottle between us, when the horses began to make restless noises. Hamilton said it was probably a prowling leopard but not to worry since the horses were well stabled. The noise kept on and we decided to investigate. He took a rifle and I the Webley, which I was seldom without. We left the bungalow for the stables, he went one way round, I went the other. As I passed a tree something made me shine the torch up in to the branches and I just saw a leopard, with shining green eyes, starting to leap. I couldn't miss at that range and put two .45' in to him before he fell at my feet. I kept the skin for some years before putting it in to a London auction house. I do not think my reactions are so fast now, some 70 years later.

This was the last cat I shot and for a very good reason. I was itching to fly again and since we had a little grass airfield and a wooden hut just outside Arusha, I thought of buying a light aircraft. Although I was doing quite well I still could not afford one. I went to discuss the problem with the Manager of the Standard Bank of East Africa, by the name of Gardener. We reached a compromise in which I would endeavour to sell some land he had in Moshi and he would lend me half of what I needed to buy an aircraft. The other half came with great sacrifice. I sold my Holland and Holland double barrelled Magnum rifle to a visiting American for a far greater figure than I paid for it and added my meagre savings to make up the balance.

The only aircraft I could afford was a fairly old high-wing Fairchild Argus with a Lycoming engine. This gave admirable downward visibility and was easy to fly. It had one very annoying feature however, that took some getting used to. The throttle was a push-pull knob, situated on the instrument panel. Conventional throttles are usually on the pilots left and are pushed forward to increase the power and backwards to decrease power. This silly little knob operated in reverse and pulled out to increase power and pushed in to decrease power. The first few hours proved quite novel when instinctively closing the throttle for touchdown I took off again with a roar. Once I got the hang of it, I began using my spare time to see further areas of the country. On one occasion I scared myself to death by flying too low over the crater of Kilimanjaro. I had gone to see whether I could spot any other easy ways to climb up the west side and became fascinated by looking down in to the bottom of the carter cone. I did not realise the strength of the downdraft on such a small aircraft until I found myself going down with insufficient power to climb over the lip. By pushing the nose down, turning steeply inside the cone and using slightly more than permitted full power I was able to spiral upwards and slip over the lowest edge of the crater wall. I never tried it again, but with my later experience of helicopters I would dearly love to have another attempt, if only I could drop off a few years.

My new toy worked well and by minor servicing it myself I was able to afford to run it. I flew to Nairobi for the major service and C of A (Certificate of Airworthiness) but apart from one forced landing, due to a blocked fuel line, I never had any trouble. I did a little instructing and quite a few trips with passengers. Two flights in particular come to mind. The first was when I offered to take up several of the Chagga tribe that I had met during my expeditions to Kibo. They were fine on takeoff, when flying straight and level and looking out and chatting about the sights below. However, directly I banked in a turn they became terrified. Hands over their eyes, crouched forward and moaning as if they were about to fall out of the sky. Directly I straightened up again they returned to normal and began enjoying the sights again. None was sick but I think that half hour added something to their lives they will be unable to forget.

The Tanganyika groundnut scheme:
'The worst fiasco in recent British colonial history' (1947–1952).

The other flight I remember well was part of the sorry story of the Groundnut Scheme. Some years after the First World War, an area known as Kongwa was surveyed and a vast underground supply of water was recorded. Nothing came of all this and somewhere in Whitehall the documents must have gathered dust.

After the Second World War an enormous scheme was thought up by the British Government to help solve the world shortage of vegetable oil. They envisaged a colossal scheme covering Kenya, Tanganyika and Northern Rhodesia of some 3,120,000 acres divided into units of 30,000 acres and on virgin land. This was for the production of groundnuts. We heard that they proposed to start at Kongwa and then go on to Urambo and Lindi, using Mikindani or Mtwana Bay as their harbour for off-loading machinery.

There was much local talk by farmers of the stupidity of embarking on such a huge campaign, especially since it was intended to recruit most of the supervisory staff in the United Kingdom. Absolutely no notice was taken of local knowledge and, when a consortium of farmers put up a paper showing that they could supply a fairly large acreage as a pump-priming exercise to prove the viability of the scheme, they were ignored.

I could write a book about the ignorance and stupidity of those managing the scheme, however, a few instances will indicate how it all went wrong. The research stations at Lyamungo (coffee), Milinganu (sisal) and Amani (fundamental research in to agriculture) all had contributions to make but were either overruled or ignored. It soon became evident that the water previously found at Kongwa had dried up and immense sums were spent in piping water for irrigation and drinking.

Raw recruits were brought out from England and housed in inadequate tin boxes without proper lighting, cooling or furniture. It was boiling hot during the day and freezing cold at night. There was a strict hierarchy of rank between those administrators and field workers and very few could speak Swahili.

Hundreds of tractors were shipped in to clear the bush. Farmers throughout the country suddenly found their trained tractor drivers deserting them for the ridiculously high wages offered to them at Kongwa. Like a vacuum cleaner working at full strength, other native labour began to be drawn to the south, leaving at risk crops that were the lifeblood of local farms and estates. Then the fun really began. The tractors used had been supplied with brass bushes and, due to the fine volcanic soil, had rapidly been ground to pulp. By the time new spares arrived many of the tractors had rusted or surreptitiously disappeared in to Indian hands. The tractors had tried to clear the land in the conventional manner and failed.

It had long been known that the most effective way to do this was the use of chain. When this was finally recognised large quantity of chain was ordered. For some administrative reason these large parcels of chain were left on the quayside and when at last they were ordered to be sent up country, most of them had been stolen. African labour, which had been drawn away from farmers by high wages, started to drift away. They returned to their little patches of land supplied by the farmers and, since they now had enough money, they would not work for anyone until the money ran out. Because of this wages policy everyone lost out and the pressure for increased pay began to infiltrate throughout the territory.

As matters went from bad to worse it was decided that Unilever should take over and they sent out one of their Directors, Sir Leslie Plummer. On his visit to Arusha I flew him over some of the areas where he could see huge tracts of wonderful, fertile ground where thousands of acres of groundnuts could be successfully grown, with local labour and expert supervision, but this was all to no avail. The only advantage I could see of this whole scheme was that it mopped up ex-servicemen who could not get jobs in England. It helped build a good deep-water harbour at Mikindani and it kept the Indian population supplied with free materials for years to come. All this time, they were burning groundnuts in Southern Rhodesia because they could not find a market.

A Horrible Task – Culling

One day the Veterinary Department rang me up and said that they had identified a bad case of rinderpest in a herd of zebra and wildebeest. These animals were a danger to the grazing Masai cattle, which could be infected. Would I join some other volunteers in a cull? I readily agreed and six of us set off for the migrating herd. As migration goes in the Serengeti, this was a small group numbering somewhere in the figure of 3,000 animals of hundreds of thousands already some way ahead. With one rifle to each lorry, we strapped ourselves to the front wing and the six lorries started off in line abreast. We shot all morning until our guns were almost too hot to hold. The herd had, by this time, split up and we each followed a smaller and smaller number until they were all either killed or dispersed to an extent where the lions or leopards would kill them off. By late afternoon the whole area was awash with vultures and, as we left, the hyenas were beginning to battle with them. It was a horrible task, but a necessary control.

Marriage and Return to England

It was now 1947. I was 24 years old and, since leaving England, I had concentrated on everything except my love life. I kept seeing Ruth Lany but, although we enjoyed each other's company, it was obvious that she did not return my feelings and, at that age, one does not hang about. At least I did not! I am not a very

Canon and Mrs Cordell, Margaret's parents.

good churchgoer, although I have a strong belief. My childhood Australian experience of attending church four times on a Sunday, wearing starched white collars and listening to uninspiring sermons, led me to driving quickly past churches or crossing to the other side of the road when seeing a clerical collar. Arusha had a little church and an Australian canon as an incumbent. He also had a wife who was to put it mildly a 'Big Bertha' both in manner and in size. I steered well clear until one day their youngest daughter, Margaret, arrived from Australia having just finished at music school in Sydney.

She was pretty, petite, intelligent and just 20. We met on several occasions and found we had a lot in common, except her mother. I imagine the reputation I had gained as a drinking companion of Judah Bloom and company had filtered through in such a small community. This, added to the fact that I never attended church, made me appear the very antithesis of someone her daughter should cultivate. However, I could not get across the fact that my alcoholic excesses were now over and that my actions had almost all been caused by wanting to keep up with what I considered were real men. As we continued to meet, so the hostility to me increased, to the extent that it affected Margaret. She was told not to see me again and when she disobeyed was, on one occasion, locked in her room. I went to see Canon Cordell to see if I could show him what a really nice chap I was underneath the veneer. I was not the hard living, hard drinking person I was rumoured to be and the short period when I had 'gone off the rails' was part of my 'apprenticeship in Africa'. He appeared to understand and I thought I had squared the issue. 'Big Bertha' must have intervened, however, for when I saw Margaret again she told me that she had been threatened with excommunication if she continued a relationship with me. This was more than I could take so, with Margaret's agreement, I told Canon Cordell in quite cool but in no uncertain words that I was prepared to book passages on a Union Castle line to England for Margaret and myself where we would get married. I think Cordell must have over-ruled his wife for, after a little while, they reluctantly agreed that I should marry Margaret in Arusha church. There was a funny twist to all this which I will come to later.

While all these boy and girl problems were being enacted I was still working very hard and, apart from my flying, I had dropped almost all the other activities which I had previously enjoyed. I had come across a young farmer on one of my visits who desperately wanted to learn to fly and have his own aircraft so I added him to my list for weekend instruction. His name was Lloyd, which I could never understand since he was meant to be of Russian birth. After several hours flying I came to the conclusion that he was too erratic to be a good pilot and his co-ordination was poor. He wanted to persist, however, and so we soldiered on, without much improvement, up to the time

Margaret Cordell.

Lloyd's Bren-gun carrier, later abandoned in attempt to go up Kilimanjaro.

I left Africa. My last words to him were not to try and go solo without further instruction and to join a flying club for some time before he considered buying an aircraft. I heard, some considerable time later, that he bought an aircraft, had managed to go solo, built up a reputation in Arusha as the 'Aeroplane King' and then killed himself during a landing. Shortly after I first met him he bought a tracked Bren-gun carrier and, having fixed a solid wooden support for cameras, we used to cruise out over the Serengeti chasing game of all sorts. He then had the hair-brained idea of climbing Kilimanjaro in it. The expedition is another long story, but the outcome was that the carrier made it to the snow line, got bogged down in scree and its rusty hulk is probably still there to this day.

When I first joined Bovill Matheson and Company I was given a bungalow some distance outside the town. This was small, with a sitting room, bedroom, kitchen and veranda. It was constructed of local mud and daub with a corrugated tin roof. There was no water, no electricity and had not been lived in for some time. It did have a magnificent view of the countryside and Mount Meru and this alone was in its favour. I had taken on one African who said he could cook and would look after the necessities of bringing water, food, paraffin etc. In the beginning the water always ran out prematurely, the food was awful and all the oil lamps smoked continuously. The only animals that seemed to like living in the bungalow were fruit bats which, as darkness came, descended in their thousands. I used to sit on the veranda with a sun-downer in one hand and a tennis racket in the other trying to protect my home. In one night I must have swatted 60 or 70 that would never join their mates. This problem ended in due course when they learned they were not wanted. My African cook's food improved and I gradually settled in to a bachelor existence. Three things then occurred, in fairly rapid succession. I was reading a book one night, in the sitting room by the dim oil lamp, when I heard a funny noise. It was like a soft plopping and seemed to come from a corner behind the table. All windows and doors were tightly shut against the myriads of insect life and I first though that something had come in during the day. This could have been anything, from an animal to a snake. I picked up the lamp and, as it lit up the table, I saw the whole wall behind it had collapsed forward in a heaving, wiggling mass of white ants. The mound must have been a foot high and was now flattening as it seeped or crawled across the floor. I yelled for the cook, who was not there, and, grabbing what I could, I decanted to the car and to the Arusha Hotel for the night. Next day I returned with a 'fundi' (carpenter) who, being a man of all trades, shovelled and brushed the white ants in to a pit of fire, re-mudded the wall, whitewashed it and repaired much of the table. Having thrown a lot of half-eaten material away I again settled in, not expecting further disturbances, but I had not counted on the cook.

One evening he asked me if he could go to the local village where there was a gathering for a wedding. After supper I went to bed and was awakened by the cook standing by my bed, his hand over his eye, moaning, "Bwana, Bwana, Shauri, Ku Piga", "Sir, sir, bad hit". I thought, stupid man, he had been in a punch up. When he removed his hand, his eye fell out and hung alongside his nose. There was a long *panga* slash across his cheek to his forehead but, oddly enough, not a lot of blood. The poor chap, before waking me up, had made me a cup of tea to soften what he thought would be my wrath. I rushed him to the local hospital where the duty doctor took him in for what I thought would be a major operation. The dispute had been caused by too much *pombi* (local beer) and over a woman. I was vastly surprised next morning to find my cook had had his eye removed and, bandaged up, he had walked back to prepare and cook my breakfast. This drama had only just occurred when I was called away for a few days. When I returned to the bungalow there was a scene of carnage. Safari ants had massed and, on their way to find another nest, had passed around, through and over the bungalow. The cook, who had rescued what he thought he could of my possessions, said the trail was solid at ten feet across and stretched far out of the garden in to the adjoining *shamba* (native farm). The house had literally been enveloped and everything eatable had been devoured. I left with no regrets and rented a lovely little bungalow right in Arusha, with all mod cons. I also, for the first time, hired myself a full staff. My cook came but did not stay long and, in addition, I had a houseboy and a gardener/driver.

I always had lunch in the New Arusha Hotel when I was not on safari and it gave me the opportunity to meet many people passing through. In particular I made friends with Dr Louis Leakey (1903–1972) and his wife who were paleoanthropologists. They were working in Tanganyika and Kenya and had made major discoveries around Lake Victoria. Mary Leakey (1913–1996) shot to fame in 1959 when she found the skull of a 1.7-million-year-old hominid (*Zinjanthropus*). Their son, Richard Leakey, grew up to also be a palaeoanthropologist, a politician in Kenya and general secretary of the South Africa party. I can only remember him as a small inquisitive little boy with bright eyes, and frequently a dirty face.

Another character was a Canadian geologist called Williamson (John Williamson 1907–1958), who came in occasionally and tended to support the bar. He was shabbily dressed and rather morose. I nevertheless befriended him, and I bought many rounds. He borrowed 100 shillings from me on the last time I saw him and I thought no more about it, or him, until one day I read that in 1940, some six years before I met him, he had discovered a diamond pipe which had surfaced in Mwadui. He was literally picking up stones off the surface and was reputed to have become a millionaire overnight. Having achieved his lifetime's ambition he proceeded to drink himself to death and eventually the Government and De Beers became the owner and beneficiary of his find for £4 million. The Williamson diamond mine at Mwadui, outside Shinyanga, is just one of the many mines in Tanganyika operating for gold, mica, iron ore, vermiculite, tungsten, nickel, platinum etc. I greatly regret that none of it rubbed off on me.

One Sunday I took Margaret out for a drive to a fairly high ridge on Mt. Meru and from there we walked to a lovely waterfall cascading down from the rain forest. I had with me a gold chain to which was attached a family heirloom. It was a gold seal made up as a belt and buckle around a stone, which on one side had my mother's family crest and on the other the coat of arms. I have no idea where I lost it, but I searched on several further visits without success. I wonder who will find it and what story will be attached to its loss? My mother never learned of its demise as I did not want to upset her.

I saw my parents in Moshi from time to time and had been ticked off on a number of occasions by my father, who had obviously heard of some of my party excesses. He did not think his job as a senior government official would be jeopardized by my behaviour, but he was very pleased when I changed my ways. Their reaction to the news of my engagement to Margaret was not one of delight however.

There was one adventure I wanted to undertake before my marriage and I had been trying to get information about the wheres and why-fors for some time. I had heard, from several sources, that down in the South, somewhere along the Ruvuma River which borders Portuguese East Africa, there were a herd of pygmy elephants. I had only shot one elephant and had no stomach to shoot another. I did want to be the first to photograph miniature elephants if they existed and, besides which, this was an area I had never visited. A friend of mine, Terry Egon, who was a policeman, agreed to accompany me and took his annual leave for the purpose. Our plans were almost set when I read in the paper that the crisis in Berlin, because of the Russian isolation policy, could lead to another world war. I also read that Air Marshal Tedder had called for ex-pilots to rejoin, in case of early trouble. I rang headquarters RAF in Nairobi and learnt that an airlift of food and supplies was about to begin from England to Berlin. The seriousness of the situation seemed overwhelming to us, living so far away and with little up-to-date news. I wrote to Nairobi and volunteered to rejoin the Royal Air Force. Nothing seemed more important. The elephants would remain small, if they existed, and my marriage could be brought forward and Margaret and I could escape the clutches of her family. So my last planned adventure did not mature and what was to follow did not exactly please me either.

The day of our marriage was hot and I was both despondent and nervous. I was despondent, since I had sold my aircraft and resigned from Bovill Matheson. I kept my promise to Mr Gardener, the bank manager, by buying his piece of land from him, since I thought I might return and build myself a house. My policeman friend, Terry, had agreed to be my 'best man' and, in return, I had given him my .318 Wesley Richards express rifle. I had the prospect of a wife but very little else and not a clue about the future.

I turned up at the church too early and kicked my heels in whatever shade I could find until I joined Terry and went in. The congregation seemed to be made up only of women. I thought all the men were working, or too frightened to attend. I really cannot remember the ceremony but I can remember the reception in the Cordell's bungalow afterwards. Again all women and practically none of whom I knew. The servants, under the eye of my new mother-in-law, served lemonade and tea. It was so hot that the beetroot sandwiches were dripping blood red on to the floor and splashing on a number of limp white dresses. After saying a few words of thanks, Margaret and I fled to the car, in which was sitting my best man. He drove us around several corners, out of sight and sound of the church, where a gathering of my friends and their wives gave us a riotous party and saw us off to Moshi, where our train was due to depart for Mombasa the next day.

My parents had gone on holiday but had left their bungalow and servants

R. C. TREATT & CO., LIMITED.

EAST AFRICAN MERCHANTS.

CORRESPONDENTS FOR
BOVILL MATHESON & CO., LIMITED.
KENYA, UGANDA & TANGANYIKA.

TELEPHONE:
MANSION HOUSE 7471.
TELEGRAMS:
"TREATT, FEN, LONDON".
CABLES:
TREATT, LONDON.

PLANTATION HOUSE,
FENCHURCH STREET,
LONDON, E.C.3.

16th February 1949.

Dear M'Kenzie Hall,

      I have just received a copy of your letter
addressed to B.M. & Co., dated the 31st January, and
write to tell you how sorry I am to hear you are
leaving us. At the same time, I wish to congratu-
late you on the line you have decided to take, which,
I am sure all will feel with me, does you great credit.
In going back to the Royal Air Force, you are un-
questionably doing your duty, and you will carry with
you my very best wishes for your future.

      You have had, I know, a pretty tough time
down at Arusha, and I am sure you will be greatly
missed.

      Wishing you the best of luck,

      I remain,

      Yours sincerely,

      EwBovill

J. M'Kenzie Hall, Esq.,
P.O. Box 36,
Arusha,
Tanganyika Territory.

*ABOVE: Letter from Mr
Bovill of Bovill Matheson
on rejoining the RAF.*

NORTHERN PROVINCE

Ref.No.C.36/1/

DISTRICT OFFICE
ARUSHA

6th April, 1948.

Dear M'Kenzie Hall,

      I am most grateful to you for the great
assistance you gave me as an Enumerator during the
period of the Non-Native Census held in February.
Your valuable work is also much appreciated by
Government.

      Yours sincerely,

      DISTRICT COMMISSIONER
      ARUSHA DISTRICT.

JSH/DZA.

*RIGHT: Letter of thanks
for assistance in non-
native census of 1948.*

for us that night. I never understood the reason behind why my parents did not attend the wedding. If they objected to Margaret they never told me. I know my father did not care for my father-in-law but that was not sufficient excuse. By the time I saw them again in England my father was terminally ill and the question was never raised. I shall now never know but occasionally the thought comes back to me – Why? Why?

Jorgen Larsen had loaned us his car and driver since I had relinquished my faithful Hudson and next morning, having delivered us to the railway station, I saw him off on his return journey. We made ourselves comfortable in one of the compartments and waited for the train to move. Just before this happened I suddenly saw Mrs Cordell coming up the platform, waddling and panting as if she had run all the way from Arusha. As the train started to move, Margaret pulled her head back from the window and sat down. Suddenly there was a 'tap, tap' on the window and, as the train gathered speed and thankfully left her trailing, I heard her repeat the words, "Don't let him give you a drink. Don't let him give you a drink". What a send off!

Apart from my in-laws, I was sad to leave Africa, even though I hoped to return. The hot days and cool nights, the sun-downer as the moon rose, magnifying and highlighting the distant snows on Kilimanjaro. The monotonous African drums intermingled with the croaks of bull frogs, incessant hum from insects and, now and then, the faint call of the larger animals staying well clear of town or camp. I had achieved a little, learned a lot and, even though at the time I did not realise it, I had grown up.

Harold Macmillan's wind of change was beginning to blow and political interference was already causing rumbles of unrest among the Africans who had sampled some of the best and worst of our western civilisations. Militant tribalism, under the guise of independence, was beginning to be felt everywhere except in the very isolated regions. The slow and sure steps that had been taken over the years by successive colonial administrators to educate, sustain and govern, were short-circuited by post-war politicians and newly created administrators, who believed that equality and freedom could be introduced overnight. We reckoned that it would take at least 50 years and, as I write this, it is now over that period and there is little to be proud of. We have pumped money in, most of which has been ill spent, stolen or used to create miniature armies with which to continue tribal battles. The vast natural resources of Africa, with exceptions, have ended up in the hands of a few mega-rich citizens by exploitation and corruption, creating a civilised way of life for an elite governing class but, by doing so, has, one by one, ruined their country's economy, ruined the agricultural potential to feed their own people and killed off the ability to sustain industries or businesses necessary to remove them from the third-world category. The West has poured billions of pounds of aid in to

Africa without adequate supervision or control. In the last 50 years the standard of living for most people in the world has improved on every continent except Africa. Superficial results can easily be seen in lavish new buildings, skyscrapers, expensive business life-styles, fancy cars. The egos of their heads of state demand total luxury, with no expense spared, yet poverty, starvation and disease increase in ever more serious ways through the urban areas and city fringes. Most of their economies are boosted by the tourist trade, on which many countries are now becoming dependent. I expect we, in our new found shame of colonial rule, will pour many more billions of the world's money in to funding more weapons, bigger armies, supporting bigger and more repressive dictatorships, creating many more Swiss bank accounts for corrupt politicians and driving successive countries to the verge of bankruptcy. Nigeria? Zimbabwe? Kenya? Uganda? Angola? And so on. I think I was probably right leaving as Mau Mau began. What a shame and terrible indictment on the 20th century as misrule, corruption and disintegration continues in so much of Africa.

Return to England and the RAF

Margaret and I spent a week in Mombasa before joining our ship, the *Empire Ken*, for the trip to England. In this time we took the opportunity of staying at the beautiful Nyali Beach Hotel, owned by Alec Noone's family. Alec was a friend of mine from East African Airways. We had a rondavel right on the beach and, through the coconut palms, could see the open-air dance floor where we danced and ate most evenings. We also visited the famous and fabulous Gedi Ruins and historical Fort Jesus.

Our ship passed through the Suez Canal, just at the time that King Farouk was in power, and pre-empted by just on 10 years my landing at De Lesseps statue during the 1956 invasion of Egypt. The battleship, *King George V,* was anchored at Port Said and we were requested not to take photographs as we passed. Since they did not tell us why, I took a couple from my cabin porthole. I afterwards found out that just at that time King Farouk was going onboard, but I still do not know why photographs were not allowed.

Since maximum use of cabin accommodation was necessary, men and women were segregated and I only saw Margaret during the day. Southampton was reached at last and, after a short stay in a hotel, I managed to find a flat in West Hampstead. It was not a very nice part of London in those days, but the rent was reasonable and access to the centre good. I then had to get a uniform and report to the Aircrew Reception Centre at Biggin Hill in Kent. I expected to drop a rank and become a Flight Lieutenant. I had been assured in Nairobi that this would be the case, but that I would soon go up to Squadron Leader. I was taken aback therefore to receive a transfer of commission from the Navy to the

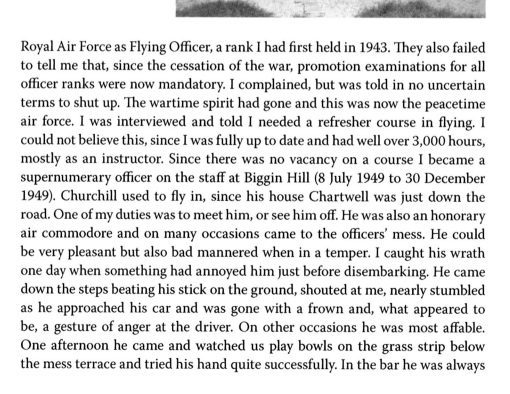

The Nyali Beach Hotel, where John and Margaret stayed after their wedding. The hotel was owned by the family of a friend, Alec Noone.

Royal Air Force as Flying Officer, a rank I had first held in 1943. They also failed to tell me that, since the cessation of the war, promotion examinations for all officer ranks were now mandatory. I complained, but was told in no uncertain terms to shut up. The wartime spirit had gone and this was now the peacetime air force. I was interviewed and told I needed a refresher course in flying. I could not believe this, since I was fully up to date and had well over 3,000 hours, mostly as an instructor. Since there was no vacancy on a course I became a supernumerary officer on the staff at Biggin Hill (8 July 1949 to 30 December 1949). Churchill used to fly in, since his house Chartwell was just down the road. One of my duties was to meet him, or see him off. He was also an honorary air commodore and on many occasions came to the officers' mess. He could be very pleasant but also bad mannered when in a temper. I caught his wrath one day when something had annoyed him just before disembarking. He came down the steps beating his stick on the ground, shouted at me, nearly stumbled as he approached his car and was gone with a frown and, what appeared to be, a gesture of anger at the driver. On other occasions he was most affable. One afternoon he came and watched us play bowls on the grass strip below the mess terrace and tried his hand quite successfully. In the bar he was always

The Empire Ken, *which brought John and Margaret back to England.*

surrounded by senior officers, but I did have the opportunity of a quick word when he asked me what I did. I said I had just rejoined and was waiting for a refresher course before making a success of my new career. He looked at me and, with a half smile, said, "Young man, don't chase success. If it's there, it will chase you," (pause) "in time". I saw him a few times after that and he always gave me a smile.

With Margaret in London I had to commute every day down to the airfield at Biggin Hill. I had therefore looked up Bill Humphries who came up with a British racing green, 3.5 or 4 litre Bentley with a strapped bonnet. This was far superior to my first Bentley and was in first class condition. It had an aluminium body, a good hood, a tonneau cover and went like a bat out of hell. I think I paid him about £200 for it, and I would have paid more. In January 1950 my posting came through for a course at RAF Finningley (now Doncaster-Sheffield Airport). I was pleased to go and spend some 17 hours flying Harvards (AT6) around, in anticipation of joining a fighter squadron. Before I had finished at Finningley, my new posting came through to proceed to the Central Flying School at Little Rissington for an instructor's course (May 1950). I protested that I was already a flying instructor and had much experience. I was told to shut up and stop whinging. I learned absolutely nothing new at Little Rissington but was now certain that I was heading for training command as an instructor. Margaret, all this time, was still in London but had enrolled at the Royal College of Music and the Royal Academy. She had made friends with other students and was obsessed with her studying. By the time she graduated, both as an ARCM and ARAM, I had settled in to my new posting in Manby in Lincolnshire (February–March 1950). This was the Royal Flying College for senior officers to refresh their flying skills and be brought up to date with current practices in both air and ground attack and, in particular, instrument flying. It was more supervision than instruction and I was not there for long. Once again I flew

Harvards but, for the first time, I had experience in Vampires and Meteors.

My next posting was to RAF Ternhill in Shropshire (No. 6 FTS in September 1950) and Margaret said she would like to join me but, since her music career was continuing, she did not want to live in married quarters. I found a flat some distance from the airfield, in a converted barn, and used one room as a studio where I installed a 'baby grand' for her. The Bentley was behaving beautifully and I had no trouble, until the day I travelled down to London to pick up Margaret. It was a Saturday and we finished work at midday. The previous day I had noticed a small weeping of water coming from the hot-water jacket that surrounded the two S.U. carburettors. I asked one of the sergeant engine fitters if he could repair it and was assured that a quick weld would seal the crack. I left it with him on Saturday morning and said I would return for it just after lunch. In the meantime four Iraqi student officers, who were receiving instruction in instrument flying, begged me to give them a lift to London. The five of us, with our suitcases, turned up at the hangar to collect the car, which was standing outside. There was no one about so we all got in and, after priming the engine, I started it up. It roared in to life all right, but I was unable to throttle back and the engine seemed stuck on half throttle. I stopped the engine, but I could not find a fault. I could not find the sergeant and decided, since time was getting on, to go and try and find a garage on the way. By slipping the clutch I was able to change gear and off we went. It was a cold day and after a little time the Iraqis had unpacked their pyjamas and had wrapped them around their heads, with the arms and legs flying out behind them. We must have looked a sight with the car roaring along and only controlled by changing down or declutching with horrible, teeth grinding gears as I missed engagement. All the garages along the way seemed shut until, after passing through 'Brownhills', I found a small garage with its workshop open. I switched off the engine, glided to the entrance and decanted my Iraqis. A very suspicious man came out but was obviously impressed by the car. I asked him if he could fix it and he said, "Of course, it is only the piston sticking in the carburettor". We pushed the car into the workshop and he asked me to start it up. I did so and, as the engine roared in to life, he put his finger in to the side opening in one of the carburettors and pushed or pulled the piston. Whatever he did caused a bang and a flash and the engine caught fire. I had leaped out but before I could stop him our expert mechanic had thrown a bucket of water over the engine, consequently spreading it even further. I have to take my hat off to the students. One student found some old curtains in a corner and this, together with their pyjamas, smothered the fire but not without a lot of shouting and pandemonium in two languages. We were now well and truly stuck and without the help of the AA I do not know how we would have got to London. I was now without a car so Margaret and I travelled back by train. I got a lift to the airfield on Monday morning and at lunchtime I went in to Market Drayton with a friend and bought the smallest and cheapest car available. It was a Fiat Topalino and a little gem. We had some marvellous times beating all over Shropshire and Cheshire without the slightest trouble and using very little petrol.

In the meantime the Bentley had been repaired. I found out that the hot water jacket had not been removed before welding with the result that the heat had caused one of the twin S.U. pistons to expand and stick. The resultant backfire of unburned fuel had caused the fire. I paid for the repair, with a little help from insurance, and managed, with Bill, to collect the car and change it for a saloon when he could find one. The Topalino had one fault. The wheels were quite small and not very strong. A knock on a curb or badly fitting manhole cover easily dented the rim and this could cause tyre wear and steering wobble. After a month or so Bill rang to say he had found just what he thought we would like. We drove the Fiat down to London and loved the car. In part exchange for the now repaired tourer, the Fiat and a handful of change, we drove back to Ternhill in great luxury in a 1927 Bentley sports saloon.

Looking back with hindsight, my two and half years at Ternhill did me little good. I logged a great deal of hours on training aircraft such as Chipmunks, Prentices and Harvards and ended up as the Instrument Rating Examiner. Although I had passed my promotion examination I was still a flying officer, and I felt the demotion bitterly. I had thrown up a good job, a promising career and an idyllic lifestyle for eight hours a day flying around in circles on instructional exercises. I had more flying hours than most of the officers gained in their whole careers, yet I had no operational experience. The Berlin Airlift had long ended and there seemed no way for me to get out of instructing. I saw little of Margaret, except at weekends and it was obvious that she was not enjoying being marooned in the countryside. To some extent this was mitigated by a number of concert engagements but this meant more separation and gradually our marriage deteriorated. One major factor in this was, I believe, largely my fault. Margaret was extremely talented and I had promised her parents that I would not prevent her from fulfilling her potential as a concert pianist. For this reason I did not want children and our sex life was therefore inhibited. We were both feeling frustrated in our different ambitions and our relationship never developed in to a fruitful marriage.

In 1952, two incidents occurred which led me to take steps to get out of Training Command. Margaret's reputation as a pianist had filtered through to Ternhill and one day she received an invitation (or was it an order?) to give a concert in the officers mess to the wives. I encouraged acceptance since I thought it would bring us a little closer to my colleagues in a social sense and be amusing for Margaret. In a similar way to our wedding, the audience consisted of all women. The commanding officer's wife, who had been a WAAF sergeant during the war, expected all the women to stand up when she arrived and departed. She also interrogated Margaret before she played and continually interrupted during the performance. Margaret was reduced to tears and felt so humiliated she walked out.

The second incident concerned me. The Wing Commander Flying was commonly known as 'Gin' Downey, for obvious reasons. He had a number of contacts in the show-business world, and he spent much of his time in their company. He called me in to tell me he had invited Ben Lyon and Bebe Daniels for the weekend. To him these were very important people and would I be prepared, since I had a Bentley, to meet them at the railway station on his behalf and bring them to his house. This seemed a friendly request and, since he was my senior, I thought (and was probably flattered) I might be included in the party. I ported their luggage in and left with his words in my ear, "I hope you looked after them?" I spent the rest of the weekend and several days afterwards trying to rid my upholstery of a perfectly vile and cloying cheap perfume.

I realised I was getting nowhere in life and seriously considered resigning from the Air Force and returning to Africa. However the 'winds of change' had already struck and independence leading to Mau Mau had bloodied the country. By chance I read an article about the communist terrorism in Malaya and the intention to use helicopters in a role of casualty evacuation from the jungle. I was immediately hooked both with the thought of going back to Malaya and the thought of flying helicopters. I was not sure how to go about it since the Air Force did not have any helicopters and therefore no training facilities. I knew the Westland Aircraft Company was building a Dragonfly helicopter and I got in touch with their public relations department. They told me they had, on order, a number of aircraft for the RAF. They believed the pilots were being trained by BEA, somewhere in the New Forest. I made immediate application, through my commanding officer, for a transfer for helicopter training and sat back to wait the result. This was in January 1953 and I did not have to wait long. In early February I was told that my application had been accepted and that I was to report to the BEA training headquarters in the New Forest on February 18th 1953. The course was to last two months and, if successful, I would be posted to Malaya forthwith. Margaret was quite pleased, and she decided to remain where she was until the course was complete. Since the posting to Malaya was an unaccompanied one she would then move to London and pick up her musical career again.

I sold the 4/6.5 Bentley, chassis VA 4096, registration number GX 2679 to Mr A. P. Maggs of Johnstone, Renfrewshire and thought I had heard the last of it. Mr Maggs was a bootlace manufacturer and had made a fortune in coloured boot and shoelaces. He apparently had five or six other Bentleys, which he kept as a hobby. He was pleased to hear that I had met W.O. Bentley in Chester and that the old man had complimented me on the condition of the coachwork and the spotless Ricardo engine. I sold it for a few hundred pounds and an excellent lunch and thought I had done very well! Almost exactly 50 years later, from the time I bought it, I came across it again. By the year 2000 it was owned by Mr Boardman-Weston, along with numerous other Bentleys he owns. We exchanged then and now photographs. It is in pristine condition and remains one of only three left. It's value, probably hundreds of thousands of pounds. Oh well! Back to 1953.

Westland Aircraft Limited 1953 – Helicopters

Just before I left Ternhill, I was told that training with BEA had ceased and that Westlands at Yeovil in Somerset had taken on the job. I therefore arrived at the factory in Yeovil on March 1st. I was lodged at the Three Choughs, an excellent small hotel, and I was fetched and returned each day by the firm's car. There were only two of us on the course. The other officer was a Flight Lieutenant Jack Maulden. We became great friends; in fact he was the only sincere friend I had made since losing Leslie Knott on a bombing raid over Germany early on during the Second World War. Our flying instructor was John Fay. John had served in the Fleet Air Arm, although I had never come across him during the war. He was a quiet, practical man, easy of manner and clear in demonstration and explanation. Jack and I, out of uniform now, were picked up at the hotel each morning after breakfast and driven to the hangar where, sitting outside, was Dragonfly (W.S.51) No. 1K. Even as I write I can recall the excitement and some of the trepidation I felt as we walked over to it. I had never been close to a helicopter before and I found it much smaller and more fragile than I had imagined it to be. Unlike a fixed wing aircraft, where the pilot is enclosed on all sides with limited view, here one had all round vision, including a view downwards past the feet. After a few minutes John Fay strolled over and introduced himself. Although Jack Maulden and I were amongst the first in the Royal Air Force to fly helicopters, the Navy had been using them for some time. John, as well as being an instructor, was also one of the test pilots for Westland. He had, in the early days, been involved in regular civilian mail runs and was the pilot responsible for lowering the lantern tower on to the Wolf Rock Lighthouse. The other instructor was Alan Bristow but, at this stage, we did not meet him or learn of his dubious reputation.

Our excitement on this day, 5 March 1953, was at first heightened when we were given our first flight and then, somewhat flattened, when it turned out to be only five minutes. In the Dragonfly the pupil sits in the front and instructor immediately behind him with dual controls. Having strapped ourselves in, John explained all the controls and then said not to touch any of the controls during this initial flight. I was surprised how solid and secure the aircraft felt once the rotors had reached their RPM. Sitting in the gold fish bowl cockpit and rising vertically upwards, after years of runway takeoffs, was quite exhilarating and the tilt forward in to forward flight, unexpected. The flight only lasted five minutes but in this time I was able to follow John's use of the rudders and (cyclic) stick, which in all applications acted in a similar manner to a fixed wing aircraft.

6 March. This time I was allowed to use rudder and (cyclic) stick, only while John controlled the power and collective pitch lever. Only ten minutes this time and I was impatient to keep going. The weather then proved my patience to the full since we did not fly again until the 31st, when again I had 20 minutes of stick and rudder. Again, in the same morning, I had another session of 10 minutes and felt ready to move on. April proved a good month, since on the 1st I started using all controls in hovering, climbing and making circuits and landings. During the next few days I learned sideways and backwards flight, autorotation, engine-off landings, spot landings and, after a pre-solo check on 8 April, I went solo after a total of three hours and five minutes. Regular flight sessions with John over the next seven weeks, and many hours of solo work covering the whole flight envelope of helicopter manoeuvres, gave me the most intensive and enjoyable period of my flying life. After eight hours instruction and 43 hours solo I was passed for operation work in the jungles of Malaya. Jack Maulden paralleled my progress and our friendship matured with our ever-increasing fascination and understanding of helicopter flight. I had great satisfaction in using my cross-country flight to go to my old RAF station at Ternhill. They had never seen a helicopter before and I caused consternation by flying around the control tower backwards.

The day before our departure from Yeovil, we were asked out for a drink by Alan Bristow (1923–2009). I mentioned previously that he was an instructor but he was also a test pilot and had a very irascible temperament. He had a habit of using his fist on both sexes from time to time. On this occasion he was leaving Westlands after an altercation with one of the directors and was about to start a business in the whaling industry with Salvesen. He wondered whether Jack and I would like to join him as pilots. We both declined. Although Bristow was able to retire to the Bahamas as a very rich man, and he went on to control worldwide interests in helicopter operations, I do not think the experiences of his future helicopter pilots proved us wrong.

Chapter Six

Malaya (Part II)

June 1953 saw Jack Maulden and I, minus our wives, on a Hastings aircraft from Lyneham via Idris, Habaniya, Maripur and Negombo to Changi on Singapore Island. We landed on the runway built by my father and other prisoners of war during the Japanese occupation. I had said goodbye to Margaret before leaving England, assuring her that immediately on arrival I would acquire married quarters. There was, at this time, a ruling that wives could not accompany their husbands by air but must travel by sea at the first available opportunity. Since Margaret was so busy with her music I had the impression that she was content for me to leave her temporarily. Our separate ways of life had caused a certain estrangement but I had every hope that this would end once she joined me in Malaya.

I am not exaggerating when I say that my whole life was about to change. I suddenly felt more alive and eager to get airborne once again. I was not to know that the next three years would bring one event tumbling on another, including tragedy, divorce, death threats, promotion, jungle rescue and, oh dear, once again instructing!

I was sent to the Army Air Observation Flight at Benta Field, outside Kuala Lumpur. The flight, part of Army 656 Squadron, flew Auster aircraft on jungle observation and communication. The idea was to give new pilots in Malaya flight experience over jungle, to observe operations, landing strips and enemy-occupied sites and to familiarise one in low-level navigation, in varying weather conditions. I spent a week flying with various army pilots at tree top level from Benta and then joined 1914 Flight at Taiping, dropping supplies to army units and surrender leaflets to the Communist Terrorists wishing to surrender. In all, about 50 hours as a passenger over impenetrable jungle gave me a pretty good idea of the task ahead.

Leaflets to encourage communist terrorists wishing to surrender, dropped from Auster Aircraft by Army 656 Squadron.

Benta Field Army Airstrip, outside Kuala Lumpur.

194 Squadron

Finally, on 23 July 1953, I joined 194 Squadron at Kuala Lumpur, equipped with Westland Dragonfly helicopters. My Commanding Officer was Squadron Leader Jock Henderson, a little wiry Scot. He was short of talk, but he ran a tight squadron of very experienced pilots. This was the first helicopter squadron formed in the RAF and had been operating from Singapore before my arrival. The main role had been a restricted one of casualty evacuation from jungle sites but this had enlarged to include taking passengers in and out and supply and communication. The squadron had Bristol Sycamore helicopters as well as Sikorsky Dragonflies but the former, in my view, had limitations in tropical conditions. I spent a little time converting on to the Sycamore, did not like it and never flew one again.

At the end of July all Sycamores were grounded. It seems that the main rotor blades, which were a series of wooden boxes glued on to the leading main spar, had, due to the high humidity and atmospheric conditions, become unglued. One Sycamore had plunged in to the jungle. As a result the Dragonflies were temporarily grounded as well. Jack and I were therefore without a job, since we were still undergoing training and there were sufficient pilots to operate the Dragonflies when they were cleared. This was the ideal time for me to gain practical jungle experience on the ground and I was assigned to the 2nd-7th Gurkhas for a 10-day patrol. Jack went elsewhere and joined an East African Regiment for a similar period.

Malayan Emergency

Here is very brief dissertation on the start of the 'Malayan Emergency'. At the end of the Second World War it was the intention of the Russians to expand communism into the Far East. China was the first to accept the concept but, in 1948, the year I left Africa, the Malayan Communist Party started a guerrilla war against the British. In the beginning the communists were called 'bandits' but later this changed to 'terrorists' and I will refer to them as CTs. The secretary of the party was Chin Peng (1924–2013), who had worked on the British side during the Japanese occupation of Malaya. He had 31 aliases and avoided capture throughout the emergency. Malaya was in turmoil after the Japanese invasion was defeated and the population of Chinese, Malays and Indians (mainly Tamils) distrusted each other. The country was near bankruptcy and ripe for takeover by the communists. They started with industrial strife and then began the indiscriminate murder of planters, miners and civilians in isolated areas. In June 1948, Sir Edward Gent, the first Governor of the Malayan Union, declared a 'state of emergency' over the whole country. There were about 5,000 armed communists up against the army, the police and the 'Special Constabulary'. This force of many thousands was not enough to contain the CTs. Sir Edward was killed in an air crash in July 1948 while on his way to London and was succeeded by Sir Henry Gurney. As the army was built up, so the CTs took to the jungle and terrorised the villagers, on the edges of the jungle, to supply them with food. Sir Henry was assassinated just before I arrived and was succeeded by General Sir Gerald Templer as High Commissioner of the Federation of Malaya. He was followed by Sir Donald MacGillivray (last British High Commissioner in Malaya 1954–57) and then by Sir Hugh Stockwell as GOC Malaya, followed by General Bourne.

My Gurkha patrol was led by a sergeant, who could speak only a few words of English. A corporal, who had a kind face and no English, was told to look after me. None of the patrol was over five foot eight inches and I towered above them at six foot two inches. I learned a lot during those 10 days, and I begin to ache all over even now when I recall the first few days. Communist camps had been seen in the Bentong area to the north-east of Kuala Lumpur and our patrol's task was to find these camps and flush out any terrorists.

The Gurkhas are so efficient. They cut their way through the jungle with their *kukris* and do not seem to notice hills, gullies, swamps, leeches, flies, snakes, centipedes, scorpions and other creepy crawlies – I did! I started sweating on the first day and I do not think I dried off the whole period. I soon got backache because, where the patrol cleared a path they could walk through, I had to continually bend in following them. By the end of the first day I could hardly straighten up and I was stiff in all my limbs. I could hardly sit in comfort, let alone lie down on the ground and sleep. While I collapsed in agony the others set up camp and brewed up tea. Their rations of rice and meat were cooked in little metal pans over a wood fire that did not seem to issue volumes of smoke. The corporal woke me every two hours (as if I were asleep) and made me walk around 10 minutes or so indicating that this would help my stiffness.

Travelling through Malaya primary jungle was quite different from travelling in Africa. For one thing, I had come across no deep jungle in Africa. Even the thick forest around Kilimanjaro cannot be compared to the wet clinging wall of foliage where every step had to be hacked out. In addition there were streams and rivers to wade through and the humidity was so high that one was continually sodden, even when it was not raining torrents.

Next day was also hell. Walk, walk, chop, chop. Saw nothing, seeming to get nowhere; I must keep walking, why? I just wanted to stop. We eventually did and I spent another broken night being woken up to exercise. Next day I felt better. I found I was able to keep up quite well and was beginning to notice things. Noises I had not listened to before began to mean something. I could distinguish animal noises from bird ones and the insects did not appear to bother me as much as before. We had only progressed about 10 miles and were still a long way from our objective. I must have indicated to the Sergeant that I was feeling a little better for we seemed to increase our speed and I found the only way I could keep up was to stop and let one of the patrol pass me and I would move on again. By the time I had got to the tail end of the patrol my little scheme had been noticed and the Corporal came and indicated that he would carry my pack and rifle to the next stop. I did not think I had any pride left but I found myself totally resisting giving up and, in fact, becoming so angry with myself that I found fresh impetus and began walking forward up the patrol again. Things got better from then on and I found I was ignoring bites and scratches; I even enjoyed a meal and slept a whole night without disturbance. I do not think I had shrunk but my backache disappeared and I found myself de-leeching myself in the evening without those squeamish feelings I first had.

On the sixth day we came within reach of the suspected camp. After a recce, we surrounded it, moved in and found it empty but not old. An amount of food was stored in boxes and it seemed that the huts were there for passing groups of CTs to stop off and recoup. The patrol destroyed every vestige of the camp and set off to return. We overshot the 10 days by one day and I am sure that this was my doing, in holding back the day-to-day progress. After arriving at base camp the whole patrol came together and, with one of the officers as interpreter, they presented me with a silver *kukri* and their congratulations to me for completing what they said had been a very hard, but routine, patrol.

Since my squadron aircraft were still grounded, I was asked if I would like to travel up to the Thailand border, to a town called Alor Star. My temporary duty would be that of Air Liaison Officer to a committee made up of the British Adviser, the Police and the Army. Even during my school days in Malaya I had never been further north than Penang. After a visit to the Air Operations unit in Kuala Lumpur, I was given a black standard Vanguard Saloon, a Webley .45 revolver and told to report to Alor Star in the state of Kedah in two days time.

Unlike East Africa, the roads in Malaya are beautifully 'tarmacked' and driving in normal conditions is very pleasant. However, by 1953, the communist terrorists had ample opportunity to set up ambushes and these occurred fairly frequently to vehicles thought to be of service origin. I was advised to drive fairly fast, only to stop in towns and villages and not to frequent quiet roads after dark. I set out on the 250-mile journey via Telak Anson, the nearest town to where my father had had his estate on the Bernam River. Onwards to Ipoh, then Taiping to Butterworth. Just north of Butterworth, the Gurkha Battalion was situated outside a little town called Sungi Patani and, since I had made friends with the brigade major, I stopped off for the night. From here on the land flattens out, rather like the fen country of Lincolnshire, and consists almost entirely of rice fields and hard-working water buffalo, seemingly led by small boys. Having had an enjoyable and uneventful drive I arrived in Alor Star and reported to the local Army Commander. I was allocated a very new and comfortable bungalow just north of the town, and I learned that the site had been the very point where the Japanese army had entered Malaya from Thailand. Just as in Africa, I had a houseboy and a cook, both Chinese in this case, and I set about organising my daily routine. This was not particularly difficult since, apart from 'morning prayers', I had little to do but remain on call should air support be required. 'Morning prayers' was the term used for a fairly early morning briefing at police headquarters, consisting of the British adviser or his deputy, the senior police officer, the senior army officer and myself. We were briefed on the previous day's action throughout the area and discussed plans for the continuation of the campaign against the infiltration over the border of CTs, the containment of villages known to harbour food carriers and sympathisers and to locate and destroy known communist bases. If air support was required it was my job to lay it on from air headquarters in Kuala Lumpur. I therefore had most days to myself but not always, as I will later explain.

Shortly after I arrived in Alor Star, the RAF told me that Margaret had a berth on a ship bringing back a Gurkha contingent from England that had been in attendance at the coronation of Queen Elizabeth II. I was pleased to be able to welcome her to a very comfortable bungalow and made arrangements to take a few days leave and fly down to Singapore to meet her on arrival. Everything seemed normal at first, after we had arrived back at Alor Star, until one day she told me she was pregnant. It appears she had met a major in the Gurkha regiment on the boat and, on such a long voyage, the inevitable happened. I think the RAF misspelt their message to me when they said she 'had a berth on a ship'. They were only out by about nine months!!

I offered to keep the child but Margaret was adamant that she wished to marry Major Burrows and wanted to arrange a divorce. To this day I do not know whether her decision was because she had had enough of our marriage, built or not built on either my absence flying or her absence on recitals. Or was it because her sense of loyalty to the father, or even shame in her disloyalty to me, made any other decision impossible? After about 10 days she left and I did not see her again for about seven years. The divorce was a stitched-up affair. It involved a hotel room in Singapore, a private detective giving evidence of adultery, my consenting to a divorce and, within months, a decree nisi. All this carried out by correspondence from one end of Malaya to the other. The shock was such that, in the beginning, it was just numbing and I did not really fully understand the inevitability of what had taken place or, in fact, who or what was to blame. In fact, for a time I must admit to almost feeling a relief to be single and free again.

As I was fairly fluent in Malay I was asked to several parties given by the Sultan of Kedah, Tunku Abdul Rahman and found him to be amiable. We spent many evenings playing tennis together and, on one occasion, sailed out to the island of Langkawi to feast on *ikan meru* (red fish); but more about that later. My duties as Air Liaison Officer were gradually increasing as CT activity in the area adjoining the border with Thailand was on the increase. To the east, the country was very difficult to police. With dense jungle spreading over rugged ground and deep valleys, the possibility of spotting and correctly identifying the exact position of communist camps was very difficult. There were, of course, no roads at all in the central areas. Jungle tracks were hard to follow and, in most cases, led nowhere. I did a little reporting of air observations where cultivated areas of terrorist clearings had been spotted but to 'lay on' bombing raids on insufficient evidence was a waste of resources and generally it was agreed to send in either police or an army patrol to identify and destroy. One had also to be very careful, for many of the cleared and cultivated areas were inhabited by indigenous Sakai aboriginals who had no contact with the CTs.

My idle life came to an end on a Thursday morning. I attended 'morning prayers' as usual and was surprised to come across a buzz of excitement. During the night a police patrol had come across and arrested a food carrier. After some interrogation he had admitted that he was taking supplies in to the jungle where a meeting of important terrorists was taking place. The area was broadly known as a route into Malaya and intelligence had heard rumours of a very important communist leader about to travel to the south. When he was shown a map the food carrier was unable to read it or identify the position of the camp. He said he would be willing to lead a patrol there but it would have to be quick since the camp was only one for transient use, and it would not be occupied for more than a day or two. The army was all for going straightaway, but distrusted the food carrier's story. The police claimed it was a job for them, since they had a fort facility near the area, and they were familiar with the Sakai tribe living nearby. My suggestion was that if they could quickly identify the site I could lay on a bombing run overnight that would obliterate the area of the camp and all in it.

This was immediately accepted and it was agreed that a small police patrol would set out late afternoon that day, aiming to get back before dawn, with the co-ordinates of the target. The chief police officer suddenly looked at me and said, "We have a pilot amongst us. Would it not be sensible if he obtained the map reference personally before recommending a bombing raid?" I could not very well refuse and, with my recent jungle experience behind me, I thought it a good idea to get some action. I togged myself out in jungle 'green', strapped on my close companion, the Webley .45 (which I had not yet fired), and was given a short-barrelled automatic rifle of which its name, after all this time, escapes me. Just prior to dusk we boarded an armoured vehicle and set off towards the border. The patrol, led by a police sergeant, were all Malays. There were about 10 in all including the food carrier, looking as sick as a dog. Unlike during the Gurkha escapade I was able to converse easily with all of them, but I did not expect what followed. We arrived at our destination early at about 11.00 pm and this proved to be a stretch of road where the food carrier would have entered the night previously. It was pitch black and as we were climbing out of the vehicle it was necessary to bunch up in order to communicate. No lights were allowed but the food carrier, who had his hands tied to the leading member of the patrol, seemed to see like a cat. We started off up a narrow track, each member holding onto the shoulder webbing of the one in front. I was somewhere in the middle and, by the time we had spent an hour or so stumbling along, I had learnt more under-breath swear words in Malay than I knew in English.

Either our eyes became adjusted or the sky became lighter because, after about three hours, we were able to discern each other even though we were in secondary jungle. Apart from the startled noises of disturbed animals, we proceeded in silence until, on an upward slope, our prisoner indicated that the camp was just ahead, on the top of a rise. By a stroke of luck we had just forded a tributary of a river which I identified as the Pha, and I was told that this led to a village called Khao Yuan, some way north. I was, therefore, able to pinpoint my position, and I hoped to verify it in full light. It was suggested that I remain behind while the patrol went forward to make sure of the camp and it's occupancy without giving themselves away. They would then return, pick me up and return as fast as possible to base. I sat down in relief, for it had been a hard night walk and first light was just beginning to seep down through the trees. I suddenly heard a faint murmur of a human voice and then a chink of metal coming from the opposite direction from where the patrol had left. I then saw a leg and barrel of a shotgun coming around the side of a tree. I leapt to my feet pointing my automatic at a startled pair of faces and shouted, "Put your hands up, you bastards". I could not, in the emergency, immediately think of the right words in Malay. It did not matter, however, since the shock was just as great for them. They both froze and dropped their guns, looking at me as if I was a banshee from hell. I had my finger on the trigger, and every time they even blinked I considered pulling it. I knew, though, this would endanger the patrol. How long we just stood there I cannot remember. Suddenly one of the patrol turned up and took over until the rest arrived, trailing an even more terrified ex-food carrier. They had found what they thought was an occupied camp and, since I had the map reference we decided to get out and back to base as quickly as we could without being seen. On the way back to the road it was quite light and I was able to get a cross-bearing on a prominent hill to confirm my previous bearings. I felt quite exhilarated and, after de-leeching myself and having a shower, I reported to the police headquarters.

By this time it was mid morning and sufficient hours had passed to make me forget the fright I had had on capturing the two CTs. I did not tell anyone that after the patrol had returned I discovered that, in all my posturing and bravado, I had forgotten to take the safety catch off. I do not know what happened to the food carrier but the two prisoners were sent for interrogation and I had the task of 'laying on' a bombing raid that night. I had previously notified RAF headquarters in Kuala Lumpur of the possible requirement and all that was necessary was to pass them the map reference. I asked the police exchange to put me through to operation headquarters in Kuala Lumpur. When they answered I asked for the duty officer and told him that the night's operation had been successful and that I hoped it would be possible to 'lay on' a pattern bombing attack that night. Having passed them the map reference and received their confirmation I hung up with the quiet satisfaction of a good job done. The next morning our meeting waited in expectation for the results of the raid but nothing happened. I eventually rang through to my headquarters in Kuala Lumpur to ask them the news. The operation officer was cheerfully dismissive, "We haven't received any map reference from you. In fact we were waiting to hear from you but in the end committed the aircraft to another target last night". My report to the morning gathering was not well received. I remember the British adviser giving an embarrassing cough, the chief police officer glared at me and the army commander muttered something about he knew he should have sent his men in. With my tail truly between my legs I went to find out what had gone wrong. It seemed that my call to Kuala Lumpur had gone through to the police operations room and not the RAF operations control, since I was using the police telephone operator. The police thought I was informing them of what I had already laid on with the RAF and took no action. There is no doubt that I had made a silly mistake but, in the end, everything turned out well. The two CTs admitted under interrogation that there was no one of importance at the camp and that they were just joining a couple of companions who were on their way to join a much larger group in the Batu Melintang area.

The final outcome therefore was two communists captured, a terrorist camp identified, a substantial saving in aircraft, explosives and manpower and, finally, one slightly demoralised and tired liaison officer. Shortly after this episode the chief police officer was ambushed on a hilly road and killed. He had only a month to serve before retirement.

One morning I received a call from a Brigadier Frank Brooks. His troops had identified a large camp in dense jungle, and they had advanced to a strategic distance, but were afraid that to approach further might warn the terrorists. He requested a bombing run in advance of his men attacking. I arranged for a night bombing raid and passed the co-ordinates of both the camp and the two run-in lights. I decided to join Brigadier Brooks, who positioned himself at the nearest lead-in light which was about half a mile from the camp. The aircraft arrived on time but, due to error, dropped their bombs short. In fact so short that we were on the receiving end of the 'tail enders'. The camp was hit successfully but Frank and I were pretending to be moles for a good 15 minutes during the raid.

While I had been waiting for Margaret to join me and, knowing that my stay in Alor Star was only of short duration, I had managed to rent a bungalow in Kuala Lumpur adjoining one that Jack Maulden had rented for his wife, who was also on her way. It was now November 1953 and I had been in Alor Star for over three months when my decree nisi came through, and I heard that my squadron had commenced operations again. I immediately applied for a return to operational flying, and within a fortnight I had packed up and was on my way to Kuala Lumpur. I had aimed to arrive about sunset, but had overstayed my welcome at Sungi Patani with my Gurkha friend and was pushing it hard when I wanted to spend a penny. This was about 30 miles from Kuala Lumpur and it was already dark. The road was straight and seemed clear. My urgency

Sikorsky Dragonfly Helicopter, Malaya, 194 Squadron, 1953–1954.

overcame the risk and I stopped, turned off the lights, got out and started to relieve myself. A sudden burst of automatic gunfire close by started me so much that, in ducking down, I wet myself which, at the time, I did not notice or care about. My revolver was in the car and in the ensuing silence I made a scramble in to the driving seat and burnt rubber in my hasty retreat. I never found out what the firing was about, but it would be a long time, if ever, before I stopped again at night on the edge of the jungle.

I settled back in to Kuala Lumpur and, as I had several friends there, joined the Golf Club and the Lake Club and spent many evenings playing tennis, swimming or attending a succession of parties. One of my friends, called Carter, was an accountant for a large firm and had been in Tanganyika at the same time as myself. His wife invited me to one of their parties, and at the end asked me to help her collect the ivory cocktail sticks which were most valuable and she did not want to leave it to the staff. For much of the evening I had been standing by an open window to keep cool, drinking and eating snacks happily, while breaking each cocktail stick in half as I finished and chucking the pieces out the window. It took me months to find suitable replacements but, for all my stupidity, we remained friends. Another difficulty I found when visiting various bungalows for hospitality resulted from the Japanese occupation. My father had to evacuate his estate extremely rapidly as the troops were getting very close. He managed to blow up the factory and burn as much of the estate as possible before having to flee down to Singapore. He had just built a new bungalow, and he had furnished it with most of the family possessions. All were abandoned and the bungalow was ransacked. I kept on finding pieces of family silver with our crest on it in various bungalows I visited. My mother was a very able water colourist and many of her pictures adorned the walls of people who had come out to Malaya after the war and bought them from various shops. It was a little heartbreaking, but I just could not go about claiming them back.

By the middle of January 1954 I was again fully up to operation standard in the Dragonfly, but had yet to carry out my first jungle sortie. Having given up the bungalow I was now living in the officers mess as a single man. I had handed the service car back and now, in my unexpected freedom, owned a new Standard Vanguard Estate. This acquisition lightened my bank account somewhat, but I was quite taken aback to receive notification that, since I was now single, I had to pay back all the marriage allowance I had received since arriving in Malaya. My appeal was turned down on the grounds that we had not taken up the official accommodation in Kuala Lumpur, even though at the time of the decree nisi I was officially married and maintaining two married quarters, albeit the army in Alor Star had supplied one.

I never forgave the RAF for this set back, but my anger was overtaken by a really tragic event. Carol Maulden had, by this time, arrived and on the 19th January I joined Jack and Carol for the evening. Jack had been flying with the army observation flight at Noble Field while I was in Alor Star but was expecting to rejoin the squadron shortly. Two days later, on 21 January 1954, I was in the flight hangar when the news came up that an Auster 6, VF 604 had been lost. I then learned that an army sergeant pilot J. Perry had sent out a brief 'mayday' and then silence. His observer was Flight Lieutenant Jack Maulden. Having obtained the general area of the crash from the army, I obtained permission to carry out a search by helicopter. Flight Lieutenant Jacques and I took off, and spent two sorties of over five hours in a fruitless search of the impenetrable jungle. On return we learned that the previous message from the Auster had said a white phosphorous grenade, type number WP 80, had fallen loose in the cockpit and was rolling around. If this had gone off in the cockpit it is hard to contemplate a more horrible death.

Without further facts we had to assume that this is what must have occurred and the possibility of finding a burnt area of jungle got us airborne again on the 22nd. This time with Flight Lieutenant Pinner we searched for another three hours at treetop level, most of the time looking for any signs of charred foliage that we might have missed earlier. In the afternoon of the same day

Auster, Malaya. This was the type of aircraft Jack Maulden was killed in.

I went on yet another search for some two and a half hours, taking Master Pilot Cox with me as an observer. We saw absolutely nothing. Much later, in March 1957, the remains of the aircraft and the two bodies were discovered by a Gurkha patrol and identified only by the remnants of medal ribbons, which had survived the fire.

On return I was miserable for Carol, dead tired from hours of searching and upset since we had formed such a firm friendship. The only other person that I had had as a sincere friend had been Leslie Knott, an ex metropolitan police officer, who trained with me, but became a navigator and was shot down on his first mission over Germany in 1942. I went back to the Mess, washed and changed, and drove in to a club in Kuala Lumpur. In my attempt to forget, I drank too much. I am told I had had

Jack Maulden, 194 Squadron. Killed Ulu Langat area February 1954

four gin-and-tonics lined up at a time and kept them coming. The last thing I remember is saying to myself, "I must go back, I'm flying tomorrow". The rest of what happened I can only repeat from what I have been told and from the newspaper cutting, which I still have. To observers I seemed quite sober when I walked out of the club, got in my car and drove off towards the airfield. Some way ahead the road took a curve to the right, around a steep little hill, but my car did not. It carried straight on up the hill but stopped before it got to the top. Then, without my permission or knowledge, it rolled to its right, from wheels to roof, to wheels from roof, to monsoon ditch at the bottom, alongside the road it should have taken in the first place. A Chinese cyclist passing at the time had the presence of mind to pull me out of the back seat and lay me on it, before contacting the police.

I woke up sometime that night in bed in a small room. It was whitewashed and dangling from the ceiling was an electric flex with a rather dull un-shaded bulb. In the corner of the table was a Chinese man either writing or studying something. I could not remember how or when I had been captured by the communists. I could only feel a tremendous anger welling up inside me. I leapt out of bed with every intention of killing my enemy. I knocked both him and the table over and conveniently blacked out. I am told the doctor called for help but had me back on the bed before it arrived. The next time I woke up, I was in a hospital ward, in pyjamas, and looking up at a very pretty nurse. I asked where I was and on being told, "You're in hospital after a car accident", I replied, "Don't be so bloody silly, I don't have accidents", I then passed out again. When I next awoke I felt 100 percent, I could not remember why I was there but I got out of bed and started talking to one of the patients in case he knew. The nurse, not the pretty one, came in and 'shooed' me back to bed saying, "Don't get up yet, you are suffering from concussion, mild amnesia and from the look of your activities last night, probably a severe hangover". She was wrong about the hangover, somehow I felt as fit as I had ever been, but they still held me in hospital for several days. By the time I was discharged, Carol had already flown home and I did not see her again until I also returned to England.

I had some time to think of all the recent events while I was in hospital and this culminated in a decision to change my way of life. I had, for a long time, been letting events lead me or at least I had been failing to take a positive lead towards my full potential. My experience in flying was probably greater than many of those I was serving with and I had proved my leadership qualities both during the war and in Africa afterwards. Now, just because I had been demoted to the rank of Flying Officer, I was pottering about like a duck with its wings clipped.

I decided to throw everything into work, and, since I now had no

*Newspaper article detailing my
road accident shortly after
Jack Maulden's death.*

Pilot hurt in road crash

KUALA LUMPUR, Sun.—An R.A.F pilot attached to 194 Helicopter Squadron here was slightly injured at 1.30 this morning when his car skidded and overturned near the junction of Treacher and Ampang Roads.

Flying Officer Mackenzie-Hill was admitted to the British Military Hospital at Kinrara.

Five or six rescuers worked for ten minutes early on Sunday morning to extricate an injured European from this car which came to grief near the junction of Ampang and Treacher roads. In the accident the driver had become pinned under the seat. His injuries were not severe.—Ng Beh Leow picture.

responsibilities towards a wife or family, I plunged in. Since I still held flying-instructor's qualifications and an instrument-examiner's category I offered my services, when not flying helicopters, to the RAF fixed-wing element in Kuala Lumpur. There were several fixed-wing aircraft available and I spent considerable time retesting pilots wishing to renew their instrument rating, giving flying revision to those in administrative postings and flying passengers to various parts of the country. My knowledge of Malaya and the Malay language came to the ears of Air Vice Marshal Scherger, Air Officer Commanding and he asked to see me. He was a rather blunt Australian and was used to getting his way. He was keen for me to take command of the Far East Jungle Rescue Team, operating in Malaya and Borneo. "Simple job", he told me, "Just train a team in your spare time and, if necessary, go in to the jungle and rescue any aircrew who

Kuala Lumpur Flying Club. The plane is a Tiger Moth.

have come down, or alternatively jump in to the area and walk out". He would not listen to my protests and assured me that the team would only be used in an emergency and I could undertake the training during weekends.

I reluctantly agreed to give it a try and so took on yet another job. This was awkward since I was already spending much of my spare time, when not on operational flying, giving instruction to civilian pilots at the Kuala Lumpur Flying Club which used the grass at one end of the airfield at weekends and in the evenings. The Club had a chief flying instructor and one Australian engineer. It had one hangar and a Clubhouse and a membership of flying and non-flying members. It was run by an elected captain and a committee and, apart from its pleasure flying, fulfilled a very important role in the community. With most roads under the threat of terrorist attacks the outlying commercial estates, of which there were many, had difficulty in transporting money to pay their staff and workers. The army was too occupied to provide convoy security and the intelligence network of CT organisations proved to be very effective by the number and frequency of ambushes of wage carrying vehicles. The flying club had therefore been approached to undertake estate drops of moneybags if and where necessary. When I arrived I found a number of keen amateur pilots carrying out a desultory hit-and-miss service with few serviceable aircraft available. Apart from a couple of private aircraft there were only three Tiger

Moths and two Austers in condition to fly. The others were all waiting for spares, which were difficult to get (mostly coming from Australia), slow to arrive and which then joined a queue while the engineer supervised repairs and certification. As far as the wages-dropping was concerned it was not only the service that was hit and miss. The dropping technique left a lot to be desired, and I hate to think of how many thousands of pounds in canvas bags were lying rotting in the jungle from overshoots and undershoots of the target.

There was a very able Sergeant Lynch working on the RAF Communication Squadron. He was both an engine fitter and an airframe fitter of some experience and it was a great day for the club when he lent his assistance to the engineer. Spares magically appeared, aircraft that had been lying in pieces suddenly appeared in pristine condition and business began to take off – literally. The club was situated at the far end of the airfield, away from the RAF establishment, and operated on a grass area well-separated from the tarmac runways. The clubhouse was situated on a little rise and looked out over the airfield to the hills beyond. There was a general lounge and bar and a well-organised kitchen. In the front was a beautifully kept grass lawn with tables and chairs and one of my enduring memories is that of sitting in the afternoon shade with cool, tomato and cucumber sandwiches and tea with fresh milk. I have spent some time describing all this since it was a little oasis where I could find peace from service regimentation and relax from an ever-increasing workload. I loved flying the Tiger Moth and, apart from giving flying displays at various events, I taught many people to fly. My oldest pupil was Brigadier Bill Grierson RASC whom I bullied into going solo. I then watched with my heart in my mouth as he took off and got lost on the circuit, but he eventually found his way back and landed in one piece.

My old friend from Alor Star, Tunku Abdul Rahman (1903–1990), who had recently become the first Prime Minister of Malaya, spent many restful hours on the lawn. I flew him around the Port Dickson area when he was looking for a house but we were both too busy in our respective spheres to play any more tennis. The Tunku later became known as 'Bapa Malaysia' (The Father of Malaysia). During the Japanese occupation the Tunku (Prince) had worked as a District Officer in the Kulim area. He got in to trouble with the

Tunku Abdul Rahman in 1956, later known as 'Bapa Malaysia' (The Father of Malaysia).

Japanese for trying to protect his people and decided to leave for Alor Star, the capital of Kedah. In 1920 he had studied law at Cambridge in England and later became leader of UMNO (United Malays National Organisation, founded 1946), where he negotiated with the British authorities on the future of Malaysia. It was interesting to learn that originally Kedah was a jungle principality in Northern Malaya which the family ruled for centuries. Founded by a Mongol chieftain who was shipwrecked on the Malayan coast the dynasty had continued through nine Hindu rajahs and 20 Muslim sultans. The Tunku always had a cheerful disposition and we got on very well, probably because he always beat me at tennis. Another 'lawn lounger' was the very amiable Hon. Richard Beaumont (1926–2010) who later became the Chairman of the gun makers James Purdey & Sons. At that time he was studying Mandarin among his other linguistic accomplishments. We had many interesting conversations on the lawn, but I was never able to persuade him to fly.

I managed to organise and bring accuracy to the wage-dropping pilots and, as a result, increased club income once trust in our deliveries had been proved to the estate managers. I instigated the redecoration of the clubhouse and our membership rose rapidly, with the restaurant and bar doing roaring business. It was therefore unfortunate that I had been bulldozed in to running the 'jungle rescue' team but this was a service commitment, and it held priority over pleasure.

I updated a manual on jungle survival and arranged for my team to go jungle bashing every two weeks. This would start on a Saturday with a return on Sunday. Whenever I could I would join them but, if not, I would brief them before departure and debrief them on return. The team consisted of 20 volunteer airmen and a corporal. They were all fit and keen and capable of sustained effort in jungle survival. They had never jumped into the jungle before however and I was hesitant to lay on practise airdrops, since this was a particularly hazardous exercise. Trees were well over 100 feet tall and tightly packed. I did not want the team decorating and dangling from the tops of trees with little chance of being rescued themselves.

The original team had been formed in Singapore in 1949. It was born as an offshoot of RAF operations in the Malayan Emergency, and it was the only known parachute-trained Jungle Rescue Team in any air force. It originally consisted of two officers and 25 other ranks – all volunteers. It was later disbanded as the original personnel were transferred to other service commitments. When Air Headquarters (Malaya) moved up to Kuala Lumpur, a Flight Lieutenant Wade offered to restart the team. One of those was SAC Machin who was now my team leader. With the increase of so many ground troops and the introduction of the RAF helicopter squadrons, this made the team less indispensable since, in many cases, troops could reach trouble spots within an hour of a disaster. However, another job of the unit was to test new military equipment for the

Dead CT and Gurkha vehicle. Terrorist bodies were taken out of the jungle for identification by police and intelligence units.

tropics and our jungle exercises were therefore worth maintaining. In all the sorties we made we never came across any terrorists but saw many animals and snakes and, on one occasion, ran in to a herd of elephants which resented our intrusion and forced us into a somewhat undisciplined retreat.

It was now the middle of April 1954 and I had first arrived in Malaya in June 1953. Ten months had passed and as yet I had not been fully deployed in helicopter jungle operations. Now everything changed. From 20 April I was airborne almost every day in troop transport or casualty evacuation. May also continued to be hectic, flying in to jungle landing zones, police forts and army bases. It is far too complicated to go in to detail here, but my log book shows that, apart from a couple of fixed wing sorties to Singapore and Butterworth, I was jungle-borne almost every day in May. Two instances however will give one some idea of the work. I was given a map reference for a jungle clearing with a request from the army to bring out a dead terrorist. It was the custom at that time to identify and record all terrorists killed or captured. Before the use of cameras this was carried out at base by the police identification and intelligence units. On my arrival over the landing zone I found the army had cut a number of trees down leaving a vertical hole in the canopy. With very little room to spare on each side of the rotor blades I made a vertical descent on to a tiny platform made up of bamboo. As I have already explained, the pilot sits in the front of the cockpit with a bench seat behind him. This made it very difficult to accommodate casualties or dead bodies and in the beginning we used wicker

S-51 Dragonfly – 'S' for Sikorsky.

'Moses' baskets and slid them in behind the pilot with the head or legs of the casualty sticking out the side of the cockpit. Before I arrived in Malaya it was the policy to cut off the heads of dead terrorists and send them back in a bag for identification. Later on we carried stretchers strapped on to the outside above the wheels but, on this occasion, we had dispensed with them. Directly my wheels touched down I slid open the door, and I indicated for the corpse to be put in. The soldiers having got clear I shut the door, opened the throttle on full power and made a vertical ascent to above tree top level. Translating the vertical climb to forward flight requires the stick to be pushed forward. This momentarily caused the nose to drop. This sudden pitching movement had the most dramatic effect. I suddenly felt a hand on my left arm and thought, "Oh my god, he's alive," I could not let go of the collective pitch lever, but I grabbed my revolver with my right hand and, in my swinging round, caused the aircraft to yaw violently. He was of course well and truly dead, but the sudden pitching forward of the aircraft had flung his arm forward on to me.

On another occasion I was asked to bring out a body from the Cameron Highlands, and I therefore positioned overnight at Ipoh. Weather conditions in this area, with ground height up to 6,000 feet, could be hazardous and we generally flew up the valleys keeping diversionary areas or any open spots in mind first, in case we were forced down by low cloud. The Dragonfly did not have full instrumentation and we therefore flew almost always in sight of the ground. Having arrived at the landing zone in the Cameron Highlands the weather was on the turn and I wanted to get away as quickly as possible. When they brought the body out to me I saw it was a Chinese female who had been shot in the stomach some time previously and was further 'on the turn' than the weather. Death has an odour once encountered never forgotten but in this case it was unbearable. I refused to have her in the cockpit and we therefore compromised by slinging her body by ropes underneath the fuselage and between the wheels. Once airborne I headed back down the valley at about 200 feet above the trees, with the corpse dangling below me. Or at least she was, until suddenly I felt the aircraft change in pitch and caught a glimpse of my cargo descending rapidly in to the trees. The weather was closing in fast and there was nothing I could do. That was the only body that ever got away from me and it resulted in the almost immediate use of sealed body bags being issued to the troops for just such occasions.

In June 1954 I learnt that my mother, who was living in Australia, was unwell, so I begged a lift in a Hastings from Singapore to Djakarta and on to Darwin. I then took another aircraft to Adelaide and a train to Melbourne. The countryside was interesting and in many ways fascinating, since the flora and fauna is unique.

I tried to persuade my mother to return to England, which she eventually did. She was suffering from old injuries sustained in India as a result of a riding accident and deep depression following the death of my father in 1949 aged 56, who had never fully recovered from his incarceration and beatings by the Japanese at Changi in World War Two.

On my return to Malaya I quickly began flying operationally again, and found less and less time for the jungle rescue team or for the flying club. An instance of one day's flying on the 16 August 1954 shows that I carried out 16 flights in one day of army casevacs, transporting troops and observation of CT camps. This totalled over seven hours of flying in temperatures well over 100° F. This intensity of work carried on through the rest of August and the whole of September. Two incidents come to mind during this time which I found amusing. The first was a flight into an area where an East African contingent was patrolling. I took some supplies in and was bringing some intelligence material out. I arrived over the area to find that they had cut an enormous landing area out of secondary jungle and long grass. They had used fire for much of their work. I could see the landing zone a long time before I arrived because of the smoke. As I touched down, the smouldering grass took on a new life and started to sprout flames as it was being fanned by my rotor blades in to a rapidly spreading blaze. Since I had a large quantity of 100-octane petrol in my tanks I was not a happy man. The Africans seemed to me to be loitering over to the aircraft with no idea of the danger. I opened the door, leant out and shouted at them to hurry if they did not want to be blown up. As my words reached them they stopped in amazement and with beaming faces rushed over to pick up the supplies while others raced around trying to beat out the nearest flames. Why? Because I spoke to them in Swahili, which was the last thing they expected to hear. I left with a chorus of 'Kwaheri Bwana Kubwa' and a somewhat singed aircraft bottom.

When I had first rejoined the Air Force in 1948 I was posted to the Royal Flying College at Manby, in Lincolnshire. My duties were to retrain and bring senior officers up to flying standard, who, after administrative posts, were returning to duties where they were expected to fly. One of my pupils was a Squadron Leader Binks DFC who, now as a Wing Commander, had been posted to Malaya to a senior operations post. He was a very distinguished wartime pilot who flew Bristol Beaufighters in 235 Squadron and then in 1943 with 618 Squadron flying de Havilland Mosquitos. He looked very like David Niven but he did not fit in to the peacetime air force. When sober he was a perfect gentleman and universally liked. After a few drinks, however, his personality changed completely to an extent where he could be indescribably rude and capable of childish and dangerous acts of which, when sober, he was either very apologetic for or completely unaware. One evening he borrowed a little Fiat 'Topalino' and, after I had invited him for a drink at the flying club, he arrived, drove up the steps in to the bar and parked at the counter. He then pushed his head through the rather fragile soft fabric roof and ordered a drink. Of course he apologised later, but that was hardly the point. On another occasion he drove his staff car up to the officer's bachelors quarters and parked half over a monsoon ditch and went to sleep. I discovered him late at night with half the car teetering dangerously over a drop of some 20 feet. By anchoring the back of the car we got him out, but next morning he remembered nothing. Just as his long-suffering wife arrived with their several children, after the long sea voyage, he out-performed himself. Sir Donald MacGillivray, the new Governor General, gave a reception to which he was invited. Binkie turned up in a somewhat dishevelled mess dress, walked up to his Excellency and said, "Hi there cock," and walked on in to the gathering. The Governor sent an equerry to find him and tell him to leave and re-present himself in the proper dress and in the proper manner. Binkie, who was never obstreperous, quietly left and almost immediately returned to greet the Governor and his lady wife with, "How do you do Sir and Lady something or other". He was not only escorted out of the reception but out of the country, to be followed by his wife and children on the next boat home.

Despite this disgrace he was given command of an air force station in

England accommodating the American Air Force. One day, on an inspection by the air officer commanding and with the whole station on parade, Binkie marched up to the air marshal, saluted, reported, "All present and correct Sir," and fell flat on his back and passed out. Following this incident and a long line of others he was asked to resign his commission and was ignominiously dismissed from the service. I next met him as a very successful restaurant owner of the 'Chicken in the Basket' at Benson, in Oxfordshire, just outside Wallingford, where, after repeated disappearances for 'drying out' and being banned from every officers' mess and most pubs in the area, he slid in to obscurity. I admired his wartime experiences immensely and his character, when sober. However, I could never understand what lay behind his 'Jekyll and Hyde' lifestyle which led to his demise as an incurable alcoholic. Tony 'Binxie' Binks died aged 89 in the bar of the Six Bells in Warborough on April 8 2005. A small plaque in the bar states 'he baled out in the Six Bells, his second home'.

One of my intermediate tasks was to fly General Sir Gerald Templer around the territory on various missions. One I remember in particular, since it was to take him to my old stamping ground in Alor Star. It seemed that the British Advisor had not been pulling his weight and the General was paying him a personal visit. Templer was in good humour when we took off, but shortly before we landed I saw him hitting his boots with his stick and seemingly fidgeting with unease. I was wrong. He was working himself up to give the British Advisor the fright of his life and a piece of his mind. Five minutes after takeoff from Alor Star I heard him say to his aide-de-camp, "That's taught the bugger a lesson he'll not forget" and a good-humoured and very approachable Commander in Chief was delivered to Butterworth.

Shortly after this, Templer left Malaya and his replacement was Lieutenant General Bourne. We flew quite a lot together as he visited the areas of his command. I found him also a very pleasant passenger and one who knew what he was up against in this strange war. He had only one arm, but this did not seem to affect him in the slightest. He also had one teenage son, and he asked me one day for a favour. Would I take his son on a few jungle sorties to give him experience? I cleared this with my squadron commander, Squadron Leader Henderson and on 1 September, having first 'kitted out' young Bourne (Michael Bourne 1937–2013) in jungle green, we set off from Kuala Lumpur for various jungle landing zones. We picked up a Brigadier Henriker for a recce and, after flying for some six hours on several missions, we landed for the night at the camp of the 2nd 6th Gurkhas. Refuelling was done from stocks of petrol in jerry cans and the use of large funnels, carried to the upper side of the fuselage. The General had told me to treat his son as flight crew, with no favours. I did just this and told him, under the eagle eye of my crewman

Corporal Plant, to do all the carrying, lifting and sweaty work necessary to service the helicopter. I then asked the officer of the day for accommodation for my two crew. He said there was a *basha* (hut), over by the Gurkha mess, which they could use, and he ushered me over to the officers' mess. I casually mentioned that one of my crewmen was the commanding general's son and the change was amazing. The word spread like magic and practically all the officers suddenly turned out and had something to say to Michael. While Corporal Plant went to the *basha*, his fellow crewman was ushered in to a room in the officers' mess with all the alacrity that goes with licking boots. I have a great regard for the Gurkhas in all respects, but this turnaround did surprise me. Even I was given increased respect for having flown the man who deigned to call General Bourne his father.

Work eased off in the middle of September and I was able to put in some fixed-wing flying and carry out some service-instrument flying tuition. I had time to give instruction at the flying club in the wonderful Tiger Moths. I also dragged my jungle rescue team out in a couple of training sessions. I did not know it, but this was to be very near the end of my time with the flying club and the jungle rescue team.

About this time I took a short break and went down to Port Dickson where there was a wonderful beach called Magnolia Bay. I stayed at the Si Rusa Inn, which almost had its legs in the water. I was surprised at breakfast, the next morning, to see a very senior officer coming down the stairs with an equally senior officer's wife. He was slightly embarrassed when I flew him shortly afterwards. On returning to Kuala Lumpur I attended a piano concert by Vladimir Horowitz who was making a tour of the Far East. A large audience assembled in the Chinese Assembly Hall to hear this famous pianist. Shortly after he started, flying insects gathered around the brilliant lighting overhead. As they burnt themselves they fell on to Horowitz to such an extent that he had to stop. After several minutes of consternation by both musician and audience, two little Chinese men appeared with a ladder, and they proceeded to tie bunches of chillies on to the casings of the lights. The event continued with just occasionally an insect falling down. I am still wondering why they did not simply move the piano a few feet away from underneath the lights.

The first two weeks in October I went back to intensive helicopter flying but, on the 14th, I was called in, together with Flight Lieutenant Jackson-Smith, a fellow helicopter pilot, to a meeting with Jock Henderson, my commanding officer, and Wing Commander Williams, the O.C. flying Kuala Lumpur. Jacko had, like me, served as a senior officer during the war and, at the end of hostilities, as a Wing Commander, had been appointed Air Attaché in Scandinavia. He had then left the service and, on rejoining, had also been demoted in rank. The first thing we were told was that from 20 October 1954 we were no longer members of 194 Squadron. Seeing our look of horror, Wing Commander Williams quickly put our worst fears at rest. We had done nothing wrong, in fact it was just the reverse. Since the beginning of the Malayan Emergency the Royal Navy had been carrying out the bulk of troop transporting, since they had the larger S.55 Sikorsky helicopters. The RAF role of casevac and communication in Dragonfly and Sycamore aircraft were restricted because of lack of carrying capacity, compared to that of the bigger naval aircraft. The Air Force had now arranged for Westland Whirlwind S.55 helicopters to be shipped out to Malaya for a new squadron to start intensive troop-carrying operations, in conjunction with the Navy and finally to replace Naval Squadron 848 who had served their time.

155 Squadron

Jacko was promoted to Squadron Leader commanding 155 Squadron and I was to be his second in command and to act as operational training instructor for all the new pilots about to come out from England. None of these new pilots had operational experience, and none had flown Whirlwinds before. Amongst other things I had passed my promotion examination and was now a Flight Lieutenant. I had last held this rank ten years previously in 1944.

The new aircraft were being flown in to Seletar Airfield in Singapore any day now. They were crated in sections and a representative of the Westland Aircraft Company would be on hand to supervise assembly and ground

Norman Jackson-Smith – 'Jacko'.

testing before first flight. Our orders were to get down to Singapore as quickly as possible, oversee the arrival and assembly of the aircraft, to air test each one and finally to fly all of them between us to Kuala Lumpur before working up as an operational Squadron. Although slightly apprehensive at the news, Jacko and I were overjoyed at having been chosen for this project, and we immediately flew down to Seletar. For the first few days, while the aircraft were being assembled, we read the pilots notes and sat in the cockpit to familiarise ourselves with the layout and controls.

On the 29th October 1954 I climbed aboard the first aircraft to be assembled, XD188. After a few minutes hovering and manoeuvring around the airfield, I felt confident to proceed with a full air test. After the little Dragonfly, the Whirlwind was a much more stable platform. It was a delight to have a full instrument panel in front of one, even though the visibility from the cockpit was less than in the Dragonfly. Leaving out all the technical details of our work in preparing the aircraft for operational work, Jacko and I took it in turns to fly each one, as it became ready, to Kuala Lumpur. By the end of November we had eight Whirlwinds in operation. Apart from the occasional troop lift I was now back in to the instructional role as each new pilot arrived. They were straight from training school, and they had little experience of the aircraft or the tropical conditions that they had to operate in.

The Whirlwind was much easier and more stable to fly than the Dragonfly, but it had one awkward fault. If the hydraulic assistance to the cyclic pitch lever failed the reversion to manual control presented heavy forces for the pilot to maintain. This was not in any way dangerous if the pilot was prepared, but continued flying in manual proved very tiring as I found out during one delivery flight from Singapore to Kuala Lumpur. I spent over an hour battling to keep on course as near to straight and level as possible. Almost immediately I introduced regular practice in manual control technique into training. It was necessary immediately to recognise the hydraulic failure, and to take firm hold of the controls, reduce speed to below 50 knots and try to land as soon as a suitable site became available. The worst and heavier forces were on the lateral movement of the collective, and this was overcome some time later by a modification using engine oil pressure to release the lateral loading. After I left Malaya I understand that manual training exercises were discontinued. I think this was very unwise, and it could cause accidents with pilots not knowing what to expect, as happened during the Suez Crisis which I will explain later on.

With one or two exceptions, the new pilots coped very well and learnt quickly. Some little way from Kuala Lumpur, the members of 194 Squadron had made a clearing in the jungle that was considered safe to use as a practice landing ground. It was small but ideal for teaching steep approaches and takeoffs, with a limited area of manoeuvrability on the ground. One hazard that had been left on purpose was a tree trunk lying across one corner of the touchdown area and each pilot was briefed about the method of avoiding this before touching down. One officer was posted on to the squadron who should never have been passed as a helicopter pilot. I will call him 'G'. I flew with him for twice, if not three times, longer than the others before I felt he could cope. He was slow in reaction and terribly heavy on the controls. The training jungle landing zone was called Ulu Langat and after arranging with Squadron 194 for its use, I arranged for a security party to fly in before using it for training. I usually took a pupil in and out myself and then, sitting beside him, let him repeat the procedure until I was satisfied he could go solo. 'G' had three exercises dual before I thought he could go into the

'... hundreds of sorties, besides carrying VIP passengers and continuing to instruct.'

John M'Kenzie-Hall piloting an S.55 Whirlwind helicopter over Malayan jungle.

clearing solo. In order to be sure, I flew above the clearing in another aircraft as he made his attempt. I saw him descend satisfactorily and come to the hover at 90° to the log. He then started to turn the wrong way before touching down. I could see the tail rotor moving inevitably towards the fallen tree, and I shouted at him to stop turning. The moment his tail rotor hit the log the aircraft spun to the right, dipped and the main rotors hit the ground with such force that the aircraft bounced on to its nose and came crashing down on its side. Fortunately and surprisingly, there was no fire and I watched as the security force helped 'G' out of the cockpit. 'G' later told me that he had not heard me calling him but his radio tested OK and those on the ground heard my message on their radio set. It took some hours before, having returned to Kuala Lumpur to refuel, while the ground force cleared a space, I was able to fly in and bring him out. It took days for the fitters and riggers to dismantle, repair and rebuild the aircraft so that it could be flown back to Kuala Lumpur. No matter how hard you try, it is not always possible to overcome inherent problems, such as a lack of co-ordination, and to turn out a satisfactory helicopter pilot. After several further instructional flights I was forced to suspend 'G' as being unsuitable for operational work.

I carried out hundreds of jungle sorties besides carrying VIP passengers and continuing to instruct. It would take too long to itemise each flight, each problem and each success. Several outstanding incidents occurred, however, and I will relate some of these to illustrate the variety of work. It was not long after we had formed the Squadron 155 at Kuala Lumpur that the requirement to commence troop lifts in to small jungle clearings was put in to practice. The Naval Squadron 848 had been carrying out these duties for some time and was lifting eight to ten troops per aircraft. Our aircraft were only fitted with Pratt and Whitney engines of 650 hp. The naval aircraft had Wright Cyclone engines of 1100 hp. When you add the high temperatures and humidity of Malaya, we found it increasingly difficult to carry more than four or five troops with full kit on a vertical takeoff. Reducing fuel capacity helped but, in the majority of cases, because of the distances involved, this was not an option. We stripped every possible item off the aircraft to reduce weight but were never able to match the naval workload. Frequently, when flying from Kuala Lumpur or other landing strips, we positioned the helicopter in to the wind and took off with a forward run like a fixed wing aircraft until sufficient lift was obtained to get airborne. By the time we reached our objective, sufficient fuel had been burned off to enable (hopefully) descent into a small landing zone. This one factor permanently restricted and reduced operational efficiency. Although pilots dressed in jungle green overalls, 'bone domes' (hard helmets) had not been brought in to the service. Just wearing a radio headset and flying with windows open, due to the heat, resulted in high levels of noise from the engine and gearbox. Many of those pilots operating in these early days, including myself, suffered permanent hearing damage from extensive periods of both low and high pitched vibration

S.55 Westland Whirlwind helicopter over Malayan jungle.

Sakai tribe visit with
Pamela Gouldsbury,
Protector of Aborigines,
near Fort Brooke.

The Sakai lived in a
bamboo and wooden
construction on stilts
called a 'long house'
and lived communally.

and noise. Apart from one or two other small technical inconveniences, the aircraft behaved well and the ground crew were magnificent in maintaining and keeping the aircraft flying under very difficult conditions.

On 22 December, 1954, I was asked to fly a Protector of Aborigines, Mrs Pamela Gouldsbury, into an area of jungle inhabited by a Sakai tribe. In accepting this job I had little idea of the long-term consequences that would result. I had already encountered Chief Superintendent Gouldsbury, as head of police in Kuala Lumpur, following my car accident, and assumed, when I heard the name, that he would also be my passenger. I was therefore surprised when his wife turned up by herself. We took off from Ipoh and flew some 40 miles in to the jungle to a police post called Fort Brooke. This was only a few simple buildings surrounded by barbed wire and manned by a small company of Malay policemen who kept an eye on the area. This made a base for patrols to operate, and it maintained supplies of fuel for helicopters. They also had supplies of trade goods for the aboriginals and hopefully prevented the CTs from coercing the Sakai into supplying them with food.

I had a Corporal Clarke as crewman and, leaving him and the aircraft at the Fort, Mrs Gouldsbury and I, together with a police escort, set out along a well-worn track for the Sakai village. When we arrived there we found some 30 women and children but very few men. The Sakai lived in a bamboo and wooden construction on stilts called a 'long house' and lived communally. They grew their own maize and vegetables and kept a few chickens. The men hunted with blowpipes and poisoned darts. Their existence was very primitive, although civilization had touched them slightly since many of them dressed in manufactured clothes and used cooking implements obtained in Malay *kampongs* or from the fort shop.

Our little delegation was greeted somewhat suspiciously until Pam distributed a variety of gifts and began talking to them in the local dialect. The men began to trickle back in to the 'long house' and we were told that, in our honour, a music party would be held that evening. Pam's job was to ensure the group was healthy, had not been upset or disorientated by the military activities and to offer any assistance that might be requested. By the time dark fell, a fire had been built and the whole company gathered around ten or twelve musicians. The musical instruments were hollow bamboo tubes of various lengths and up to six inches in diameter. By holding them vertical and beating them on the ground a thumping rhythm was produced. The musicians sat on one side of a circle of men who maintained their positions, but who beat their feet and swayed to the music.

Inside the circle all the women, except the very old, gathered and began dancing in a slow undulating motion, rather like a partner-less slow waltz. With the firelight flickering on their faces and bodies I could not help thinking of the European version of a witch's coven. The beat gradually increased in tempo and, as it did, so the women danced faster. Pam and I must have watched for over two hours and I was just about to suggest that we call it a night when Pam said, "Don't go, it's just about to get interesting". The beat had now increased to a degree where the rhythm was almost a steady flow of sound rising and falling. The dancing women were now in a state of frenzy with their limbs violently flexing in all directions and their heads jerking in an agony of ecstasy. Suddenly one fell down and began writhing on the ground. Immediately one of the men broke ranks, rushed into the circle and dragged the woman out. As each woman collapsed they were dragged out of the circle. The music increased in tempo but, as more women collapsed, the circle of men became smaller until some of the men began to take the place of the women and began their version of the dance. It was well into the night and the fire had burnt itself out before the party ended. Pam explained to me that the hypnotic effect of the music and movement caused a physical collapse that was not harmful. It apparently had a therapeutic effect on the dancers but not on the musicians, who must have had very tired arms. All I had was a headache and an ever-lasting memory of a ritual fire dance. I made several further expeditions with Pam in to the deep jungle and will come back to our ongoing relationship later on.

A different type of dance in Kuala Lumpur caused much amusement. Jacko and I, with several squadron members, went to a dance in the Eastern Hotel in Kuala Lumpur. This was really out of bounds to the military, since it had an unsavoury reputation. To dance, one purchased a ticket and generally bought a drink for the girls who swarmed around us. We bought the tickets and the drinks but did not dance. Jacko, however, fell for a beautiful looking brunette, and had a couple of dances with her before we all left for another port of call. A few days later we were sitting in a restaurant when the brunette came in. Jacko immediately went over, re-introduced himself and bought her a drink. We were all killing ourselves with laughter because Jacko did not realise that he had picked up a transvestite and, although as far as I knew he never saw her again, I am pretty certain he never knew that 'she' was a 'he' and none of us ever put him wise!

In February 1955 I was asked to assist A Company 1st Battalion, the Royal Hampshire Regiment. One of their patrols in the Kluang area of Jahor had a serious casevac to be lifted out, or a doctor taken in, preferably the latter. I picked up Captain Lichenstein and flew into an area of very dense jungle. It would have taken days to walk out of an area where the patrol was operating. They had dynamited an area of 200-feet-high trees for me to descend into, but when I flew overhead I was appalled. The hole I was supposed to descend into was very small and irregular stumps up to 12 to 15 feet high were sticking up at various points.

Photo taken by Captain Grey when Captain Lichenstein was lowered to treat a soldier.

It was therefore, completely impossible to land. It would have taken too long to make the landing zone larger and my only alternative, other than aborting the mission, was to descend vertically in the hope that the tree canopy would not be pulled in to the rotors. Captain Lichenstein would then be lowered by rope. The trunks of the surrounding trees were so close to my rotor blades as I descended that there was no room for manoeuvrability. It was a case of vertical descent, like a lift, and then of coming to a hover just above the slivers of the remains of blown up trees. These shattered trunks were standing like stalagmites up to 15 feet high, but one or two seemed even higher on the perimeter of my hover. My crewman, Corporal Plant, threw out a rope and the doctor slid down about 20 or 25 feet to the jungle floor. I have been in some pretty small and dangerous places in my life but never in one as potentially catastrophic as that trip. A Captain Grey took

Difficult descent into a jungle clearing.

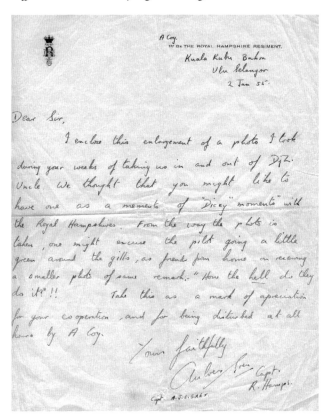

A letter of appreciation from Captain Grey, of A Company 1st Battalion, Royal Hampshire Regiment, who took the above photo and the one on the previous page.

photographs of my efforts and, following a splash in the newspapers, he sent me two framed photographs of me amongst the trees, which even today I find it hard to believe. It turned out that one of the soldiers had suffered a leech, which had entered through his trousers and penetrated up his penis. This had become so swollen and dangerous that his life was in peril. He was operated on in time and survived this experience. No comment.

A new Squadron Leader "H" had arrived the previous month to take over the squadron from Jacko Jackson-Smith. I had hardly seen him for the first two weeks but it now rested for me to break him in to the new job. He had no experience of jungle operations and very little helicopter time, although I never saw his logbook. After converting him on to the Whirlwind I spent considerable flying time introducing him to jungle operations and to the limitations of the underpowered engine. I was sorry that Jacko had been replaced because he was, in my opinion, a better operational pilot than our Squadron Leader "H". Between then and early May 1955 I carried out over 100 operational sorties, a few civil training flights and one or two instructional night flights in the Harvard. Air Vice Marshal Scherger had by now been replaced by Air Vice Marshal Kyle, who was not so pressing with the idea of the Jungle Rescue Team. As a consequence I was able to ease off, and then I pleaded operational necessity to hand over the team to another officer. During all our period of intense jungle training the team had never been called out to a rescue. My only satisfaction, and that of the team, was that, had an incident occurred, we were very well trained and equipped to do the job.

I mentioned previously that, because of lack of engine power, we had stripped the Whirlwinds of all unnecessary weight. This helped but, in general, hampered the loads we could carry. Two off-the-record incidents took place which amused me, but which might not have been officially approved. The first happened when an army patrol wished to cross a river, which was in spate. They had a collapsible boat which, because of the current and turbulence, they could not use, but which they needed on the other side for their return. I devised a way to take the boat over without overloading the maximum weight allowed. Using a log as a pivot and a plank as a see-saw I put the boat on one end and fully kitted troops on the other end. By counting each soldier and multiplying by 200 pounds (the average weight used to calculate troop passenger load) I was able to add this figure to my known fuel load and calculate whether I could carry the boat. After ferrying all the soldiers across I was able to take them their boat after lashing it underneath the fuselage. The second incident occurred a little later on when I lifted a baby elephant across a turbulent river. The patrol was trying to save it, since its mother had been accidentally shot. I used the same method of a massive log balanced in the fork of a tree with quite a few soldiers climbing up a rope to the other end. We got it balanced before a couple of soldiers fell off. With sufficient fuel left to get me back for refuelling and, using the same sling, the baby elephant was lashed under the fuselage and transported across, but got its feet wet in the process.

In the middle of May, rioting began in Singapore. This, it was claimed, had nothing to do with the Emergency but with a workers' strike that was threatening to paralyse air and road transport and a large number of industries, including schools. The Commissioner for Labour, Mr Goodwin, believed it was more political than industrial and that it had to be contained by all means: 40,000 strikers rioted violently and there were many fatal casualties. The Chief Minister supported Mr Goodwin and agreed that the pattern of action by the strikers followed the communist technique. I was instructed to position myself at Pearl Hill Police Station (on top of a hill in Singapore) and provide air cover and information for riot control. For five days I flew at low level over the city carrying police observers, VIPs and voice loud speakers. On one of the early flights I had an engine failure and the only open space was a tennis court. Thank goodness it was a fairly large one and the nets and posts were down. Although I had practised hundreds of engine-off landings on the airfield, this was my first real emergency since I learned to fly helicopters. I was pleased that there was no damage and, after the ground crew had arrived and fixed the engine, I was able to fly out again and continue the operation. This forced landing had been due to a fuel blockage and I thank my lucky stars that it had not happened over the jungle when I would surely have been killed. [Editor's note: John M'Kenzie-Hall suffered three engine failures during his RAF career. Nowadays, in peacetime, the RAF has awarded an AFC for engine-off landings which saved lives. For example: RAF News report that Flight Lieutenant Ben Wallis was presented with the Air Force Cross by the Duke of Cambridge at Buckingham Palace for saving the lives of his crew on board his Merlin helicopter after engine failure in 2018].

After five days I returned to Kuala Lumpur, and I flew some 50 further sorties. I carried out many instructional hours before our Squadron Leader sent me to Kluang in command of a flight. This area, just north of Singapore Island, was amongst the worst areas for terrorist activity and the army was intensifying its work to contain and eliminate the problem. To show the intensity of our work, I carried out 11 troop lifts on 21 June and 12 troop lifts on 22 June. This meant flying continuously, except for refuelling, from dawn to dusk. This was equalled by the other pilots on the flight and we moved hundreds of troops from landing zone to landing zone as well as carrying out recce flights and casevacs.

I was recalled to Kuala Lumpur on several occasions to fly VIPs, since I was the authorised pilot. One of these flights nearly ended disastrously but it had its funny side. Lord De L'Isle and Dudley, then Secretary of State for Air, accompanied by the C. in C. Far Eastern Land Forces (FARELF), came to Kluang and wanted to be taken to a jungle landing zone. We duly departed with my VIPs in rather uncomfortable canvas seats in the cabin. Lord De L'Isle had with him a civilian departmental minister whose name I cannot remember and did not record. He was of ample proportions and had found the canvas seats particularly uncomfortable. While waiting for Lord De L'Isle to finish his visit I asked my fat friend, with baggy shorts and very white knees, whether he would like to fly up front with me on the way back. The navigator's seat was wide and well padded and he was glad to accept. Since he was not active enough to climb up the outside I asked him to enter the cabin, push up the seat from underneath and climb in to the cockpit up the steps. While he was doing this I started the engine and engaged the rotors while I waited for my passengers to approach. All the aircraft were equipped with dual controls and the collective pitch and throttle control lie to the left and parallel with the navigator's (or co-pilot's) seat. I watched as the seat rose and his head appeared through the hole. He started to climb the couple of steps in to the cockpit when he got stuck. He forced himself up, however, and as he rose he caught the pocket of his shorts under the collective pitch lever which also rose. Raising this lever is the operation for taking off to the hover. This, the aircraft quite properly proceeded to do, but, not having sufficient rotor revs, started hopping like a rabbit, but sideways. He continued to climb up and I was pushing madly down on the collective and yelling to him to climb down again. Something had to part and it did. My downward force split his pocket along the seam and left him with only one leg covered. We settled down on all four wheels again about 20 yards from where we started. I do not think Lord De L'Isle ever knew how near he was to being stranded in the jungle. My fat passenger was more concerned with his loss of dress and dignity than with the danger, which I do not think he appreciated.

Shortly after this little episode I was back at Kluang when the army informed me that they had captured a terrorist camp and that a list found there catalogued those to be targeted and eliminated. It contained my name. For the next few days I was looking over my shoulder wherever I went, but my attention was suddenly diverted by an urgent request from the medical authorities. There had been an outbreak of smallpox on a little island off the East Coast called Pulau Tioman. Because of time lost in getting the news over to the mainland, it was thought that a serious epidemic was likely. Could I please take over a medical team immediately? This island was some 40 miles out from the coast, and it rose to some 1,000 feet above sea level. This was another first for me, since I had never flown over water for such a distance. Just north of my route, and some distance seawards from a town called Kuantan, the Japanese Air Force had sunk the battleship *HMS Prince of Wales* and the battle cruiser *HMS Repulse* on 10 December 1941. Under certain lighting conditions these can still be seen sitting on the seabed and remain a memorial to the 840 crew that died in December 1941 (the Japanese attack on Pearl Harbour had taken place just three days earlier). The flight was uneventful and gave me useful experience for what was to come in 1956.

Based in the Kluang area was a company of the South Wales Borderers and I had quite a lot of contact with their commanding officer, Lieutenant Colonel Miers, if I remember his name correctly. We had undertaken a number of troop lifts for him and when he asked if I would fly a Father Christmas to his camp on 25 December I was only too pleased to oblige. This went down very well and shortly after this he asked me for a particular type of immediate operational support. He had received information that a large number of CTs were gathered at a known jungle camp and he was about to go in after them. However, there was an escape route to the north that he could not cover and this is where he sought my help. If I could hover, or move slowly over the area to the north, it would almost certainly block any escape in that direction, since the terrorists would assume we were putting down troops to cut them off.

Flight Lieutenant Hicks had just come down to relieve me after I had been some five months at Kluang and he mentioned that there was possibly a decoration awaiting me at Kuala Lumpur, or so he had heard! He now joined me in this little operation for Lieutenant-Colonel Miers. We positioned ourselves over the map reference at precisely the time agreed and, flying low over the treetops, we made a lot of noise for about half an hour and then returned to base. The army had a great success and captured or killed a number of CTs and their report to Army Command led to my undoing. Since my part had been little more than a fly over, I had not thought it necessary, or had the time, to put it through Kuala Lumpur Headquarters as an operation to be approved. Lieutenant-Colonel Miers in his report, however, had praised our effort as an important part of the success. However, when this reached the ears of Air Vice Marshal Kyle he knew nothing about it. This obviously embarrassed him, but in my view he over-reacted. Officers commanding an isolated detachment should be allowed a modicum of independent authority in an emergency operation, and should not be tied down to an administrative source at a distant headquarters.

As a result I received a full portion of his wrath for not obtaining prior approval. After a few days I returned to the Squadron in Kuala Lumpur. I carried out two flights with General Bourne and one with General Hamilton and on 22 January 1956 I carried out my last flight in Malaya. Two things happened, of which one pleased me and the other still annoys. The first was that I received an assessment in my logbook as 'Exceptional'. I believe I am the first helicopter pilot to receive this assessment of ability. The second was that I heard that our Squadron Leader "H", having decided after my *faux pas*, that no one person in the squadron deserved a decoration, awarded the DFC to himself as representative of the whole squadron. I said 'goodbye' to the flying club, sold my car and flew back to England in February 1956 via Karachi.

In January 2000 my son James returned from touring Malaysia and Borneo. I was delighted to hear of his adventures, but, oh dear, how things have changed in the space of 50 years; even more so since as a small boy, in 1927 I had arrived in Singapore by sea in to a bustling dock of other liners and cargo ships. The first impact of the oily, salty, tarry smell of the docks in high temperature and humidity was exciting enough as one disembarked in to the busy custom sheds. This was followed by the first sight of rickshaws, seating two, pulled by a coolie (trishaws had not yet evolved) running through the streets lined with shops and stalls and pushing through hordes of people of all colours and nationalities. The intermingled smells of people (the babble of many languages), produce, flowers and over-ripe fruit as one bounced along in a chain of rickshaws to the Raffles Hotel, where we always stayed, is a never-forgotten memory. After two days of shopping we then crossed over the causeway to the Malay States by car which, in my father's case, was an American 1926 Nash Open Tourer with lovely wide running boards. In Kuala Lumpur there were no buildings much over three or four storeys, and there were wide-open spaces, many covered by stalls and bazaars, where the noise, smell and excitement were magnified especially to a small boy. Kuala Lumpur, the capital of Malaya, was hardly a city, more like a large town with the railway station being the biggest and main feature. There were very few hotels and most people travelling through stayed in government rest houses.

James arrived in Borneo in December 1999 and was driven to one of the Hilton Hotels. After Christmas, in a hotel in the jungle, he sampled a bit of jungle walking, a few nights in a 'long house' and some river trips. He then flew to Singapore, stayed at another Hilton with a view of all the other sky scrapers and shopping malls and, like all good tourists, he bought a drink at Raffles, before visiting the Tanglin Club. After Singapore, he went by train to Kuala Lumpur. KL has been transformed into another New-York-style city now, boasting tall buildings such as the Petronas Towers rising 88 floors – 375 metres (1,230 feet), making them the tallest twin towers in the world.

Then James went on to Penang, where a few vestiges of the 1920s and 1930s buildings remain. His return of 15 hours by air, to Heathrow, with one stop at Abu Dhabi, is the modern equivalent of five weeks at sea in 1936. Having seen his photographs, I realise that the country I loved will never be revisited by me. I might just as well visit Birmingham or the Shard in London and stay at the various Hiltons. Malaysia is now so consumer-orientated, air-conditioned and politically controlled that it seems to me that visitors will now only get a smidgeon of the East as it was. Of course the same old smells will remain to excite at least one of the senses and, even with air conditioning, a change of shirt several times a day will still be necessary if one gets out in the sun.

Chapter Seven

England (Part III), JEHU, Cyprus and Suez

My flight back to England in 1956, and the stop at Karachi, was a shock. We spent the night at the Beach Luxury Hotel which had been, just prior to independence, equivalent to a large marbled palace. Three short descriptions will illustrate the change and I hope by now a further change has taken place. As we were shown to our rooms it was necessary to scrape past the various cars parked in the corridors. Wooden ramps had been laid up the ornamental stone steps and there was a distinct smell of garage. Each room was en-suite but, where, in the past, a comfortable ceramic loo had been fitted there was now a hole in the floor, which necessitated a squatting position. When the chain was pulled (in this case knob) there was a sudden deluge of water which inevitably caught one's shoes or feet. The first time I tried it I tripped over trying to skip clear. The cocktail bar was still elegantly furnished and the barman was scrupulously dressed in a red and gold uniform with jewelled turban. I suddenly noticed a rat running along one corner of the counter, and I nearly knocked over my glass in my excitement to tell the barman. He just smiled and indicated that he knew it was there. There were four or five of us in the room and, when someone asked him why he was not doing anything about it, he just shrugged and said that if he killed that one there would be another one to follow. I did not linger over my drink but had a fitful night expecting to see rats climbing on to the bed whenever I stirred. So much for the sudden post-war change to independence!

JEHU

A cold, windy, drizzly day in winter is not exactly the best time to return to England. I had been so long away that I had lost touch with many friends. I now had no wife, no home, no car and no idea what the RAF had in store for me. I

Joint Experimental Helicopter Unit (JEHU).

stayed in London for about two months and had time to visit some old haunts before being posted to Middle Wallop in Hampshire. The airfield there had been a wartime fighter base for the RAF, but it was now under Army control as a training school for AOP pilots. Shortly before my arrival, a new unit had been formed to evaluate and experiment with helicopters prior to the formation of an Army Air Corps. This was known as the Joint Experimental Helicopter Unit (JEHU). I joined the unit at the end of May 1956 and was pleased to find that many of the pilots from my old squadron were there, including Jacko Jackson from 155 Squadron, now relegated back to Flight Lieutenant. Our commanding officer was an army colonel by the name of J. F. T. Scott and his second-in-command was a Squadron Leader Kearns, both of whom had surprisingly limited operational experience of helicopters, although Kearns had an instructor's qualification. JEHU consisted of a mixture of RAF officers and ten army officers. Most of this integral force had operational experience in either Sycamores or Whirlwinds and, in a number of cases, both. I had only been at JEHU for less than a month when I was asked by the Air Ministry to carry out Whirlwind trials in Cyprus. This operation had been asked for by Field Marshal Sir John Harding, the Governor of Cyprus. It seemed that the squadron of Sycamores stationed there were being operated by aircrew with insufficient knowledge of tropical conditions and several aircraft had come to grief. It had been found that Sycamores were not operating successfully in the tactical requirement for mountain flying at heights up to and above 6,000 feet. More training was being carried out and more Sycamores were on their way but the need was evident for large troop-carrying helicopters. I arrived in Cyprus as a passenger on the first overseas flight of the new Beverley Transport Aircraft. Packed in its stomach was a Mark 2 Whirlwind Helicopter together with a representative from the Westland Aircraft Company, Mr Chant. Once the helicopter had been unloaded and assembled I was able to carry out a successful air test and assess the mountainous terrain. I then commenced a series of weight lifts at all heights in all weather conditions.

Cyprus

The temperatures in Cyprus in summer were little different to Malaya, but the humidity was much less. The winds, however, were stronger and continually changing direction over the scrub-covered steep slopes of the mountainous regions. By reducing fuel, I managed to carry up to five fully laden troops to a reasonable height but this proved dangerous in the hover for, with no ground cushion on the slopes, any change of wind led to loss of lift and required more power. Unfortunately the Mark 2, at full throttle, could not hold its position out of wind and, with the turbulence, I had some nasty moments. In my final report I had to state that the payload required in the conditions prevailing would not be practical with this mark and that, although individual troop lifts might be successful, full utilisation would almost certainly result in accidents. This would be the case particularly if pilots were not fully experienced in mountain flying.

While I was in Cyprus I had the pleasure of being blown up. One day I was driving back to the airfield at Nicosia when I passed an Army Captain, trudging through the dusty red road in the heat of the afternoon. I stopped and offered him a lift, which he was more than glad to accept. His name was Captain Worthington and, his Land Rover having broken down, he was walking back to his unit. I drove him back, via the RAF for a shower and drink, to his base. A few days later he rang to thank me, and asked whether I would like to join him on his boat, which was moored beside the police station at Kyrenia Harbour. I thought this a pleasant diversion and shortly afterwards I drove down to the harbour (now Turkish territory). Imagine my surprise when his boat was a cruising yacht of large dimensions and Captain Worthington turned out to be one of the brewing family. His crew had brought the yacht *Fieldfare* to Cyprus for the honeymoon he expected to enjoy following his forthcoming marriage. My next invitation was for dinner. On 13 August 1956 I duly drove down to the yacht ready for a pre-dinner drink before eating. We were sitting up on the deck enjoying the cool of the evening, when there was an enormous bang and the yacht began to sink on its moorings. It ended up pinned to the wall of the quay by its moorings with its decks awash. Alas, no drinks! EOKA [Editor's note: *Ethniki Organosis Kyprion Agoniston* (EOKA) was a Greek Cypriot nationalist guerrilla organisation that fought a campaign for the end of British rule in Cyprus) had slipped by the police station and attached a limpet mine to the hull.

Suez

I returned to JEHU on July 15th, having left the Whirlwind with the Sycamore Squadron. I heard later that, although it was only used for low-altitude work, it had crashed badly. Shortly after I returned to Middle Wallop, word came through of the political problems concerning the Suez Canal. While I had been in Malaya in 1955, and during the early troubles in Cyprus, the Soviet Union was supplying arms to Egypt. This had all the makings of a major conflict in the Middle East. Suddenly, in July 1956, Gamal Abdel Nasser, President of Egypt, nationalised the Suez Canal. Churchill had become prime minister again and Anthony Eden was foreign secretary. Following Churchill's resignation, Anthony Eden became prime minister. Selwyn Lloyd had been made foreign secretary in

The pleasure of being blown up: the attempt to sink Captain Worthington's yacht Fieldfare *with me on it!*

December 1955 and had been involved in diplomatic journeys around the world, trying to mediate with all concerned. While all this was going on the chiefs of staff, Dickson, Boyle and Templer, had been discussing a possible takeover of the Suez Canal, since Nasser's action was a breach of international law and the Canal was of the utmost importance between east and west.

At the end of September 1956, JEHU was instructed to prepare itself for flying onto an aircraft carrier. No reason was given but we all knew fairly well what the situation was. JEHU commenced its retraining by carrying out elementary deck landings at Middle Wallop, by marking out the size of a ship flight deck. Since I had had much experience of deck landings in the Fleet Air Arm during World War II, I was dragged in to help. We embarked in *HMS Theseus* at Spithead, on

Westland Whirlwind helicopters of the Royal Navy taking the first men of 45 Royal Marine Commando into action at Port Said from HMS Theseus.

1 October, with 12 aircraft. We carried out full operational training for about 10 days before returning to Middle Wallop to await results. In October we were ordered to carry out more continuation training at sea, this time on *HMS Ocean*.

We sailed on 27 October, from Devonport to Malta, with 45 Commando Royal Marines on board with us. As we reached Gibraltar, Squadron Leader Kearns and I flew to the Rock and brought back the news that we were at war with Egypt. On the way back to the carrier the aircraft lost servo pressure and went in to manual. This took Danny completely by surprise. I do not believe he had practised this mode of heavy control flying previously. There was little to worry about and with two of us co-ordinating the controls we returned without difficulty. Malta was reached on 31 October where we joined *HMS Theseus*, carrying the naval element of helicopters. These two carriers gave us 21 aircraft for the assault.

It had first been planned that we would be used for casualty evacuation, but this plan had earlier been dropped. Instead, it was proposed that we would lift 45 Commando, via Ismailia, to a point behind Port Said, to capture a couple of bridges. This plan too was dropped. Shortly before we departed it was learned

The Suez Crisis (operation Musketeer) 1956. With a French hospital ship in the background, HMS Theseus is shown with Westland Whirlwind helicopters of the joint RAF/Army unit which operated alongside Royal Navy helicopters from her flight deck.

A helicopter view of the attacking fleet.

that the French had already captured the bridges. We were therefore told that our task would be to follow up the sea-borne assault and land our troops on the beach by the statue of De Lesseps. Since this was to be the first occasion in military history in which helicopters were to be used in a full-scale assault, we were all slightly nervous. I was kept awake on and off all night, since my bunk was close to the lift and this banged and scraped each time it carried aircraft and stores to the flight deck. We assembled just before dawn for prayers and went on deck to see plumes of black smoke arising in the distance from Port Said.

At about 6.00 am on 6 November 1956, I took off, together with the five other Whirlwinds as the first wave. I was carrying six Royal Marines and flying in low, over the water, at about 75 knots to the beaches. Since the port was still being attacked from the air by Sea Hawks and Wyverns, it was a little frightening suddenly to see rockets and other missiles passing very close at high speed and ships exploding in front and to each side. The turnaround time was about 10 minutes and on my first lift I landed in thick drifting smoke, some yards from De Lesseps statue. As the Marines disembarked one was wounded and I had him back on board and in sickbay some 15 or 20 minutes after he first left the carrier. I think I carried out six or seven trips before the attack was completed and, in all, JEHU and the Navy lifted 415 marines and 25 tons of equipment in the two and a half hours of the assault.

We then lifted out the RAF ground personnel to Gamil airfield, which had been captured in the first assault by army parachutists. This was our base during our stay. Our work then consisted of forward-area reconnaissance, casualty evacuation and communication. A little way along the shore from Gamil airfield stood a number of holiday chalets right on the beach. JEHU moved into these, and they soon wished they had not. They were filthy, and flies covered the tables, walls and windows like black cloths. Even after we had spent hours cleaning up and spraying, the flies returned. Having accepted the inevitable, we made ourselves as comfortable as possible when off duty. One of the pleasures was being able to walk down the steps straight in to the sea, and swimming took up most of our leisure time. Having passed through the Suez Canal several times in the past, I was not particularly enthused with Port Said and during our stay I never went into the town. Plenty of rumours reached us

Our beach-side chalet a little way along the shore from Gamil airfield.

Debriefing at El Gamil – L to R: Maj R. V. Waters R.A., Flt Lts M'Kenzie-Hall [in sunglasses, partially obscured] and Stewart, Capt. J. Garry RASC, Flt Lt J. Johnson, Capt. R.N. Harris RASC (seated), Sqn Ldrs Panter and the 2IC Sqn Ldr Kearns.

The dispersal at El Gamil Airfield – note distant rows of oil drums used by Eqyptians to block runways.

The helicopter dispersal at El Gamil airfield with the air traffic control building, and in the foreground discarded parachutes and air drop containers.

of chaos that accompanied the army takeover, and some of them were probably true. I was told that, because of the mass of shipping involved, the planners had allowed the tanks to go in early, but their ammunition was still out at sea and the tank crews were straddling the streets and using small arms and Very pistols. Unlikely, but it sounds very like the environmental planners of today!

I can only tell of my own experiences while at Gamil and, operationally, and these were quite exciting. One of my first flights was to El Kantara, about a third of the way down the Suez Canal. We found the French had already been there. It was obvious to us that very little work would be required to retake the whole of the canal down to Suez, if the opposition was similar to that which we had already encountered. Just north-west of Gamil airfield and out to sea was a small island containing a radar station. We flew out and occupied it, finding all personnel had fled but very little equipment destroyed. I found a picture of Nasser in one office which I took as a souvenir but have since lost. On 18 November I was flying over Lake Manzala when I saw a *felucca* sailing north-west. As I watched, a number of figures on the deck seemed to have weapons and then they all disappeared below decks. I reported this immediately and returned to the airfield where I picked up five Argyll and Sutherland Highlanders and caught up with the *felucca* again, amongst some sand banks where there was a small mud building. I flew directly over the boat, came to a hover, forced it to beach and then landed quite near the hut. Directly the Argylls disembarked, the Egyptians came out with their arms up in surrender. Having accomplished my task I returned to Gamil. I understand that 18 Egyptians were captured, together with a machine gun and 3,000 rounds of ammunition. I believe the noise and size of the Whirlwind almost on top of them must have scared them to death. Had they resisted there surely would have been one dead pilot, five dead troops and one destroyed helicopter. God was on my side that day.

Our fly-blown accommodation on the beach had now become a dump for empty bottles, since the heat and long evenings had raised our consumption of beer and alcohol considerably. Jacko (Jackson-Smith) and I decided to solve the problem, since no further supplies were available from the stores brought over. We collected all the empty bottles, loaded them in to crates and hitch-hiked them to Nicosia in a Valetta (like a Dakota). I can still remember the background rattle every time the aircraft hit any turbulence. While I purchased a fresh supply Jacko went off to get rid of the bottles which, in those days, were returnable. He came back very pleased with himself having persuaded the NAAFI to take the lot by saying that they had been purchased from them in the first place. This little white lie recouped some of our expenditure and no one went dry up to the time of our departure from Port Said.

The military campaign was proceeding satisfactorily and we were 20 miles

Logbook No.6 commendation – 'Flying Ability Exceptional' – Suez 1956.

down the canal when threats from America (President Eisenhower), the UN and Russia caused the campaign to halt. An order was given therefore to cease fire. The American Sixth Fleet were, by this time, close by to intervene if we did not obey and Eden had already decided that there was no recourse but to comply. Our unit continued at Gamil for two weeks before being recalled to the United Kingdom.

During our time at the airfield, the salt had begun to corrode the magnesium alloy of the aircraft fuselage. John Coombes, the Westland Aircraft Engineer, had been with us throughout the operation and he was now very concerned about the gradual deterioration of the aircraft. It was decided to fly the six Whirlwinds to Cyprus. The official history of JEHU was written in 1961, some five years after the event. Many of the mistakes in it were because the document was obviously compiled by those who were not at the scene or from hearsay. In the section describing the evacuation from Port Said it states, "The six Whirlwinds were embarked in *HMS Eagle* on 22 November and, on reaching Cyprus, were flown to Akrotiri." In fact, the aircraft were flown from Port Said directly to Nicosia and then on to Akrotiri. Halfway over they all landed on *HMS Eagle* for a short re-fuelling stop before proceeding. My passenger was Mr Coombes, who had asked to fly with me. I often wonder whether the six Whirlwind pilots who had carried out the first carrier-borne helicopter assault were also the first to fly that number of single-engine helicopters over a vast area of water and to fly in formation for so long. Perhaps this is a paragraph for the *Guinness Book of Records*?

From Cyprus we boarded a tank landing craft for the journey to England. This was a cramped, stuffy voyage with a full complement of tanks giving the ship a pitching and rolling motion. The only comfort I could get was up on deck in a sheltered corner. The Bay of Biscay was terrible and we nearly foundered when some of the tanks shifted, giving us an alarming list. We arrived at Devonport on Christmas Eve 1956 to find the opposite of a return of the conquering heroes. Having since read the full political story, from the British and French point of view, I am convinced that we could have turned the canal debacle into a success had it not been for the United States' political intervention and the world trade in sterling. This was our own money which, at a fixed exchange rate, we were being obstructed from withdrawing from the International Monetary Fund by the United States Treasury.

Meeting June

The anticlimax of my return to England was soon overtaken by another dramatic event which, once again, changed the direction of my life. Routine had begun to settle in to JEHU again and I was still the Operation Training Officer. Having sold my car before going to Suez, I now bought a Jaguar MK VII. In those days this was the poor man's Bentley and I spent my spare time roaming the local hostelries and travelling up to London, where I had several girl friends. One weekend, in Salisbury, I ran into Pamela Gouldsbury, whom I had last encountered as a Protector of Aborigines in Malaya. She and her husband had now retired and were living in a little village called Martin, just outside Salisbury. They invited me, on several occasions, to drinks and, on one occasion, I took Jackson-Smith along. Amongst others, we met Philippa Gouldsbury, Pam's sister-in-law. I learned that the Gouldsbury family had been in India as tea planters for the Glasgow company James Finlay on the Seetagundi Estate in the Nilgiris, the neighbouring estate to my family's tea plantation. Indeed they had old photographs of my family. The result of all these communal meetings was an invitation to a hunt ball and I was to be sure to bring Jacko.

Jacko and I togged ourselves up in full mess dress and drove down to Martin village. Since Philippa was almost my height I expected to partner her, and this I thought was confirmed when we arrived and I met her friend who was Jacko's height. She was introduced as June Steele. The girls went up to change and during this time they must have discussed our various merits. When they eventually emerged down the stairs and joined us, June, being the shorter, made a beeline for Jacko, as she told me afterwards, thinking Philippa was my partner. At the first opportunity Philippa hissed at June, "You've got

Walter Henry Medhurst, June M'Kenzie-Hall's great-grandfather, was a missionary, author, printer and translator in China.

ABOVE: W. H. Medhurst in conversation with Choo-Tih-Lang attended by a Malay boy.

RIGHT: Title page of one of W. H. Medhurst's publications, 1842.

the wrong one". To the surprise of Jacko, June turned to me, leaving the way open for Philippa to move in.

June had been married to an army officer in 1945 when she was 20, but was now divorced. Although she was only 5'2" to my 6'2" we immediately took to each other and had a wonderful hunt hall. After some dancing we found ourselves sitting half-way up the grand staircase talking, talking and talking! Her father had been a prisoner of the Japanese – so had mine; she had been sent to England to be educated– so had I. We found common ground on so many subjects that we only just managed the last waltz. Next day we spent hours walking in the countryside and finding a great deal of compatibility balanced by an individual outlook on life gained through our various experiences; hers in the Philippines and in India and mine in Australia and Malaya.

June was born at Iloilo in the Philippines on 2 June 1925, the third daughter of Walter and Doris Medhurst Saul. The Saul name comes from County Down, Ireland, where there is a village called Saul near Downpatrick. The Medhurst name comes from the Reverend Dr Walter Henry Medhurst (1796–1857) who spent his life as an LMS missionary printer in Malacca, Penang, and Batavia and, after the First Opium War, he established a London Missionary Society mission in Shanghai in 1843, where he helped translate the Bible into classical Chinese and the New Testament into the Mandarin dialect of Nanking. Robert Powell Saul married Medhurst's daughter Martha Medhurst in 1849. Their son George Medhurst Saul (1851–1928) was born in Liverpool and went to the Philippines and married Damiana Robles Y Figuerroa (widow of the American consul Loring) and established an import-export business under the name Hoskyn & Co, Merchants, which was the first department store in Iloilo. George and Damiana had five sons, one of whom was June's Father, Walter Emil Medhurst Saul, who was also born in the Philippines. My wife June was named 'Barbara' after a golf course and 'June' after the month she was born in, and she preferred to be known as June. She was one of three sisters: Pat, Penny and June. They departed the Philippines in 1931. Her father remained in Iloilo to run the family business but was captured by the Japanese and put into Santo Tomas prison camp in Manila where he was badly treated and malnourished.

The three Medhurst Saul sisters were called the 'three disgraces' by 'uncle' Cecil Ferrers (not really a real uncle but the wicked 'Uncle of Baddesley Clinton'), whom they met on board the boat to England, and they remained friends with the Ferrers thereafter.

The three sisters became Londoners and were educated at home by a home tutor, not a governess as June was careful to point out.

Their mother, Doris, one of five children was from the Tennent family, so

June M'Kenzie-Hall (née Medhurst-Saul).

'The Three Disgraces' – June (centre) with her sisters Pat (left) and Penny (right).

they had lots of Tennent relations. Tennent family Christmases were held at Tyttenhanger Lodge, Uncle Monty and Aunt Hester's Prep School at Seaford, East Sussex. The three sisters were either lodged in the sanatorium or the dormitories. About 21 members of the family gathered here pre and post World War Two.

June was confirmed at St Paul's Cathedral on 13 July 1940 aged 15, by the Bishop of London, Dr Fisher (later Archbishop of Canterbury). This was the darkest period of World War Two for London in particular. No wonder the inscription in her prayer book given at her confirmation, read: 'May your future be always as bright as June'.

Her parish church was All Souls, Langham Place. The vicar Earnshaw Smith and his family became close friends. All Souls was bombed in December 1940.

June matriculated two years early as she was put in for the same exams as her two sisters 'just for practice' and got a distinction. She was very good at Latin. Post-war she was destined for Cambridge to read theology. That did not happen.

During the Second World War they remained in central London, at Sussex Gardens and went about their education, popping in, when necessary, to the air-raid shelters on the way to their various activities during the bombing. An often-told anecdote was when a bomb landed close by, they dived under the table and a deaf relative remarked 'did someone drop something?'

June was too young to go off to work but her sisters went to war. First the eldest Pat to the WRNS and spent the war at Bletchley Park (she never spoke about what she did, but now we know it was the top-secret home of codebreakers, as depicted in *The Imitation Game* film starring Benedict Cumberbatch as Alan Turing).

Henry Hemmings' inscription.

Penny joined MI5 (The War Office, Intelligence Service) in 1941 and worked at Blenheim Palace. One did not just join MI5, and I believe the first to join was her cousin, Pam Tennent, very early in the war. MI5 recruited by introduction and, I think, it was quite common for members of the same family to enter the secret intelligence world.

June would join MI5 just after the war. She said it was her university. She was known under her married name, June Steele. I would like to quote from an email from Henry Hemming, the author of the 2017 book: *M. Maxwell Knight, MI5's Greatest Spymaster*. In the copy he sent June, inscribed 'For June, also known as Stainless Steele', he wrote 'What a courageous, dedicated and talented woman she must have been to work under John Bingham and Maxwell Knight in MI5'.

She was too discreet to reveal her work but I know she enjoyed it and particularly admired her agents in the field for their courage. This was the period known as 'The Cold War'. We get some idea from the John Le Carré novels who based some of his characters on a combination of Maxwell Knight and in particularly John Bingham, who was partly the template for George Smiley. June's boss was John Bingham. I wish I knew more.

My decision on whether to consider marriage was further complicated by several factors. I had been seriously thinking of going over to Canada, where a large helicopter company called 'Okanagan' was advertising for pilots at very high wages and superior conditions of living. By 1952 Okanagan Helicopters Ltd had become the largest commercial helicopter operator in North America and one of the largest in the world. A friend of mine at JEHU, called John Shaw, had already joined them and reported very favourably on the work in the Northern Territories. It is extraordinary how sometimes, after a lull, everything comes at once. Following a weekend in London, I returned to Middle Wallop to find that I was required to report to the Air Ministry in London for an interview. I was given no information on what it was about, but I had some trepidation since officers were generally posted without being consulted. Since returning from the Suez campaign I had been busy as the Operational Instructor for the unit. My experience as a naval pilot had enabled me to train both the RAF and army pilots of JEHU in the techniques of landing on aircraft carriers, prior to Suez. The commanding officer of JEHU, Colonel Scott, was particularly pleased with my work and, once again, I had my log book endorsed as 'exceptional'. I had been called in a hurry just before Suez to carry out operational trials in the mountains of Cyprus, and I had received kind words from the governor. This then might be another such assignment, but why call me to the Air Ministry? I was soon to find out.

In London I was interviewed by an air commodore, whose name I have forgotten, who informed me that I had been asked by the Captain of The Queen's Flight, Sir Edward Fielden, to visit him at RAF Benson in Oxfordshire. Since I had been operational flying overseas for some years I had little knowledge of TQF, except that they flew the Royal Family in somewhat dated Vickers Vikings. This was an aircraft I had never flown, besides which I was now wedded to helicopters which, in my view, were going to play a very important part in future service operations. The air commodore did not enlighten me further, except to say I had been highly recommended by a previous commanding officer and that, since I was the only name put forward by the Air Ministry, I should feel rather privileged. At this point in time I felt more confused than privileged. I did not really want to stop operational flying, with so many overseas opportunities in the offing. Having refused all staff and administrative duties over the years and changed services twice, I was still somewhat surprised to have been chosen as a candidate.

In my book *Hoverhawk: the personal story of the first Royal Helicopters* (2017) I have described at some length my meeting with Sir Edward Fielden, or 'Mouse' as he was universally known. Suffice to say here that, after discussing my experience at some length, his dossier on me looked fairly comprehensive. We progressed to subjects far removed from flying even talking about continental drift! At the end he explained his ambition to bring helicopters onto the flight and to inaugurate a service for the royal family for short and medium flights in the UK and Europe. If I accepted he would like me to join The Queen's Flight and to undertake the whole programme of acquiring the right type of helicopter and to undertake the testing of the new aircraft to be custom built for the royal duties and to command the unit, once formed. He also added that, in addition, I would be appointed as flying instructor and personal pilot to Prince Philip, Duke of Edinburgh. Not only did the thought of the task seem overwhelming but the knowledge that I was to join and hopefully become one of the elite of a small group, chosen as the best pilots in the RAF, was exciting but devastating to contemplate.

I had to accept the challenge, but little did I know of the difficulties and disappointments that such an undertaking would bring before success was achieved. After unbroken years of build-up to a full operational role we flew not only the royal family but foreign royalty and heads of state from all parts of the world. More of this later but, at this time, I was involved in saying goodbye to my very good friends in the experimental unit of the army. We had formed the initial nucleus of the forthcoming establishment of the new Army Air Corps, and we had marked our success by carrying out the first carrier airborne assault by helicopter in history.

This was not the only goodbye that I had to make. I had a number of girl friends in London and, as I moved further in my feelings for June, I felt it important to end these relationships as soon as possible. This was carried out over several rather entertaining weeks which were not without upset and tantrums. June never knew when to expect me and I could not explain my nefarious shedding activities without giving the wrong impression. I somehow think that my attitude towards women in that period was partly due to my feeling of inadequacy after my failed marriage and, in some ways, a form of carefree revenge to prove my masculinity.

I now had just a month to go before I joined The Queen's Flight and I was on leave and free of all commitments. I asked June to marry me with some trepidation, since I had little money, no car (having sold it prior to Suez) and my only asset being an area of building land in Moshi, Tanganyika, which I had hoped to develop. I realised also that, equally, June's trepidation of another marriage was not only strong but in many ways fearful. We were both afraid of making the same sort of mistake again. The knot was finally tied in the Brompton Registry Office. There was nothing glamorous here. We stood before a funny little man who gabbled through the brief ceremony at such a pace that it was difficult to follow him. Since I was looking over his head and thinking 'Oh God, what have I done' he sharply reminded me that I had to say 'yes' or 'I do. Then it was all over. June's mother was the only person attending and, at the end, the little man asked where my witness to the marriage document was. I had not thought of this so we solved the problem by hijacking someone outside the Registry Office. I cannot remember him in any detail whatsoever or what we paid him. Why did we not have a church wedding? The horror of my first wedding in Tanganyika and the fact that we were both divorced made us decide otherwise. It was not until the late 1950s that divorce became semi-acceptable. In certain circles of the air force the stigma was apparent up to the late 1960s. Apart from this, I had only a limited time before my new appointment which I wished to take up as a married man. The air force, erroneously, believed that an appointment carrying responsibilities bore more

June M'Kenzie-Hall (née Medhurst-Saul), 1945

weight with a married officer. In this case, very unusually for me, I went by the book probably because it suited me!

I knew June worked at the War Office and she had obtained leave to coincide with mine. Our honeymoon was very short and somewhat of a disaster. The adage 'you pay for what you get' comes to mind here, since we had little money and no transport. Pre-war, with my father in Malaya, we had lived at Avonside, a house on the banks of the river Avon, at Stratford-on-Avon. I knew that the house had been taken over by the Ministry of Defence during the war and that we had left a number of suitcases, from our return from Malaya in 1936, in the cellars. I had come across an advertisement for a hotel called Avonside in

Stratford-on-Avon and naturally assumed that this was our old abode, turned in to a hotel. I looked forward to renewing my acquaintance with Stratford, remembering how I used to strap my ice skates on in the front porch, step over the garden and skate up the river to the newly built Shakespeare Theatre.

To get to Stratford we had to have a car and my sister-in-law, Pat, offered us her A. C. Sports car for the period. I gladly accepted and, after a quiet wedding breakfast, we set off from London. Old sports cars, however illustrious in the past, have a habit of teaching one a lesson. This A. C. was no exception. A few miles out of London the clutch pedal snapped off at the floor boarding and, of course, at the first stop the car stalled in top gear without a means of release. Not to be beaten, and determined to show resourcefulness, I bought a broom handle from a local ironmongery shop and bound this to the stump of the clutch pedal stalk, beneath the floorboards. On the command 'push', June pushed down and I changed gear. On the command 'release' she let go of the handle and we engaged gear. We continued until another change of gear was required when we repeated the process. With some inevitable failure in coordination, but still honouring our marriage vow, we eventually arrived at Stratford-on-Avon. I thought I remembered the way to Avonside, which lay past the theatre, past the Dirty Duck pub, past the church and on the left. We found it quite easily, only to be told that the Shakespeare Company had taken over the building when the war ended, as a hostelry for theatre employees and the various tour companies playing there.

After some difficultly we found another 'Avonside'. It was a bed and breakfast house, not quite a hotel, outside the town but at least on the river side. We made the best of it. It was not what we had expected, but then many things in life never really live up to expectations. With a new clutch installed we finally returned to London, June back to the War Office and I to RAF Benson.

Chapter Eight

The Queen's Flight

Although The Queen's Flight was a lodger unit at RAF Benson it was an entirely separate unit based at one end of the airfield and its area was strictly out of bounds to all but TQF personnel. It had a wing of two-storey offices along one side of the hanger, but entry to the hanger or workshops was guarded day and night. Before a royal flight, following preparation, the particular aircraft was also individually guarded until it was positioned for departure. I came across all this security directly I arrived at TQF. The warrant officer in charge wanted to see my identity card and even then was reluctant to show me around until after I had made myself known to the adjutant. The executive and aircrews occupied the second-floor offices with Sir Edward Fielden at one end who was looked after by a senior civil servant acting as his secretary.

There were two empty offices between the secretary and the flight adjutant. These were to be occupied by me later but, at the time, formed a barrier between Sir Edward and the adjutant, which no one dared to breach unless invited. The aircrew room was at the other end of the building and it was here that I had my first introduction to the aircrews who manned the Viking aircraft. They were each made up of pilot, co-pilot, navigator, engineer and radio operator. The commanding officer of the unit was a wing commander who had his separate office next door to the adjutant. However, since he was also the senior pilot, he was invariably in the crew room in connection with the planning of forthcoming flights.

I had rarely seen so many heavily decorated officers all together in one unit. DFCs, AFCs, CVOs, MVOs, DFMs etc. were all well distributed and I felt a little shamefaced with only my campaign ribbons on display. My only consolation was in the realisation that since I had travelled the world, from theatre to theatre, I probably had more flying time as an instructor and more experience of flying, in its many forms, than most of them.

TQF Dragonfly helicopter which had been lent by the Central Flying School.

My promotion had not yet come through, so I arrived as a Flight Lieutenant in June 1957 with the rank I had previously held in 1943 before transferring to the Fleet Air Arm of the Navy. The cool and enquiring welcome I received was quite understandable. All the crews were in a state of flux and uncertainty. Sir Edward had decided to phase out the twin-engine Vikings for the new four-engined de Havilland Herons. These required only a pilot and navigator, so the engineers and radio operators were being faced with redundancy. Those about to depart had little interest in helicopters and of those remaining only one officer, Allen Lee, knew anything about them! He, together with Brian Trubshaw (future test pilot of the Concorde) had some years previously taken a course on the little Hoverfly helicopter, and he had made a couple of experimental flights with Royal Mail. This had not been a success and the trial was discontinued. Allen Lee, however, had returned for a second tour of fixed-wing flying on TQF and he had been the pilot responsible for bringing back Princess Elizabeth and Prince Philip from Kenya on the death of her father, King George VI. He was now leaving for flying duties in Vietnam where, tragically, he was shot down and killed shortly after arrival.

There was a Dragonfly helicopter on the strength of TQF which had been lent by the Central Flying School at RAF Little Rissington. It had been used on a couple of occasions to fly Princess Margaret (an abortive flight with a forced landing) and the Queen Mother. It was highly unsuitable and I could never understand why Mouse ever agreed to its use. I can only assume that since larger rotary wing aircraft were not available at that time he pushed for this as a prelude to persuading the Air Ministry to finance the considerable cost of establishing a custom-built unit of helicopters to complement the fixed wing element.

On my first meeting with the commanding officer, Wing Commander Hyland-Smith, I was put completely at ease. He explained that he knew nothing about helicopters and that, with the intensive work schedules and intricate forward planning necessary for the Viking flights, he would have to leave me very much on my own. Mouse had not involved him in this new phase and most of the other officers had little idea of what my role was to be. It was understandable in that helicopters were only just beginning to play an established role in the RAF, with most of their early activity being overseas. There seemed to be general feeling amongst transport aircraft crews that helicopters were frail, unpredictable, prone to engine and airframe failure and lethal if the engine stopped. It seemed that one of my first tasks was to enlighten not only them, but many others responsible for the safety of the Royal passengers, including Mouse. He, although firm in his determination to use them, was always a little anxious on the affect that any serious incident might have on TQF and, of course, on his reputation. Because of this separate role and operational complexities it was agreed that, instead of operating through the commanding officer, I would have direct access to Mouse. Hyland-Smith agreed, but this was not always the case with those who replaced him.

On the question of rank and status within the flight, Hyland-Smith must have sensed my ill-ease, for he explained his outlook. Discipline within the tasks to be undertaken should be recognised. That said, since all the aircrew had been chosen primarily for their experience, expertise and standard of performance, they were all considered to be equal. Having spent most of my career finding that the opposite viewpoint prevailed, in all the services, I was immensely pleased. My meaning of 'opposite viewpoint' needs explanation and I will try to do this without it appearing to be a matter of 'sour grapes'. I had served under many good senior officers but, in my opinion, a small number were mere passengers with limited flying experience whose attitude towards junior officers was imperial, without consideration and whose whole service career was spent living by the book (keeping their noses clean) and keeping in with their superiors, without questioning and, in many cases, failing to appreciate either factual or moral issues. An officer's career could be curtailed, or seriously affected, by one bad comment in his annual report. Such reports, written by those you got on with, or by those you did not, followed you relentlessly throughout your service life.

For the first few weeks after joining TQF there seemed little to do except re-orientate myself by flying around the area in the Dragonfly. This little aircraft, although sensitive to control and fairly unstable in flight, took me back to my early days during the Malayan Emergency when I spent so many hours flying over deep jungle, bringing back dead and wounded communist guerrillas and many of our own servicemen.

At this time, Mouse was away on a long, foreign royal trip, so I occupied the rest of my time in getting to know the aircrews and the servicing personnel on the hangar floor. From the small gang that looked after my helicopter to the many engineers, riggers, carpenters, wireless mechanics and stewards etc, I found all to be absolutely first class and wholly dedicated to their work. There was an attitude on the hangar floor of immense pride in everything they did and woe betide anyone who let the flight down.

Since no one seemed to know anything about Mouse's plans for incorporating helicopters, and the secretary could give me no previous correspondence to read, I decided to prepare a paper for Mouse on his return. The idea was not to pre-empt any strategy already decided but to show my ideas in such a way that Mouse might appreciate.

I did know that, after much hard bargaining with the Air Ministry and particularly those controlling the service estimates, agreement had already been reached for the provision of an initial two large helicopters based on the American Sikorsky S-55. Almost as soon as I picked up my pen to start I had a call from the secretary, Ralph Dawson, to attend 'Mouse', who had just returned. This was my first meeting with him since my arrival at Benson and I was not altogether happy with the outcome. It was quite apparent that, knowing little about the operation of helicopters, he had accepted advice from quarters in the Ministry that also seemed to be ignorant of the necessary provisions vital for the safe and comfortable transport of Royal passengers. Apart from this, he had further news affecting me personally.

There had been an arrangement for some months that when Prince Philip wished to fly to an engagement in a helicopter, the Royal Navy provided one of their aircraft from a VIP squadron based at Lee-on-Solent in Hampshire. The pilot, Lieutenant Commander Spreadbury (whom I knew quite well from Malaya) had been selected for this duty and his role had been expanded recently to cover other royal passengers who were realising the advantage of shorter journey times and a more convenient mode of travel. Until such time as our own aircraft began to appear, Mouse wished me to accompany every helicopter flight carrying royal passengers, not as the pilot but as navigator. He did not seem to recognise the difficulties this would cause. He was quite blunt in telling me he had been dissatisfied with this temporary arrangement with the Fleet Air Arm, since part of his responsibility had necessarily had to revert to the Navy. Once having instigated a flight he never knew at any stage where the aircraft was until completion of the flight. He also never received a post-briefing report covering the journey. From this date, and this had been agreed with the Navy, I was to be in command of every flight but not as captain (pilot) of the aircraft. My responsibility, however, covered the pre-flight planning, the briefing of those receiving the royal personage and regular communication with TQF during all stages of the flight. With an almost dismissive gesture, he handed me a scrap of paper saying, "Here is a map reference. Pick up Prince Philip and take him back to Buckingham Palace". As I went out of the door he casually told me, "I have arranged for a whole sheet to be laid on the lawn and you will probably see policemen hiding in the surrounding trees". I had been thrown in at the deep end and left to get on with it!

Since I knew Ted Spreadbury, I immediately phoned him. He told me that the flight had already been laid on, the necessary flight plan filed and that he had been told of the new arrangements. I was to join him at Lee-on-Solent on the morning of the flight.

This was the first difficulty. I was in command, albeit not as captain of the aircraft, but I had had no part in any of the arrangements. I had not vetted the landing area, had no idea of the safety arrangements at the map reference or at Buckingham Palace. I had never met Prince Philip and had no briefing on protocol. I was now to be fully responsible for the safety of the Queen's Consort in an unknown aircraft to an unknown destination. I flew down to Lee-on-Solent on the appointed day to find that the aircraft we were to use was an American Sikorsky S-55 with an American Wright cyclone engine which once started was very reliable. However, we were delayed some time before leaving since bits of the cabin were lying all over the ground. A hydraulic fluid leak had occurred and was being repaired and there was not an alternative aircraft available. Fortunately we had allowed time for such an event and while we waited Ted briefed me. He had not been to the site where we were to pick up the Prince but he felt sure it would be suitable. He had been into Buckingham Palace a number of times, and he described the procedure with Prince Philip for all his flights.

Prince Philip would make the decision on whether to fly or not when he walked out to the aircraft. I would be standing by the cabin door with Ted in the pilot's seat. I would salute the Prince and, if he decided to pilot the aircraft, Ted would quickly climb over to the co-pilot, or navigators, seat. The Prince would climb up the steps in to the cockpit and start the engine. At this stage I would assist any passengers into the cabin, remove the wooden steps, stow them inside and climb in. Should the Prince not want to pilot it I would assist him and any passengers in to the cabin and rush around the nose of the aircraft and climb up in to the co-pilots seat. While all this was going on Ted would have started the engine, engaged the rotors and, once I strapped myself in, he would take off.

I have explained all this at length since such makeshift arrangements did not appear to me to be adequate either for efficiency or for the occasion.

The other problem concerned starting the engine. This was by cartridge, which, when inserted in to the breech and triggered, caused a rapid turnover of the engine. If properly primed it would start. However, if the cartridges were damp or the engine was at the wrong temperature or poorly primed there would be a 'whoosh' as the engine turned over and then silence. In the event of running out of cartridges the whole flight would have to be aborted. In my book *Hoverhawk*, I have described how embarrassing this starting procedure could be on occasions, but not on this particular one.

It was a lovely bright morning when we finally took off from Lee-on-Solent, with little time to spare. On this, my first royal flight. I navigated to the map reference which was a large country house where the Queen and Prince Philip had been enjoying an incognito weekend. I made sure that positioning reports were sent en route, and I reported our arrival. This was at a field next to a very large house and indeed a sheet was laid out, just as Mouse had described. What he had not told me was that there were one or two stones holding it into position. As we came in to hover it took off like a banshee, fortunately flying away from us towards a contingent of policemen hiding in the nearby trees. As for fire precautions, there were none, except for a small, lonely fire extinguisher sitting by itself some distance away.

We stopped the engine and I climbed out to wait at the cabin door for the arrival of the Prince, while Ted stayed in the cockpit. After a short while a number of people came to a little gate leading in to the field. They were obviously saying goodbye and would wait there for the departure. I noticed a young girl, in a white blouse and what appeared to be a gym slip, detach herself and cross the field obliquely to the aircraft on the opposite side to where I was standing. I lost sight of her as she crossed behind the aircraft and was apprehensive that she might well harm herself on the very hot and obtrusive exhaust pipe, which protruded from the other side of the cabin at waist height. I could see that the Prince had not moved from the group, so I rushed around the nose of the helicopter to remonstrate or at least protect the young lady. I came face to face with the Queen. I am not sure who was more surprised, but I certainly know who was the most put out. Before I could even think what to say she gave me a lovely smile and said, "I hope I am not in the way. I think my husband is about ready to leave". I muttered something inane and watched her walk back to the gate. That lovely smile remained with me for years, until I received it again on being honoured by a private audience with Her Majesty in the formal surroundings of Buckingham Palace.

With great informality Prince Philip came over, acknowledged my salute with a nod, handed me his hat and proceeded to climb up in to the cockpit. Our flight back to the garden of Buckingham Palace was uneventful and, on arrival, I was relieved to find that a proper 'tee' had been pegged out on the lawn and a fireman with fire extinguisher was in attendance. We returned to Lee-on-Solent where I picked up the Dragonfly and flew back to Benson.

This first royal flight brought home to me not only the fact that new custom-built aircraft were necessary but that the whole procedure of initiating flights, vetting sites, communicating with those receiving royal guests, i.e. individuals, organisations, companies, civil dignitaries and the various royal residences, needed reorganisation. More important still was introduction of proper flight procedures and above all safety precautions, both in flight and on the ground. This latter requirement was vital, since many of our sites were isolated areas without adequate local assistance or services. It was a matter of picking up my pen again and establishing a pattern that Mouse would agree fitted all the requirements and standards enjoyed by the fixed-wing elements of TQF.

It had now become obvious that the new aircraft would not be available for some considerable time and that in the interim it would be necessary to continue using the naval aircraft. Mouse had indicated that he envisaged an ever-increasing use for helicopters, with eventually an overseas role in conjunction with the new de Havilland Heron aircraft, which had now arrived. By this time, June had arrived at Benson and we were installed in a little house on the outskirts of the airfield. We were extremely lucky to find, not only a couple to help in the house and garden but I inherited a most useful and diligent batman. At this stage the thought of not having enough to occupy myself faded away. In between a slowly increasing programme of royal flights, I was producing a dossier of procedures and aircraft requirements for the future. I made visits to every site prior to a royal flight. This included communication with and, in most cases, meeting the people concerned with hosting the royal visitor. In many early cases I participated in mock pre-programmes, even to the extent of eating the food of the proposed menu. I was also able to advise, in general, on the protocol required for the various passengers I was to carry.

When I first arrived at TQF there had been only one Land Rover available whose main task was to deliver the red carpet to London airport for the arrival or departure of the Viking aircraft. I was told that I could use this for the lawn at Buckingham Palace when it was not otherwise engaged. This was wholly unsatisfactory since I required personnel that not only could prepare the site and landing tee but who were also qualified to carry and use the necessary fire equipment. This illustrated the low priority given to helicopter operations. I argued successfully for my own Land Rover, then another one and finally a third. These were to be equipped with foam and powder and manned by trained firemen. Eventually radio was installed for communication with arriving and departing aircraft.

In the beginning I was supplied with a staff car and driver to visit the various sites prior to pre-planning a flight. This was unsatisfactory in many ways. It took up too much time and did not allow me to orientate the necessary flight path at low level or to assess the approach in to the chosen landing area. The obvious answer was to use the Dragonfly, but there was some resistance to the idea of the noise and safety aspects in bobbing up and down all over the country in to built up areas and centres of towns and cities. I put this to Mouse who used his considerable influence to persuade the necessary aviation and civil authorities to allow me unrestricted access to any site in the United Kingdom. In these early days, helicopters were hardly known to the public and rarely flew over or into built-up areas except in emergencies. In order to prevent the public ringing the police or 999 with panic reports, I always contacted the local police prior to my flight and generally found a 'bobby' present when I landed. This was generally useful, since I was able to discuss with him the area security for the forthcoming royal flight.

My landing sites covered factories, private gardens, commercial enterprises, city car parks, government establishments, hospitals, football and other sporting fields, and particularly many new public enterprise schemes. It also covered, where necessary, all military and civil airports. Having visited and approved a landing area and briefed all concerned, I would return to Benson to prepare a flight itinerary received from Buckingham Palace. This involved a complicated process of notifying an extensive list of addressees, including all civil authorities concerned, the Navy, the central meteorological office, the 'Notice' to airman (NOTAM) and to arrange with Ted Spreadbury to file a 'flight plan' on the appropriate day. I also had to arrange for local police presence and the fire and ambulance services to be on standby. These procedures were always picked up by the local press and invariably meant large crowds on arrival and positive measures had to be taken to keep the landing area clear and the aircraft guarded.

The need for me to fly down to Lee-on-Solent to join Ted for every royal flight meant that the Dragonfly was essential and had to be permanently serviceable. I was fortunate in having a first-class maintenance crew and I spent what little time I had joining them on the hangar floor.

I have gone to some length to explain some of the initial arrangements which I undertook in addition to participating in each royal flight. Until very much later, when I was able to build up administrative trained staff and additional aircrew, I was very much a one man band and fighting to keep my head above water while awaiting our own aircraft for the unit. Interruptions were not slow in coming. The Dragonfly being such a versatile machine was thought by other members of the flight to be a useful taxi. Squadron Leader Tom Bussey, the senior engineering officer, would ask me if I could fly him over to the de Havilland factory for a meeting. Squadron Leader Brian Stanbridge would ask me to lift him over to White Waltham where he was to join Prince Philip for a training flight in a Devon (DH.104) which was hangared there. Mouse would suddenly decide that he wanted to go somewhere in a hurry or the deputy captain, Air Commodore Mitchell, wanted me to give him some dual instruction.

I was very conscious that Wing Commander Hyland-Smith was allowing me complete independence, but the sharing of the crew room was causing problems with the growing problem of administrative paper work that was accruing. Once again I appealed to Sir Edward with immediate results. I was installed in one of the empty offices between the CO and the adjutant, supplied with a telephone and told that this would remain my office. It could also be used as a crew room for the helicopter unit when the new aircraft and their crews arrived. One more step forward and a mountain left to climb.

I was not happy with the Naval Sikorsky helicopter, its equipment or its reliability for continuing in a broader role for carrying other members of the royal family. There was no alternative however, in the immediate future. Neither was I happy in shouldering the full burden of responsibility, for several years, while awaiting the arrival of the custom-built new aircraft.

Although I was rapidly promoted to Squadron Leader, I was still playing a lone-wolf role which was singularly different from the other aircrews. Their work consisted of flying royalty from one aerodrome to another, along prescribed airway patterns. The captain or deputy captain accompanied every flight and were the only officers to associate with the passengers. I was privileged to play a different role altogether. Not only did I meet all my passengers but I gradually got to know them. I visited all the royal residences and was frequently invited inside. In these early days, because of aircraft weight limitations and therefore fewer passengers, I occasionally had to act as an extra equerry during a visit. This was particularly so with the Duke of Gloucester and I used to carry a little silver flask containing 'Angostura Bitters' in my pocket since he liked it with his gin and few hosts supplied it. The Queen Mother graciously showed me around the Castle of Mey and regularly invited me in to the Royal Lodge, Windsor for an after-flight refresher. These are a couple of examples of how my work differed completely from the other aircrews. I always remember, rather embarrassingly, the occasion when, on a visit to a very large organisation with the Duke of Gloucester, I had to leave the luncheon table to prepare the aircraft for the next stage of the flight. Since no one should leave the table before the royal guest,

The first lineup of TQF Helicopter section. Peter Wilson is on extreme right. Ron Kerr is in naval uniform, Ralph Lee and Ron Crompton-Batt as navigators. John M'Kenzie-Hall is second from the left.

some 40 heads turned to look at me in silence as I rose to my feet and proceeded to walk from the bottom of the table to the top where protocol decreed that I asked the Duke, through the host, to excuse me. This was granted and as I left the stentorian voice of the Duke rang out, "That's my young pilot, he tells me I have got to go". My embarrassment hastened my exit. However, that incident was some way ahead, and while I was still using the naval helicopter, Ted Spreadbury was replaced by a Lieutenant Kerr. He was an Australian and a very different character to Ted. I would be dishonest if I said we got on. Although he was an adequate pilot, he was, in my view, undisciplined, unreliable and unsuitable for the team I hoped to build up in the future. His careless attitude in general led to several mishaps that could have been serious. Some of these are described in my book *Hoverhawk* and I will not repeat them here. However, on one occasion his actions precipitated a degree of poor airmanship which led eventually to my leaving the Royal Air Force on medical grounds. I will come back to the problem of Lt. Kerr and his position with TQF later on.

After years of operating from Lee-on-Solent, Sir Edward gave me the good news that the new aircraft were about to start construction at the Westland aircraft factory at Yeovil in Somerset. In addition to my existing duties I was now to liaise with the company in the production of two aircraft and when completed accompany them to Boscombe Down. I was then to participate in the schedule for fully flight testing and acceptance programme. Since I had been originally trained at Westlands and knew the company employees quite well this was very welcome news.

At the same time Mouse, having accepted that the time for bringing in additional helicopter aircrew was fast approaching, arranged for the Dragonfly to be replaced by the much larger Whirlwind S-55. This was a similar aircraft to the Naval Sikorsky but much underpowered. I would now be able to carry out my proving flights with a navigator, give him the opportunity to train in this method of transport and prepare for the arrival of further pilots and navigators who would also need orientation and training.

Life has a way of balancing events between good and bad and this welcome news was tempered by a change of personnel. Firstly W/Cdr Hyland-Smith had been replaced by W/Cdr Dickie Wakeford (I refer to him as 'Dickie' with some reserve since he retired as Air Marshal Sir Richard Wakeford, KCB, LVO, OBE, AFC). In those days, as part of the team, one could not have worked with a nicer, more competent and understanding commanding officer. He fully appreciated my task, never interfered and always showed a supportive attitude. He fully accepted that I worked directly through Mouse and I was always very careful to keep him fully informed of progress until the time came to fully integrate the helicopter unit with the fixed-wing unit under one commanding officer.

However, the number of royal flights was increasing and the workload on Mouse was becoming too much for him to accompany each flight personally. He already had a deputy captain in Group Captain Dennis Mitchell, but even this was proving inadequate.

Sir Edward had been in charge of 'The King's Flight' and then 'The Queen's Flight' since their inception in July 1936 and now had thoughts of retiring and this meant change. Over the years he had much opposition from forces inside the Air Ministry to maintaining what was potentially a private air force unit inside the pattern of air force provision or command. It was quite obvious that many in the upper echelons of the RAF wished to see an end to this small empire and, like the proverbial cat, had been waiting a long time to spring.

To paraphrase a famous saying 'This was not the end of TQF but the beginning of the end' when Dennis Mitchell was promoted to Air Commander and departed to command Cranwell. In his place arrived a new group captain. I will call him 'S'. There are few people who have caused my hackles to rise as much as this officer. I make no excuse in setting down my personal opinion of

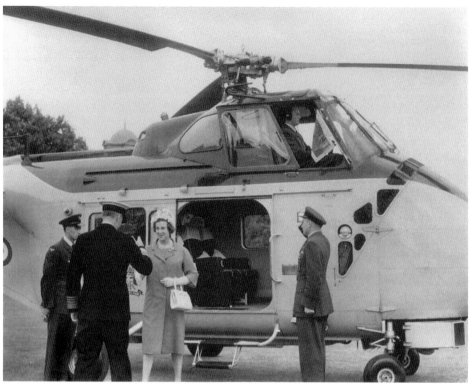

The First Royal Flight in Hoverhawk I, XN 127's first royal passenger: with Princess Marina, the Duchess of Kent, from Kensington Palace to Papworth Hospital, Cambridgeshire on 23 February 1960. This was the first time Kensington Palace was used as London landing zone.

him which has not changed over the years. He oozed charm but there seemed to be no sincerity about it. His work of deputy captain consisted mainly of seeing to the welfare of royal passengers on their arrival, accompanying them on the aircraft and giving the formal salute on debarkation. As a career officer he embodied everything that air force regulations require. As a human being he lacked adaptability and humility. He was the first officer, in my opinion, to build up resentment among the aircrew due to his continual interference in the previous smooth running procedures under the commanding officer. Ralph Dawson confided in me, shortly after the new group captain arrived, that he was continually interrupting Mouse in his office and that Mouse had told him, in no uncertain terms, to make any excuse to keep him at bay. His frequent sorties into the crew room proved quite disruptive, since he expected everyone to acknowledge his presence as a senior officer for what generally turned out to be a question of not having enough to occupy himself. On a personal level he began by ordering the adjutant to arrange for me to take him home or fetch him by helicopter. Out of courtesy I did this on several occasions in the beginning

A garden departure: Queen Mother's visit to Althorp to visit 7th Earl Spencer, with Lady Fermoy in attendance. Lady Fermoy and Earl Spencer were the maternal and paternal grandparents respectively of Lady Diana Spencer. Helicopter XN 127 on 6 July 1961.

The Queen's Flight 1962 – helicopter section, with named officers.

but by dint of convenient excuses for unserviceability, necessary proving flights and heavy administrative work he eventually found it more convenient to use his staff car and driver.

Possibly in retaliation 'S' called me in one day and suggested that it might be in my interests to take a flying instructor's course at the Central Flying School, Little Rissington. It was such an incredible suggestion that my first thought was that he was trying to ease me out for someone else. He had not mentioned this to Mouse, and in fact he had no authority to mention it to me. I could only reply that if he would look up my service record he would see that my instructor's qualifications included the Central Flying Schools of both England and America, that I was an accredited civil flying instructor on both helicopter and fixed wing aircraft and had some 12 years experience as a flying instructor in Training Command. I never heard another word on this subject during his tour of TQF.

After some time, another deputy captain was appointed to join in attending royal passengers on fixed-wing flights that were still increasing. It was not long before a third group captain joined the flight. Because of weight limitation I was unable to carry them and, in any case, I considered their role for helicopter flights quite unnecessary, since the navigator was quite capable of opening the doors and saluting on arrival and departure.

With this bureaucratic overweight at the top there was a distinct change in the general atmosphere and relationship amongst the air crew. The relaxed attitude of the previous regime under W/Cdr Hyland-Smith and W/Cdr Wakeford faded noticeably.

My work was not greatly affected at this time and I was delighted when I was able to replace the little Dragonfly with the much larger Whirlwind, for training expected navigators and pilots in their role, prior to receiving the new Whirlwind Mark 8s from Westlands. My first navigator to aircrew was Flt. Lt. Ralph Lee, DFC.

Since he had never flown in helicopters, and he had spent his career in multi-engine transport aircraft, my first task was to orientate him to rotary wing operation and in particular to low-level navigation without radio aids on the majority of flights. He took to it like a duck to water and we clicked as a team from our first meeting. I had complete confidence in his ability and he never seemed to doubt mine. At first our flying together was limited since if I was not flying down to Lee-on-Solent for a royal flight, I was down at Yeovil with the new aircraft and then on to Boscombe Down for the flight trials. However, he was able to accompany me on all proving flights and these took us to all parts of the United Kingdom including the Scottish Isles and the Hebrides.

A month or two before the new aircraft were ready my second pilot arrived

Wing Commander R. G. "Dickie" Wakeford, commanding officer of TQF and Squadron Leader John M'Kenzie-Hall.

in the shape of Flight Lieutenant Peter Wilson. Once again it was a good match and, since Peter was already a fairly experienced helicopter pilot, I just had to give him a rapid orientation onto the aircraft before he and Ralph Lee were able to team up for continuation flying while I was away.

Domestic life hardly existed for me at this time since I was away so often. It was also not much fun for June for, although she had help in the house, there was very little company for her since we did not really know many people locally. In addition, there was the anxiety, shared by all air-crew wives, towards the safety aspects of our work. To complicate matters further, June became pregnant with our son, James, and in May 1958, the day he was born, I had to be away on a royal flight.

From 1949, when my father died, my mother had been living in Australia where her two sisters were, but had been hoping, for some time, to return to England. When I returned from the Far East I arranged for her to return to London where she was able to reside in a hotel in Hampstead. She was not well, however, and I thought that it would be advantageous, both for her health and her small income, if she came down to us at Benson. Very unfortunately this did not work out, for she needed constant care and, with June looking after a new baby and me frequently away, there were the inevitable upsets. The doctor advised that my mother should go in to a nursing home and, although we tried this, it was not successful and she eventually went to London to live with my sister. It was doubly unfortunate that when she died, shortly afterwards, I was unable to attend the funeral since I was once more on a flight with the Duke of Gloucester in Germany.

Prince Philip and a Near-Catastrophe

When I look back, I am amazed how a small piece of wire, slightly thicker than fuse wire, could have had such a devastating affect on my future life. Not only did it wreck my career in the Royal Air Force, or any possibility of civil aviation, but it resulted in permanent disability for the rest of my life. In November 1958, Prince Philip had agreed to visit two RAF airfields in Lincolnshire which had, for some time, been equipped with Bloodhound surface-to-air missiles housed in underground ballistic-missile silos pointing east. They were situated to the south and the north of the Humber, which made a road journey via the Humber Bridge particularly lengthy, while a helicopter could shorten the journey by several hours.

I decided to position the naval helicopter at RAF North Coates the day before, in order to give us time to visit both airfields and make the necessary arrangements. The weather was not particularly good, but the forecast for the next day seemed reasonable and the distance over the Humber, at low level to RAF Patrington, was quite acceptable. Next day, 19 November 1958, we joined our aircraft, Whirlwind WV 219, an hour before Prince Philip was due to arrive by car and would drive to where we would be parked on the runway apron. There was still a coverage of low cloud, but overnight sea mist had crept inland and visibility had decreased. I had asked Ron if he wanted to make a weather check earlier on but he had thought it unnecessary, since the mist had not thickened. About 35 minutes before we were to position ourselves on the apron to await Prince Philip's arrival, Ron decided, after all, to make a quick weather check and would return to meet me at the positioning point, before the Prince arrived. Despite my caution he took off and vanished from sight at the boundary of the airfield. He radioed the control tower that visibility was reasonable and that he was returning. I was listening for his engine when, to my consternation, I was told that Prince Philip and entourage was arriving early. I tried to contact Ron, but I received no reply. I rushed over to meet the Prince who made it quite clear that he was not pleased that the aircraft was not in position. A couple of minutes after our scheduled take-off time Ron appeared and touched down in front of us. Prince Philip, who disliked being kept waiting, announced that he would not fly the aircraft and proceeded to climb into the cabin. Not wanting to waste any more time I closed the cabin door, and I hurriedly went around the nose to climb up in to the navigator's seat. I am explaining all this at some length since the consequences were caused by the failure to carry out the operation in a disciplined and professional manner.

Immediately I gained my seat Ron lifted off and went in to forward flight. I had not had time to strap myself in and with one hand holding the maps I shut the sliding cockpit window before putting on my headset. I noticed, out of the corner of my eye, that the window was vibrating rather more than usual and had slipped off its catch. I reached forward to re-latch it when the jettison safety wire broke and the window came away from its bottom runner. I dropped my maps to reach for it when, to my horror, the top began to ease away from the frame. With both hands I grasped the front and rear of the window just as it caught the airflow and completely broke away. Since I was not strapped in, the window, which was a curved plastic sheet, acted as a parachute in reverse and began pulling me out. I jammed my shoulder against the frame and hooked my right leg under the instrument panel while trying to avoid fouling the cyclic control stick. One might ask why I did not just let it go and continue windowless to our destination. All this happened in seconds and as my headset and maps vanished seawards, my first thought was to prevent the slip stream from carrying the window backwards in to the tail rotor. We were about 100 feet over the icy waters of the Humber and as the window rotated with the airflow I was now twisted in an almost face down position with my hands tending to freeze around the rim as I hung on. If we lost the tail rotor we would almost certainly lose the Prince Consort, since no one could survive a crash landing in freezing sea water even if we survived the impact.

I cannot say my whole life appeared before me in a flash, but the consequences of what might happen highlighted my agony. Press headlines, courts of enquiry, ending of TQF concept of helicopter royal flying. The strange thing was I never thought of my being killed, I just got madder as I got colder. Ron knew what had happened, but he had no other choice but to continue on course for a landfall and the rest of the short flight to RAF Patrington.

We touched down on an area of ground that was fairly dry where Prince Philip disembarked, but which was soggy and muddy on my side. I had let go of the window panel as soon as the wheels touched and tried to climb down the side of the cockpit. Unfortunately, my frozen fingers could not grip the handholds properly and I fell the last foot or so in to a puddle. I presented myself at the door with the usual formal salute when the Prince alighted to greet a multitude of senior officers. He looked at my uniform and said, "What happened to you?" What did I reply? Perhaps I should have said, "Sir, I have just saved your life plus your passengers from a watery death. I am cold, dirty and thoroughly sick of a

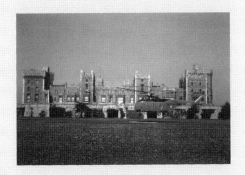

HOVERHAWK

THE PERSONAL STORY OF

THE FIRST ROYAL HELICOPTERS

BY

J M'KENZIE-HALL MVO

From: Captain Ben Tracey,
Assistant Equerry to H.R.H. The Duke of Edinburgh

BUCKINGHAM PALACE

18th October, 2017

Dear Mr M'Kenzie-Hall,

The Duke of Edinburgh has asked me to thank you for so kindly sending a copy of your memoir, "Hoverhawk: the personal story of the first Royal helicopters".

The memoir is a splendid record of your seven years with The Queen's Flight from 1957 – 1964. Chapter nine's 'Near Catastrophe' with the safety wire has been read with particular interest, as you may imagine! The memoir is an enjoyable and amusing read, and a welcome reminder of past times.

I hope your subsequent civilian career in aviation proved as fulfilling and full of interest. Thank you again for taking the time and trouble to write.

His Royal Highness sends his warm best wishes.

Yours sincerely,

Ben Tracey

John M'Kenzie-Hall, Esq., MVO

BUCKINGHAM PALACE, LONDON, SW1A 1AA
TELEPHONE: 020 7930 4832, FACSIMILE: 020 7839 9432

The Queen's Flight,
Royal Air Force,
Benson,
Oxon.

November, 1958

Sir,

I have the honour to submit a report following the Royal Helicopter Flight
from North Coates to Patrington on Wednesday, 19th November, 1958.

2.   Due to forecast conditions of fog en route to North Coates, during the
period immediately preceeding the Royal Flight, I thought it adviseable to
position at North Coates on the 17th November, 1958.

3.   A proving flight to orientate Lt. Kerr with the route took place on the
18th November, Fog persisted throughout the day.

4.   On the morning of the 19th November, I ensured that the helicopter was
positioned by 0810 hours and proceeded to the Control Tower with Lt. Kerr.

5.   Weather report actuals for the area gave visibility as approx. 200 - 300
yards, with the fog rising to approx. 1000' and clear sky above. The possibility
of an improvement in the visibility to within the limitations by 0915 hours was
thought to be good.

6.   At 0840 hours Lt. Kerr had completed the warm and run up of the engine when
the fog started to clear and visibility improved. At 0845 hours Lt. Kerr
suggested that the take-off and check visibility from our planned flight height   I
told Lt. Kerr to on the ground by 0900 hours and remained in the Control Tower
to await his decision and to liaise with A/C operations.

7.   At 0855 hours we contacted Lt. Kerr by radio and asked for his decision.   He
said the visibility was suitable for the Royal flight and this information was
passed on to I/C Operations.   I then proceeded to the landing point, expecting the
aircraft to arrive immediately.   At no time did I expect it to leave the circuit.
When it had not arrived by 0905 hours, I returned to the Control Tower as was told
the aircraft was due in 3 minutes.   At 0911 hours I again went to the Control Tower
by before reaching it the Royal Party arrived by car approx. 4 minutes early.   At
this same time I could hear the helicopter and returned to the landing area to await
its arrival.

8.   After supervising the Royal Party on board the helicopter I climbed into
the co-pilots seat and Lt. Kerr took off.

9.   As we moved into forward flight the bottom half of the co-pilots sliding
door came away from its runner.   This door is a jettisonable one with the normal
release on the top and it was imperative to prevent the airflow from getting
underneath and blowing the door off.

10.   I managed to get my hand outside and hold the door in at static position
until after the landing at Patrington.   During this interval before the return
to North Coates, we put the door back on its runner which appeared to be inadequate support should any undue strain be applied to the door at its most forward
point of travel.

11.   All our take-offs and landings were on schedule times.

I have the honour to be,

Sir,

Your obedient Servant.

(J.B. MACKENZIE-HALL)
Flight Lieutenant

Air Commodore Sir Edward Fielden, K.C.V.O., C.B. D.F.C., A.F.C.,
Captain of The Queen's Flight,
Royal Air Force,
Benson,
Oxon.

My accident report to Captain of TQF Sir Edward Fielden of Prince Philip accident.

Farewell to TQF at RAF Benson, 7 February 1995: John M'Kenzie-Hall in conversation with Prince Philip who typically quips "Still alive I see!"

badly maintained naval aircraft and the carefree attitude of the pilot". I merely said, "Sir, I slipped when climbing out". The Prince, half turning towards the group of officers all standing to attention in their pristine uniforms said, rather acidly, "Oh, I see", and was whisked away.

My right leg was extremely painful, my shoulder was throbbing and my left arm was numb. While I dried out my uniform in a nearby hut, Ron replaced the window, which was undamaged, and renewed the safety wire. Prince Philip's equerry, Squadron Leader John Severne, returned to see whether we were ready for the return trip. Some 40 years later, after he had served a term as Captain of TQF, had risen to Air Vice-Marshal and gained his knighthood, he read of this incident in my book and admitted to me that no one on the aircraft, apart from Ron, ever knew of what had occurred. Ron never referred to it except to say, "Why did you not let the window go?" Mouse Fielden received my formal report of the incident and I imagine filed it. He never referred to it again except to remind me that any leakage of the event to the press would result in a public enquiry and untold damage to the concept of the future use of TQF helicopters. My injuries lay dormant for some time but in due course the wasting of my shoulder muscles and the severe pain in my hip made the result of that trip quite evident, but only to me!

I can truthfully say that, despite the affect on me, I now feel fully vindicated in my actions since I have a report in 1989 of a helicopter cockpit window hitting the tail rotor and all nine passengers being killed in the ensuing impact with the ground.

In September 1959 I had spent some weeks at RAF Boscombe Down in Wiltshire to carry out, in conjunction with the test pilot, all the flight procedure necessary before the new aircraft could be certified for their role. A full explanation of these procedures is given in the appropriate section of *Hoverhawk*. When the two new aircraft had received their certificate of airworthiness they were returned to Yeovil for a final spit and polish before being delivered to TQF.

In November 1959, two years after having acted as navigator on all royal flights, I flew down to Yeovil with Ralph Lee and 'Dickie' Wakeford in one of the new aircraft. Peter Wilson, carrying Tom Bussey, the engineering officer, followed in the second aircraft. This was the official handing over of the aircraft and the Westland Aircraft Company had laid on a fairly impressive ceremony. Gathered in front of both aircraft, they handed over the log books and documents, made the necessary speeches and then, for the benefit of the Press, watched as Peter and I became airborne and flew in a formation display. We were then entertained to a splendid celebration lunch before flying back to Benson for Tom Bussey to give the aircraft a thorough primary inspection to TQF standard.

After all the difficulties of the past two years I could hardly believe that at long last we were about to begin the incorporation of helicopters and fixed wing aircraft into combined programmes under one roof. There was still some time to go before we could use the aircraft operationally. I also had our own training and orientation to carry out on new systems of control and updated flight systems including Decca navigation. A second navigator, F/Lt Crompton-Batt was posted in and that just left a third pilot to make up the initial team. Because the navy had supplied an aircraft and pilot for all the royal flights previously, Mouse had been persuaded to agree that a naval pilot should be accepted as the third pilot. I was not overjoyed to find that they had named Lt. Kerr who, after a period, duly arrived at TQF. I was elated that my period of navigation with the naval aircraft had finished and that my continual journeys down to Lee-on-Solent were no longer necessary.

In a sense our roles were now reversed as Ron Kerr became the third pilot in our section and, of course, lost me as a navigator. I converted Ron onto the new aircraft and considered him to be an excellent pilot in handling and airmanship. I was, however, unsure whether I could come to terms with his careless and undisciplined attitude towards the standards required for TQF, both on and off duty.

I had now flown with Prince Philip as his instructor in the new aircraft and found him well above average as a pilot and quick to adapt. However, it was obvious that without a great deal more regular flying practice, which was impossible in his case, he was always going to need a fully qualified and experienced pilot to fly with him. This was particularly so in a helicopter since reaction time in an emergency, such as engine failure, had to be in seconds before the situation of further flight became irrecoverable. This required regular continuation training in engine failure, engine-off landings, instrument flying, manual control or loss of hydraulics etc. Not sufficient of this was practiced by Prince Philip to bring his reactions up to an automatic reaction which would ensure the safety

A thank-you letter from Earl Mountbatten.

of the Queen's Consort. Since we no longer had use of the Naval Sikorsky, I had to spend a lot of time with the Prince who was, at this time, the greater user for his many and varied appointments. The arrival of Ron solved this problem as I gave him back to Prince Philip as his personal pilot while Peter, and I could concentrate on all the other royal and VVIP passengers, leaving me more time to cope with the growing administrative arrangements.

I became increasingly busy in flying all the members of the royal family but predominantly the Queen Mother, the Duke and Duchess of Gloucester and Princess Margaret on their home and overseas trips. Peter also fully took his share. Amongst my foreign royalty and VVIP's, to mention but a few, I flew his Imperial Highness the Shah of Persia on a highly secret operation, the King of Norway, King Hussein of Jordan, King Baudouin of the Belgians, the Supreme Allied Commander of Forces in Europe, the American Defence Secretary, the Italian President, the President of Finland and all the Chiefs of Staff of the Royal Air Force. I was extremely fortunate that, despite English weather, I never had to cancel a trip and, due to the exceptional servicing, had no engine or airframe failures in the new TQF Mark 8 Whirlwinds.

Social life was limited but, in the beginning, I played tennis and appeared rather lamely on the football field from time to time. Cordial invitations to the Royal Garden Parties, Royal Ascot, Trooping of the Colours etc., all duly arrived and June and I attended where we could, but unfortunately, this was not very often. It was nice to receive Christmas cards from the Queen and other members of the royal family each year and I felt especially privileged when I departed in 1964, after seven years on TQF, to receive personal photographs and letters from the Queen and Prince Philip and all the senior members of the royal family.

One day June and I saw an advertisement for a one-day sale of country-house contents in a little village of South Stoke, bordering on the river Thames. We had been collecting furniture and antiques for some time and we decided to attend the sale. The house was called 'The Elms' and, built of stone, was originally a small Georgian house in some four acres. It had been called 'The Salt Box' but had been trebled in size with large stable blocks and saddling rooms. While we were upstairs we heard a couple saying, "Who would be stupid enough to buy a house like this?" The original rooms were unspoilt Georgian dimensions and the extensions, although considerably larger with high ceilings and elegant marble fireplaces, fitted well in relation to the whole building. At the back was a little copse of beech which bordered a number of magnificent elm trees. The beech trees had been planted in a circle and pruned to provide a private amphitheatre of lush grass leading to a rather dilapidated but well-built conservatory. June and I lingered in this little oasis, not wanting to let each other know that we had fallen in love with the whole house and garden, knowing that we could not really afford it on a squadron leader's income. It sounds silly today, in the 21st century, to think that in 1960 we were in awe at the asking price of £5,000 for a four-bedroom, Georgian house with the addition of a fully fitted extension of a further four bedrooms with kitchen and bathroom, all sitting comfortably in landscaped gardens with thatched summer house. It had beautiful views over uninterrupted church lands. There was only one drawback, which never worried us. At the back of the house, but at some distance, ran the main line railway from London to Oxford. This was blocked from our view by the massive stable block which had, in its time, served a large number of horses and their respective carriages.

By haggling over the dilapidated conservatory and cutting off an acre of garden we had the price reduced to £3,975, and took out a mortgage for £3,000. We were able to raise the deposit by the sale of my plot of land in Tanganyika, East Africa, and a small short-term loan from my mother-in-law. Just to show the absurdity of economics in the time scale, if sold today it would probably fetch, because of its situation, in the region of four to six million pounds. We moved in and although there was a lot of decoration required we felt immediately at home. We had inherited a gardener by the name of Mr Allum, who kept the upper lawns, rose gardens, drive and hedges immaculately. In one corner of the stable there had been left a perfectly serviceable Ford Pilot saloon in good order, which we gave to Mr Allum in appreciation of his dedication to the garden and willingness to carry out the innumerable odd jobs that such

We named our house at South Stoke 'Kilhendre' after the ancient estate the Edwards family once owned in Shropshire.

Top left: Ancient Kilhendre Hall, prior to 1794.

Bottom left:. Kilhendre Hall 1794–1934 (now demolished).

a property entailed. Since both our families had lost their entire possessions when captured by the Japanese in Singapore and the Philippines respectively, we set about exploring salerooms and, when we could afford it, antique shops for furniture. Our cleaning lady, a Mrs Coggins, had loyally followed us to our new home, now renamed 'Kilhendre' (after the ancient estate my family once owned in Shropshire) and she caught a bus to us once a week, without fail. Our only loss was that of my batman who could not travel from the airfield to us. However, since these personnel were being phased out of the service, we would have lost him anyway.

The first difficulty to arise was the telephone which was a party line shared with another property. Since I had responsibility to supervise royal flights at all hours it was necessary for my telephone to have immediate access and maximum security. Sir Edward Fielden, when told of my problem, used his authority as Air Equerry to the Queen with immediate result. Almost next day I had a personal line granted to me with direct access to Buckingham Palace and through it to other necessary contacts. In fact, my first incoming call was a personal one from the Duke of Gloucester who was upset by a press report that he hated helicopters. This was after a recent trip where I had taken both the Duke and Duchess on an extended tour. He rang to assure me that the report misquoted him since he had only said he disliked the helicopter engine noise and he was upset that I might think he did not appreciate the valuable service we provided. A little while after we had moved, in word must have spread around that we had acquired or were renting a large old house fairly close to Scraces Farm which was Sir Edward Fielden's home. One afternoon Lady Fielden drove up, rang the bell and, introducing herself, asked if she could use our telephone. Was it just an inquisitive visit to see the house? Since she was well off her direct route home, and her telephone call was only local, we could only surmise her purpose.

One of the upstairs bedrooms needed repapering and, with lots of hot water and elbow grease, we removed several layers of Victorian flowered wallpaper. During the scraping off of the last sheet, we came across the whole wall covered in Christmas and birthday cards addressed to 'little Ernie'. These were dated over periods in the late 19th century and were obviously decorating his nursery at the time. We were intrigued about 'little Ernie' and, with great care, removed as many as we could. June opened the front door one day to be greeted by a small, well dressed, elderly couple. They said they were in the area for a short time, and they asked whether it would be possible for them to see the house where her husband had been born. June's imagination took the better of her and she burst out, "You're not little Ernie, are you?" It was and although I did not meet them, I understand that they were overjoyed at being shown over the house and at seeing the Christmas cards. It is no good living in the past and regretting decisions made when the reasons have faded. Our beautiful dream house is no more and the thought of its demise is still a recurring sadness for both of us.

My physical condition had reached a point where, having accomplished the task of establishing a helicopter section, I finally acknowledged the fact that the increasing pain in my leg and arm was affecting my enthusiasm for flying and being continually on call. The thought of leaving TQF and returning to a desk job in the regular air force had little appeal for me and I decided to consider early retirement and, hopefully, seek fresh fields in civil aviation. I had been approached several times about senior jobs in Greece, New Zealand, Abyssinia and Canada to start up embryo organisations with the ever increasing popularity of helicopter travel. I felt sure that a good rest would help me recover the full use of leg and arm again and, having made the decision, presented myself for a medical prior to taking the final step of resigning my permanent commission.

What I thought would be a simple examination turned out to be anything but. Over several weeks I attended various clinical departments and even a psychological one where they questioned my motive for wanting to retire early.

After all this they told me that I had nerve damage to my left arm, a wastage of muscle in the upper arm, which was the cause of pins and needles and pain in my left hand. They also considered that the severe pain in my right leg should be operated on without delay. This was before modern hip replacements were available and I was advised that I would have to undergo a McMurray osteotomy which meant operating to twist the hip socket to a position where it could be pinned by an internally introduced splint, thereby relieving the pressure and, it was hoped, the pain. I believe Sir Edward Fielden, who by now had retired from TQF but was still the Senior Air Equerry to the Queen, intervened. I was told that Air Commander Lewis Mackenzie-Crooks (1909–1992), Surgeon to the Queen, had agreed to undertake the operation at the RAF hospital at Halton.

While all these arrangements were taking place, June and I had come to a decision to put the house on the market. When the news got out we were approached by a small delegation from the village of South Stoke imploring us not to sell to a developer, who almost certainly would build new houses on the site to the detriment of the village and its approaches. I gave this undertaking and very shortly afterwards found what we considered a suitable buyer. He was a director of a large brewery conglomeration just outside Wallingford and both he and his wife were enchanted with the house. Although we did not sell for as much as we could have got, we were satisfied that we had not let the village down. Before I went in to hospital we bought a much smaller house in Wallingford and June and James settled in. We considered that when I had recovered we would possibly be going abroad and that the house would bring in a useful rent as well as giving us a toehold in England.

A number of years later we, like little Ernie and his wife, were in the vicinity of Kilhendre and decided to visit it. As we turned the corner of the main road I saw that the beautiful row of Scots pines, which ran along the high bank approaching the drive-in gates, had gone. Then we saw the gates had gone and been blocked. We drove on to the back gate leading to the stables. No back gate and no stables. A small entrance gate led over a flower garden to a new bungalow. Still unbelievably shocked, we decided to call on the owners only to be further dismayed to find that where our house and gardens had been there were now lots of new bungalows with entrances leading from the village sports field that had bordered our vegetable garden. The owners of the bungalow we had called on could not understand why the grass and flowers in the garden were not doing very well. We had to tell them that their patch of ground was over the old stable and probably the beautiful stone-tiled 18th-century flooring was still intact, having been covered over by the builders. We were then devastated to learn that, after a short stay, the couple we sold it to re-sold it at a vast price to a developer and moved on.

Reverting to TQF and my departure to the RAF hospital at Halton, I was duly operated upon and woke up to find myself in thick plaster from my ankle to my chest. Although very well looked after, I stayed this way, in the ward, for three months before being transported to RAF Headley Court, Leatherhead. This was a rehabilitation centre in a grand old mansion house and, unlike most government establishments, had retained its opulent furniture and fittings and could not have been more comfortable. They eventually chipped away my plaster to reveal a very white and flaccid looking body that only moved with slug-like speed. Massage, water exercises, physiotherapy and luxury living helped me, in my mind and spirit, to focus on walking again. After a further three months, I learnt to walk with a stick. The only drawback was that my right foot was slightly shorter than my left and, like Charlie Chaplin, pointed at 30° to the right. After some time I was able to dispense with the crutches and, using a couple of sticks, to visit other patients who were much worse than I was. One of these was Air Marshal Tedder who was next to my ward. He was the one who was instrumental in encouraging me to re-enlist in the RAF and leave Africa in 1948. To see him in the last state of his illness was very sad and I remember his great fortitude in accepting the ultimate end. Just after Christmas of 1963 I was discharged from Headley Court with a built-up shoe and the advice to keep straightening my foot. The shoe I dispensed with after some time because of discomfort, but try as I might I have never been able to point both feet in the same direction without severe pain. The real crunch came when they categorised me so low medically that flying as a pilot was completely ruled out. I could not conceive that remaining as a senior cripple in the Air Force would help my promotion or my attitude toward service life. I felt, therefore, that I had made the right decision to retire, but I felt unsure how this set back might affect my future employment.

While at Headley Court (which catered for a few civilians as well as RAF officers) I met a grey-haired, elderly lady who had spent many years in India with the Church Missionary Society. She was completely dedicated to relieving the poverty and misery, which was unchanged, if not worse, following India's independence. I was most impressed by her practiced and Christian outlook, particularly concerning the outrageous shortcuts taken politically to justify the handover. I remember this happening in East Africa shortly after the Mau Mau episode where many of the African peoples (less often educated in the West and living in the cities) implored us to stay on awhile for a period for education and training, in agriculture and fiscal control, to be eased in before being left in the hands of partly educated and greedy activists. Since my great-grandfather, my grandfather and my father had all served in helping to develop the agricultural industry in Southern India, I felt a sentimental attachment to a country I had

Squadron Leader John M'Kenzie-Hall, The Queen's Flight.

only passed through. My time in Malaya and Africa had given me a good practical knowledge of the Malay and Swahili languages and I had mixed with, and understood, the unfound aspirations of Tamils, Chinese, Africans, Malays and even the aborigine Sakais. I thought that perhaps I might help, in some way, to counter the legacy of the worst that so called 'western civilisation' had left them. Having discussed the idea of going to India we though it advisable to enquire in to the practicalities of giving ourselves to missionary service and whether, at our age of early 40s, we would be wanted.

We made an appointment in London with the Church Missionary Service who seemed very keen to talk to us. We duly presented ourselves for interviews and were ushered in to a very plush office just off Smith Square and spent some time talking to a young, well-dressed young woman who, from her conversation, had never been abroad, let alone to India. She seemed very keen on recruiting us straightaway and this was particularly so when she learnt that June had spent some time in South India where her then husband had been a coffee planter.

My service pension income was another point in our favour since this would support the salary she was prepared to offer. This was to start at £300 per year and, within this sum, June was required to join in the work in a subsidiary capacity. We would have to find our own housing and it was mandatory that our son, James, be educated at our expense in India. Leave would be granted only every three years but the first leave had to be spent in India learning the language. She then asked an elderly, grey-haired lady who was on leave to come in and meet us. Her dedication to her work was quite apparent but she looked as if a square meal or two might revitalise her. What they paid her after a lifetime of service can only be imagined. Our well-dressed young interviewer then told us that she had a vacancy in New Delhi for the provision of a maternity hospital. As we left this lavish, centrally heated building, I could not help feeling desperately sorry for my elderly fellow in Headley Court. She must have been another 'Mother Teresa' to give her life in poverty to such a wealthy organisation who blatantly took advantage of those who were apparently determined in their wish to help those in need, at whatever cost to themselves; an admirable trait but one I did not share. They obviously had no idea of what they were letting themselves in for. I admit to never having been a saint but I have not been a complete fool either.

Having given India a very clear miss and returning to Wallingford, to hobble about the house on a couple of crutches, we came to a conclusion on our next move. Since I found that, once I could get in to a car, I had little difficulty in driving, we would go to Europe for a drive-about and head for a destination of Portugal and the Algarve. We calculated that with my tiny pension, topped up by the rent of the house, we could camp our way through France and Spain down to Faro and the sun. This would give us our first holiday since we were married seven years previously, and it would also give us time to consider our future and that of education for James, who was nearly six years old.

We sold our car in exchange for a camper van and, having let our house, started on a new adventure which I hoped would help in wiping out that lifelong boyish ambition to be an 'aeroplane driver'. Although I had travelled the world I had only flown over Europe for limited visits and had never been a tourist. I hoped that, on this adventure, a little culture might compensate for the empty feeling that had been haunting me since leaving hospital.

Portrait of John M'Kenzie-Hall in 1976.

Postscript

by James M'Kenzie-Hall

My Father intended to complete a final chapter of his life story but he only managed to briefly sketch out an overview which I present below under the title 'A Change of Life and Circumstances'. The year 2018 was my *annus horribilis* with the death of my Mother on 18 January 2018, and my Father 10 months later on 7 November 2018.

My Father had a rich and remarkable life and did much service for his country. I am fortunate to have his memoir and his eight logbooks recording his 14,000 flying hours. My only regret is that his greatest act of heroism on 19 November 1958 was never officially recognised during his lifetime.

John and June in 2007.

The unfinished chapter...

A Change of Life
and Circumstances

A fter our extended holiday driving through France, Spain and Portugal in
1964, we ended up buying a small house in Andalucia outside one of the
white villages (*Los pueblos blancos*) called Alhaurin el Grande, in the mountains,
29 kilometres from Malaga. We owned 'Casa Rustica' until 1972. Our dream of
living abroad, perhaps like the Durrells in Corfu, quickly evaporated with the
practicalities of both earning a living and educating our son James.

I came home from Spain early and joined the National Federation of
Housing Societies (1964–71) and eventually became its Deputy Director.
I saw my role to place the voluntary housing movement in a position where
it stood firmly between the public and private sectors of national housing
production, while maintaining its traditional social service towards people
in need. Successive governments have failed miserably to improve Britain's
housing situation, while well-constructed houses and flats at a moderate price
are increasingly difficult to find because of ever-rising costs in land, labour and
materials. Where can people in need of homes turn to find help? Whether they
are the ordinary wage-earners or one of the unfortunates of our society in a
spiral of poverty and homelessness, as brilliantly shown in the 1966 Ken Loach
film *Cathy Come Home* – how can they find a way to procure a home of their
own – on their own terms?

In 1971, my book *Low Cost Homes to Rent or Buy: an introduction to the
function, formation and operation of Housing Associations and Societies* was
published by Robert Hale. It described in detail the various categories of
housing associations and societies which catered for a whole range of housing
need, from houses for young families to sheltered homes for the elderly. The
reader was taken step by step through the formation, registration, financing and
management of a housing association or society, and some basic aspects of law

and housing legislation, together with the help that could be obtained from local authorities. I saw the voluntary housing movement as a way to open up a new horizon of hope for those who were looking for somewhere to call home. The book made waves and was held up in both Houses of Parliament as a definitive textbook on the function, formation and operation of housing societies and associations and an example of a good idea as the voluntary housing movement offered a third or middle way between public and private housing to people who found themselves unable to afford to rent or buy or were not eligible for council housing. The voluntary housing movement represented not-for-profit housing associations that provided homes with the following advantages:

1. Low cost property either to rent or buy.
2. Little or no capital outlay.
3. No qualifying requirements on account of age, marital status, size of family etc.
4. Full value for money due to the non-profit element.
5. Design requirements of accommodation in the control of founder members.
6. The opportunity for creating or retaining a community spirit through social service.

One should not run away with the idea that here is a method of getting something for nothing, or that the way lies open for anyone to solve their housing problem overnight. The origins of housing associations began in the 1830s when a group of people joined together to form the *Labourers' Friendly Society,* subsequently calling themselves the *Society for Improving the Conditions of the Labouring Classes.* This was the first collective group specifically to plan and build houses, reasonably separated from each other and provided with adequate drainage and waste disposal services. This forward thinking approach to health meant that the member-householders avoided the severe cholera outbreaks of 1849 and 1854. This association amalgamated with the Peabody Trust, which is still one of the oldest and largest housing associations in London, owning and managing more than 55,000 homes across London and the South East, housing over 111,000 residents.

The foreword to my book was written by George Jellicoe, 2nd Earl Jellicoe, past president of the National Federation of Housing Societies. He wrote: "… we can take no pride in Britain's housing. Many of our fellow countrymen live in conditions which are completely unworthy of an advanced community… one of the greatest challenges to which this nation must respond is that of making certain that every family in this country has the opportunity of living in conditions fit for civilised human beings".

After the publication of my book and apart from my day job, I spent more and more of my own time volunteering, was appointed onto dozens of committees, and advised both houses of parliament on housing. A chance meeting at the RAF club led to a long collaboration with Johnnie Johnson and Douglas Bader in establishing and running the Johnnie Johnson Housing Trust. Both successful wartime fighter pilots, they did not need to enter the housing field, but both felt a need to help others and they lent their celebrity names to a good cause. ■

"JOHNNIE" JOHNSON HOUSING TRUST LIMITED

Registered under the Charities Act
Registered with the Housing Corporation, No. L 1231
Registered under the Industrial and Provident Societies Act 1965
VAT Registration No: 453 1473 61

Chief Executive's Office

Chief Executive & Secretary
Air Vice-Marshal J.E. JOHNSON
C.B., C.B.E., D.S.O., D.F.C., D.L.

ASTRA HOUSE,
212 MOSS LANE,
BRAMHALL,
STOCKPORT,
CHESHIRE SK7 1BD.

Your Ref:

Our Ref: JEJ:CO

Telephone: 061-440 9696
(5 lines)

8th February 1989

J. M'Kenzie-Hall, Esq., MVO, MRAeS, MBIM, FFB,
Ravens,
Lancombe Lane,
Pitcombe,
Bruton,
Somerset. BA10 0PG.

Dear John.

Returned 12/2/89

Your £1 Share in "Johnnie" Johnson Housing Trust Ltd.
Share Certificate No. 6

It is some time since we last met and I hope this letter
finds you in good health.

In April of this year, I am retiring from the Trust and
handing over to Jim Lunney who was my Housing Manager for many
years, and naturally I am trying to tie up all the loose ends
before I go.

Although you have not involved yourself in Trust affairs for
some time, your name still appears in our Share Register and it
would help me if you would be good enough to sign the attached
and return it to me in the enclosed stamped addressed envelope.

All good wishes.

As ever
Johnnie.

Chapter 9 was intended to be the last chapter in my Father's memoirs. Unfortunately ill health in 2018 prevented this. However he had already sketched out the main points as follows:

1. Return to England from Spain.

2. Course at Hendon: senior management.

3. Getting a job.

4. National Federation of Housing Associations.

5. Cost Rent & Co-Ownership as assistant 1957 Housing Act (*see point 7*)

6. Interviews and recommendations to Ministry of Housing.

7. Housing Corporation: Des Wilson & Skelton ex Officio board. Housing the Homeless and Shelter.

8. Visits to sites, travelling, hours of work & promotion to Deputy Director.

9. Lectures – individual & national: to Liberal Party and British Council.

10. Articles published & Television appearances (Horace Cutler: against high rise). BBC Panorama.

11. Publication of book Low Cost Homes to Rent or Buy.

12. National Twilight Exhibition.

13. Restructure of NFHA.

14. Approach by Housing Corporation.

15. Offer of Directorship of NFHA.

16. Other Associations.

17. Procedures for forming Associations etc.

18. The Times article on Housing Corporation, upset Housing Corporation.

19. Infopress non-executive Director (Tony Peck).

20. Partnership with Geoffrey Edwards: BOAC, BA, BBC, ITV. Maplin paper.

21. Partnership: V to Land, STOL.

22. Board of NFHA.

23. Peter Black and Omnium.

24. Omnium Group build up.

25. Housing Corporation: manoeuvres and campaign intimidation.

26. Johnnie Johnson & Douglas Bader friendship & cooperation.

27. NAVH: reformed. Director & Vice Chairman.

28. Housing Corporation interference.

29. Personal housing in Spain & eventually Dolphin Square.

30. OMNIUM debacle and character assassination by Housing Corporation: resignation as advised too costly to sue for defamation, so retired early.

31. Qualifications.

32. London Centre: Princess Alexandra, Lady Joan Vickers, Lady Susan Hussey, Lord Strathcona.

33. Co-Ownership Committee. Chairman Lord Strathcona & visit to House of Commons with Lady Young to see Housing Minister.

34. Advice to House of Lords.

35. Advice to House of Commons.

36. Evidence to House of Commons: Housing Corporation & Voluntary Housing including Scotland.

37. Evidence to Race Relations Committee

38. Evidence to Conservative Back Bench Committees.

John M'Kenzie-Hall's medals.

Appendix

Obituaries, Portraits and Skeleton Family History

John M'Kenzie-Hall:
Honours and Membership of Professional Organisations:

Member of the Royal Victorian Order

Fellow of the Faculty of Building

Associate Member of the Royal Aeronautical Society

Fellow of the British Institute of Management

Member of the Guild of Air Pilots and Air Navigators

Public Service Commitments (Voluntary):

Trustee & Deputy Chairman: The London Centre Trust

Trustee: St Stephen's Hospital Trust

Trustee: Kensington & Chelsea Geriatric Day Hospital

Trustee, Past Chairman & Founder Member: The Johnnie Johnson Housing Trust

Council & Committee Member: National Association of Voluntary Hostels

Council & Committee Member: National Federation of Housing Associations

Executive Committee Member: Servite Houses Ltd

Executive Committee Member: Riverhead Housing Association Ltd

Committee Member: Bromley Federation of Housing Associations

Consultant: Stonham Housing Association Ltd, a Home Office sponsored charity.

John M'Kenzie-Hall, 1942.

The Hall family coat-of-arms.

John M'Kenzie-Hall's MVO: Member of the Royal Victorian Order.

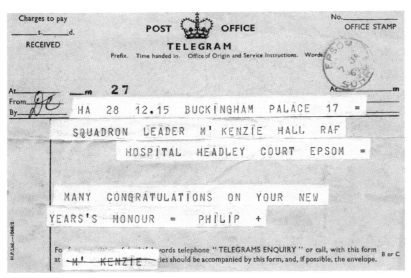

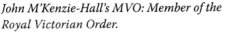

Congratulatory telegram on his MVO, from Prince Philip.

John M'Kenzie-Hall with his son James M'Kenzie-Hall in 1960.

John M'Kenzie-Hall's Obituary in The Telegraph, 21 December 2018

John M'Kenzie-Hall
Helicopter pilot who carried troops into dense jungle in Malaya, then served with the Queen's Flight

SQN LDR JOHN M'KENZIE-HALL, who has died aged 95, flew helicopters on operations in Malaya and during the Suez crisis before forming the helicopter section of the Queen's Flight.

In 1957, the Captain of the Queen's Flight, Air Vice-Marshal Sir Edward Fielden, asked M'Kenzie-Hall to set up and run a helicopter section, which was to completely change the pattern of travel for the royal family, although early helicopters were regarded in certain quarters as slightly suspect where safety was concerned.

Squadron Leader John M'Kenzie-Hall, The Queen's Flight.

At that time the Queen's Flight had no helicopters of its own and aircraft were supplied by the Royal Navy's 705 Squadron based at Lee-on-Solent. In the early months of his duties, M'Kenzie-Hall flew as navigator on all naval helicopter flights which carried members of the Royal family.

One flight in November 1958 led to a near-catastrophe when a naval helicopter carrying the Duke of Edinburgh and some of his personal staff took off from RAF North Coates in Lincolnshire to cross the Humber estuary to RAF Patrington.

Over the water, M'Kenzie-Hall noticed that the sliding cockpit window by his seat, which was also the escape hatch, was vibrating on its runner and had opened slightly. The restraining safety wire had snapped and there was a danger of the window jettisoning itself and hitting the tail rotor resulting in a catastrophic crash.

He grabbed hold of the loose window before it broke away but the airflow exerted a strong pressure as it opened further and, despite being in considerable pain as he braced his arm and right leg, M'Kenzie-Hall managed to hold on to it until the helicopter could be landed.

On his return to RAF Benson he submitted a full report to Sir Edward Fielden, who decided to keep the whole incident confidential but determined that helicopters would be under his direct control in future.

He immediately put M'Kenzie-Hall in charge of all future helicopter flight arrangements, which included overseeing the introduction to the Queen's Flight of two Whirlwinds.

From early 1960 the helicopters were able to provide lawn-to-lawn service to members of the Royal Family, landing at all the royal palaces and winching mail and passengers to the Royal Yacht Britannia during the Queen's Scottish Isles cruises. The helicopters were also used extensively for visits where airports were not available.

M'Kenzie-Hall was in command of the helicopter fleet for a further seven years and on retirement was appointed MVO [Member of the Victorian Order].

John Edwards M'Kenzie-Hall was born in Tasmania on 7 June 1923 and educated at Trinity Grammar School, Melbourne. He volunteered for the RAF and trained as a pilot in the US. Assessed as above average, he was posted as a flying instructor to No. 1 British Flying Training School at Terrell Air Force Base in Texas.

He returned to Britain in July 1944, transferred to the Fleet Air Arm and served on 891 Squadron, the first to be equipped with the US-built Hellcat night fighter.

When he was demobilised in 1947 he spent a year in Africa before returning to join the RAF in 1948. For the next four years he was a flying instructor.

In 1952 he transferred to helicopters and was posted to 194 Squadron based at Kuala Lumpur and flying the Westland Dragonfly in support of army patrols operating against the communist terrorists in the jungle.

Flying troops into remote jungle clearings and evacuating casualties was his main task. The helicopter force was in great demand and on 16 August 1954, M'Kenzie-Hall carried out 16 flights in seven hours. He also volunteered to command the Far East Jungle Rescue Team.

In October 1954 he joined the newly formed 155 Squadron, equipped with the more capable Westland Whirlwind. The helicopter's primary role was as a

M'Kenzie-Hall piloting a Whirlwind to lift troops out of the tall trees in Kluang District, Malaya.

troop carrier. To reach the deepest and most inaccessible areas, men of the SAS were parachuted into the jungle to select a site for a helicopter landing zone.

Using explosives and heavy cutting tools, an area was cleared to create a "chimney" in an area where the trees could be 250 ft tall. M'Kenzie-Hall took his helicopter into these areas and descended in the 'chimney', with minimal clearance for the helicopter's rotor blades, to land troops before evacuating any injured soldiers.

His logbook was annotated 'exceptional pilot'".

In May 1956 he joined the Joint Experimental Helicopter Unit based at Middle Wallop. He was conducting trials in Cyprus in September when he was instructed to prepare to fly onto aircraft carriers.

By 31 October, M'Kenzie-Hall's and 11 other helicopters landed on *Theseus* and headed for Egypt. At 6am on 6 November he flew men of the Royal Marines in the first wave of the Suez invasion, landing a few yards from the De Lesseps statue at Port Said.

During the day he made another six lifts during the three-hour assault. The unit then moved to Gamil Airfield and a few days later the Whirlwinds flew back to Cyprus.

His seven-year period with the Queen's Flight marked the end of his service career. His right leg had been damaged during his efforts to retain the helicopter window during the flight across the Humber and he spent months having treatment and rehabilitation.

In 1964 he joined the National Federation of Housing Societies, becoming its deputy director. He spent the remainder of his working life helping the voluntary housing movement to establish housing associations and sheltered homes for the elderly, and his book Low Cost Homes to Rent or Buy (1971) became a standard work of reference.

He also helped fellow pilots Johnnie Johnson and Douglas Bader to set up their own charitable foundations and served as a founding director of the Johnnie Johnson Housing Trust.

In 1957 John M'Kenzie-Hall married June Steele (née Medhurst-Saul). She died in January this year and their son survives him.

John M'Kenzie-Hall, born 7 June 1923, died 7 November 2018. ■

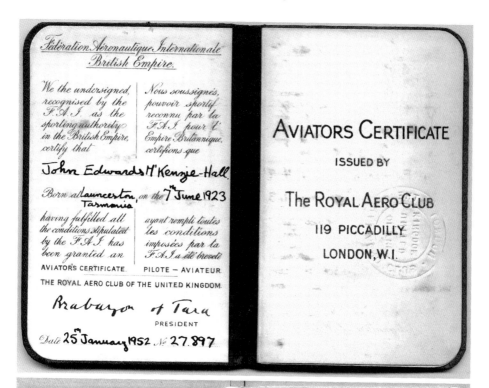

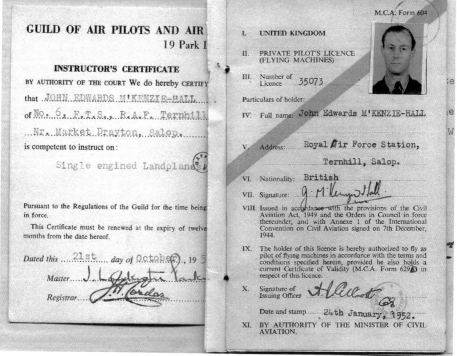

Pilot licences

The last ever photo of John M'Kenzie-Hall taken in Summer 2017, beside the grave of his great-uncle John Hay Edwards.

Jungle hero and Royal pilot

SQUADRON LEADER John M'Kenzie-Hall, who has died aged 95, was tasked to form the helicopter section of The Queen's Flight in 1957 having flown helicopters on operations in Malaya and during the ill-fated Suez crisis.

Born in Tasmania, M'Kenzie-Hall trained as a pilot in the USA and, after gaining his 'wings', he remained a flying instructor until July 1944 when he returned to the UK and transferred to the Fleet Air Arm and served on 891 Squadron, the first to be equipped with the US-built Hellcat night fighter.

When he was demobilized in 1947 he spent a year in Africa before returning to join the RAF in 1948. For the next four years he was a flying instructor.

In 1952 he transferred to helicopters and was posted to 194 Squadron based at Kuala Lumpur and flying the Westland Dragonfly in support of Army patrols operating against the communist terrorists in the jungle.

Flying troops into remote jungle clearings and evacuating casualties was his main task.

The helicopter force was in great demand and on August 16, 1954, M'Kenzie-Hall carried out 16 flights in seven hours. He also volunteered to command the Far East Jungle Rescue Team.

In October 1954, he joined the newly formed 155 Squadron equipped with the more capable Westland Whirlwind. The helicopter's primary role was as a

troop carrier. To reach the deepest and most inaccessible areas, men of the SAS were parachuted into the jungle to select a site for a helicopter landing zone.

Using explosives and heavy cutting tools, an area was cleared to create a 'chimney' where the trees could be 250 feet tall. M'Kenzie-Hall took his helicopter into these areas and descended in the 'chimney', with minimal clearance for the helicopter's rotor blades, to land

troops before evacuating any injured soldiers. His logbook was annotated 'exceptional pilot'.

In May 1956 he joined the Joint Experimental Helicopter Unit based at Middle Wallop. He carried out trials in Cyprus and in September was instructed to prepare for flying onto aircraft carriers.

By the end of October, he and eleven other helicopter crews had landed on HMS Theseus and headed for Egypt. At 6 am on November 6, he

flew men of the Royal Marines in the first wave to land a few yards from the De Lesseps statue at Port Said.

During the day he carried another six lifts during the three-hour assault. The unit then moved to Gamil Airfield and a few days later the Whirlwinds flew back to Cyprus.

In 1957, the then Captain of The Queen's Flight, Air Vice-Marshal Sir Edward Fielden, asked M'Kenzie-Hall to set up and run a helicopter section, although early helicopters were regarded in certain quarters as slightly suspect where safety was concerned.

At that time The Queen's Flight had no helicopters of their own and aircraft were supplied by the Royal Navy's 705 Squadron based at Lee-on-Solent.

In the early months of his duties, M'Kenzie-Hall flew as navigator on all naval helicopter flights, which carried members of the Royal Family.

One flight led to a near catastrophe when a naval helicopter carrying Prince Philip and some of his personal staff, took off in November 1958 from RAF North Coates in Lincolnshire to cross the Humber estuary to RAF Patrington.

Over the water M'Kenzie-Hall noticed that the co-pilot's sliding cockpit window, which was also the escape hatch, was vibrating on its runner and had opened slightly. The restraining safety wire had snapped and there was a danger of the sliding window jettisoning itself and hitting the tail rotor which would result in the loss of the helicopter.

He grabbed hold of the loose

window before it broke away but the airflow exerted a strong pressure as it opened further and, despite being in considerable pain from bracing his leg and arm, M'Kenzie-Hall held on to it until the helicopter could be landed.

On his return to RAF Benson he submitted a full report to Sir Edward Fielden who decided to keep the whole incident confidential but he was determined that helicopters would be under his direct control in future.

He immediately put M'Kenzie-Hall in charge of all future helicopter flight arrangements, which included overseeing the introduction to The Queen's Flight of two Whirlwinds.

From early 1960 the helicopters were able to provide lawn-to-lawn service to members of the Royal Family landing at all the Royal palaces and winching mail and passengers to HMY Britannia during the Queen's Scottish Isles cruises. The helicopters were also used extensively for visits where airports were not available.

M'Kenzie-Hall was in command of the helicopter fleet for a further seven years and on retirement was appointed MVO.

His seven-year period with The Queen's Flight marked the end of his Service career.

His right leg had been damaged during his efforts to retain the helicopter window during the flight across the Humber and he spent months having treatment and rehabilitation. He died on November 7.

Obituary notice in RAF News.

I saved Philip from deadly helicopter plunge

By **Marco Giannangeli**

A Daily Express article about the helicopter incident in which my father saved the life of the Duke of Edinburgh by hanging on to a broken sliding door, which prevented it from hitting the tail rotor. My Father never said the words attributed to him – that is tabloid invention.

PRINCE Philip escaped death in a helicopter crash thanks to a quick-thinking RAF pilot, it has emerged.

On November 19, 1968, five years after Queen Elizabeth II was crowned, the 37-year-old Duke of Edinburgh visited RAF North Coates, Lincolnshire, and left in a Sikorsky Whirlwind bound for RAF Patrington across the Humber estuary.

In the co-pilot's chair was ace Australian pilot RAF Squadron Leader John M'Kenzie-Hall, who died last month aged 95. After take-off the officer noticed his side window vibrating and that the

retaining wire had snapped. Describing the incident later, he said: "My immediate reaction was, 'Oh God, the tail rotor might not benefit if this flies backwards.'

"Every helicopter pilot knows if the tail rotors blades are lost by impact the aircraft will lose directional flight and there is nothing the pilot can do to alleviate total disaster.

"As this discomfiting thought flashed through my mind I was looking down at the freezing grey waters of the Humber estuary. "Just as I tightened my fingers around

the front edge the slipstream beat me to it and the window came so far off the runner that I could not slide it into its lock.

"I was just able to twist in my seat and grab hold of the back of the window as it broke free. The airflow acted like a parachute in reverse, and started to rotate with it and me. To prevent myself being dragged out of the aircraft I hooked my right foot under the instrument panel but... had to keep my leg painfully to its right.

"With my hands beginning to lose all feeling because of the cold, my thoughts came

in flashes – 'Can I hold on?'"

The craft landed safely but his fingers were so numb that when he tried to climb down from the cockpit he missed his handhold and fell.

"As he [Philip] climbed out he gave my muddy uniform a rather quizzical look and asked, not unkindly, 'What's happened to you?'"

It took the Squadron leader seven months of intense physiotherapy to recover from his leg injury.

Last night a spokesman for Prince Philip said: "The Duke of Edinburgh was saddened to hear of the death of John M'Kenzie-Hall."

CLOSE CALL: The Prince boarding at RAF North Coates

CLARENCE HOUSE
S.W.1

21st March, 1963

My Dear Squadron Leader —

Queen Elizabeth The Queen Mother has
asked me to tell you how sad she is to learn
that you are shortly retiring and that you
will therefore no longer be Captain of the
helicopter in which Her Majesty has made so
many journeys.

Queen Elizabeth felt that she would
like to give you a photograph of Her Majesty
as a token of her gratitude for all that you
have done on her behalf.

This I am sending to you herewith
accompanied by an expression of Queen Elizabeth's
very sincere good wishes to you for the years
ahead.

Yours very sincerely,

Martin Gilliat.

Squadron Leader J.E. M'Kenzie-Hall.

From: Brigadier Archie Miller-Bakewell
Private Secretary to HRH The Duke of Edinburgh

BUCKINGHAM PALACE

6th December, 2018

Dear Mr M'Kenzie-Hall,

Thank you for your recent correspondence, notifying The Duke of Edinburgh
of the death of your father, Squadron Leader John M'Kenzie-Hall. This has been a
very sad year for you, following the death of your mother in January. I am sorry.

The Duke of Edinburgh has asked me to write and send his condolences to
you. I do hope the Thanksgiving Service for your father went smoothly today, and
that it gave a welcome opportunity to reflect on his life and to meet those with
whom your father had worked – in his worldwide postings with the RAF, with The
Queen's Flight and the National Federation of Housing Societies.

This letter comes with Prince Philip's warm good wishes.

Yours sincerely,

Archie Miller-Bakewell

James McKenzie-Hall, Esq.

BUCKINGHAM PALACE, LONDON SW1A 1AA
TELEPHONE: 020 7930 4832   EMAIL: archie.millerbakewell@royal.gov.uk

AIR MINISTRY

WHITEHALL

LONDON S.W.1

17 February 1964

Dear Squadron Leader M'Kenzie-Hall,
I have it in command from The Queen

to convey to you, on leaving the Active

list of the Royal Air Force, the thanks

of Her Majesty for your long and valuable

services.

May I take this opportunity of

wishing you all good fortune in the

future.

Yours
sincerely,

Squadron Leader J. E. M'Kenzie-Hall.

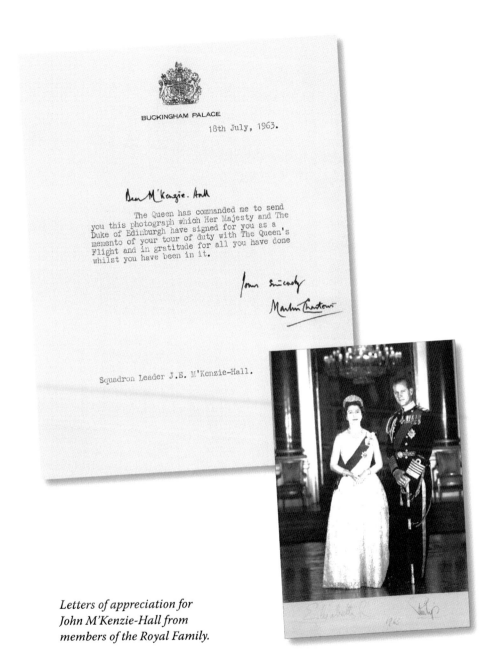

BUCKINGHAM PALACE

18th July, 1963.

Dear M'Kenzie-Hall

The Queen has commanded me to send
you this photograph which Her Majesty and The
Duke of Edinburgh have signed for you as a
memento of your tour of duty with The Queen's
Flight and in gratitude for all you have done
whilst you have been in it.

Yours sincerely

Martin Charteris

Squadron Leader J.E. M'Kenzie-Hall.

*Letters of appreciation for
John M'Kenzie-Hall from
members of the Royal Family.*

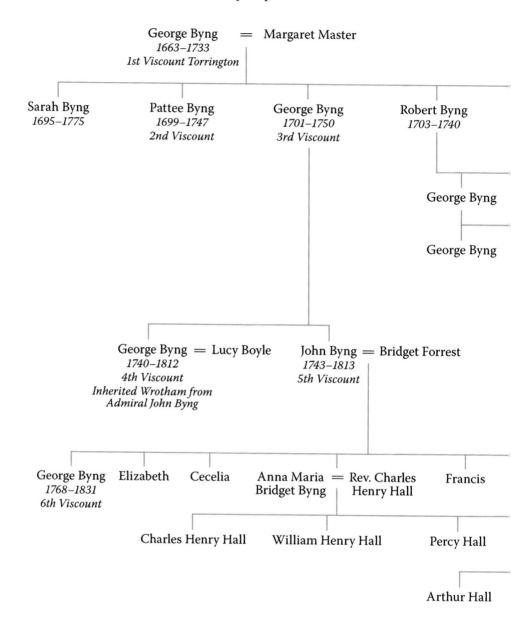

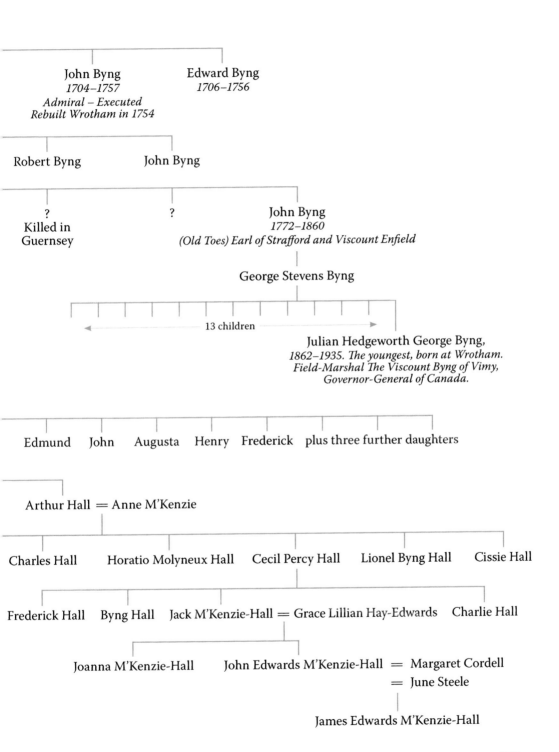

John Byng
1704–1757
Admiral – Executed
Rebuilt Wrotham in 1754

Edward Byng
1706–1756

Robert Byng

John Byng

?
Killed in
Guernsey

?

John Byng
1772–1860
(Old Toes) Earl of Strafford and Viscount Enfield

George Stevens Byng

13 children

Julian Hedgeworth George Byng,
1862–1935. The youngest, born at Wrotham.
Field-Marshal The Viscount Byng of Vimy,
Governor-General of Canada.

Edmund   John   Augusta   Henry   Frederick   plus three further daughters

Arthur Hall = Anne M'Kenzie

Charles Hall   Horatio Molyneux Hall   Cecil Percy Hall   Lionel Byng Hall   Cissie Hall

Frederick Hall   Byng Hall   Jack M'Kenzie-Hall = Grace Lillian Hay-Edwards   Charlie Hall

Joanna M'Kenzie-Hall   John Edwards M'Kenzie-Hall = Margaret Cordell
= June Steele

James Edwards M'Kenzie-Hall

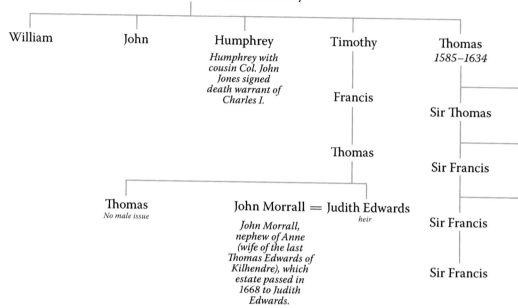

A short summary of my mother's family was given in a letter written to my mother (Grace Lillian Hay Edwards) by her uncle, John Hay Edwards. I have inserted Edwards II and III in brackets for clarity. – *John M'Kenzie-Hall*

Brattles Grange, Brenchley, Kent
15 November 1922

'To begin with I will make passing reference to comparatively contemporary matters. I will refer to your father as George, as I go.

Father (George Hay Edwards II) died in his 98th year. When a boy his tutor was George Spencer, father of the famous Herbert Spencer. He was first articled to a lawyer but not liking the law he and young Herbert Spence studied civil engineering. The latter gave that profession up and became the famous scientist and great English philosopher. They continued their friendship up to the latter's death.

Our father was associated with Joseph Locke, the famous engineer with whom he constructed several English railways. The most important perhaps of father's work was the making of the first railway in Normandy. We mostly lived in Paris where I had my early education together with my brothers and sister Charlotte. He subsequently joined his uncle, Thomas Allom, the famous Artist in partnership as Architects and Civil Engineers, afterwards retiring on a modest fortune, which was largely broken in the great Baring Bank collapse in 1890.

He always used to say that he retired too early. He was an intelligent man, well read, a dear good father, blessed with excellent health up to within a fortnight of his death in his 98th year. Our dear mother predeceased him by very many years. Charlotte, my eldest sister, was also a

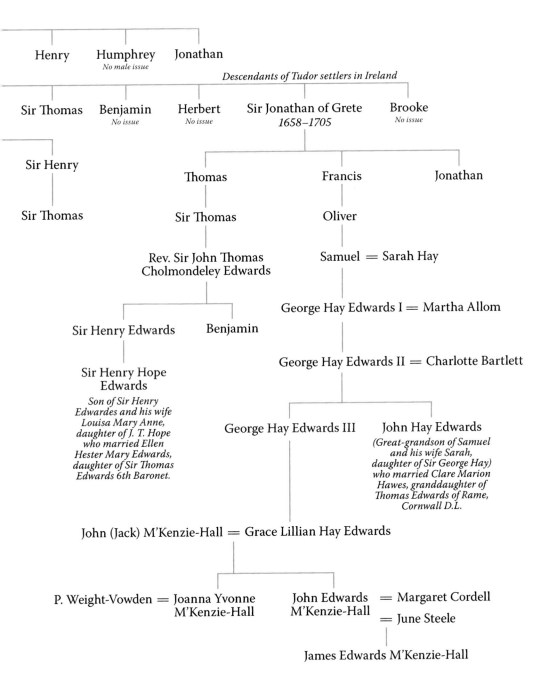

great favourite and much sought. She was a brilliant pianist and very entertaining and loveable, much in request at concerts and among friends.

George, your father (George Hay Edwards III), trained in his father's office, emigrated to Australia (feeling the profession was overcrowded in this small country) when I was comparatively a child. Fred was articled to Surveyors and followed George or possibly to New Zealand first. That would have been a good combination with a brother in civil engineering. I fear he was too restless to succeed very much poor fellow.

John (myself) wanted to be a soldier, but as it would have to be cavalry, money was not forthcoming, had to be content in later years with Officers Volunteers R.E. I was articled to underwriters at Lloyds (shipping assn. With insufficient capital to do enough business I joined other concerns and eventually a Partnership. On the whole successful with various contracts and land dealings. Retired with a very modest fortune.

Your Aunt Amy married Rossel and their children were Humphrey and Ruth.

Now I can merely give males in descent of the Edwards family as a skeleton incomplete and those males only known to have lived continuously up to a time or continued the Homes of their predecessors for the purposes of links in a chain, otherwise it would of course take a bulky volume and much research. The history of the Edwards of Salop is one of the earliest recorded in English history. So far as it is traceable with accuracy it begins with Tudor of Trefor (afterwards Tudor Trevor) Earl of Hereford. He was born at Pengworn in Chirkland, Co Denbigh about 874 AD and died about 948 AD.

Among the nobles who founded great Houses he bears a high place, nor are there many among the descendants of the Royal Tribe of Wales to be compared with him in wealth or power and territory and nobility of character. The title of the Earl of Hereford continued in the family for many years until the Saxons wrested the Kingdom from the Britons and conferred the same on the Saxon nobility.

After a long series of ancestors who married with the daughters of the Prince of Wales, of Cornwall and of Powis (before England was united under one Sovereign) was 'Madoc' the first to drop the suffix, 'Ap' and assume the surname 'Edwards', living in the time of Henry VII. Some of his family were possessors of Chirk, Duddleston, Oswestry and Whittington about the time of William the Conqueror.

Returning to Tudor Trevor to show the direct line of descent, his great-great-grandson was Rhys Sais who had three sons. The eldest was Tudor, the second Elidor and the youngest Iddon. Tudor was the progenitor of Henry VII founder of the Tudor dynasty and Iddon was the progenitor of your father's family. Descended from him (Iddon) was the above named Madoc Edwards, Co. Salop. From him was descended Hugo Edwards (leaving out all intermediary names of forefathers) joint founder of the Shrewsbury Public School (Edward VI). Hugo had five sons, the last of which was Thomas. He had three sons, his last being Thomas, Kings Body Knight, created first Baronet by Charles I with precedency over all Baronets thereafter (1644). One of his brothers, Humphrey, was against the King and with Col. John Jones, also of the blood of Tudor Trevor, and married to Oliver Cromwell's sister, were Commissioners at the trial and signed the Death Warrant of Charles I. Humphrey, Thomas's second son, died unmarried before the Restoration took place. Col. Jones, upon the Restoration, returned to the Edwards family home Kilhendre for safety, where he was seized by the Parliamentary forces, tried and executed on 17 October 1660.

Kilhendre was held by the Edwards family for over six centuries, finally passing to Judith Edwards who married John Morral. It was almost demolished in 1790 and subsequently rebuilt by the Morral family who acquired the Estate.

Sir Thomas Edwards's descendant (through intermediaries of course) was Samuel Edwards who married the daughter of Sir George Hay, Lord of Admiralty and Chancellor of Worcester. Their son named George Hay Edwards, whose son was also George Hay Edwards (my father), his son being George Hay Edwards and your father.'

John Hay Edwards

Charles Henry Hall

Charles Henry Hall (1763–1827), dean of Christ Church, Oxford, was the son of Charles Hall DD (1718–1774), dean of Bocking, Essex, and chaplain to Archbishop Secker, and his wife, Elizabeth, daughter of Robert Carsan, a Lambeth surgeon. He was admitted on the foundation at Westminster School in 1775, and was elected thence to Christ Church, Oxford, and matriculated on 3 June 1779. His career began well: he won the chancellor's prize for Latin verse with 'Strages Indica Occidentalis' (1781) and the English essay for 'The use of medals' (1784); he graduated BA in 1783, MA in 1786, BD in 1794, and DD in 1800. From 1792 to 1794 he was tutor and censor of Christ Church; among his pupils was Peter Elmsley. In 1793 he served the office of junior proctor.

On 29 August 1794, Hall married Anna Maria Bridget (d. 1852), third daughter of John Byng, fifth Viscount Torrington. He thus vacated his studentship at Christ Church and was presented to the college living of Broughton in Airedale, Yorkshire. In 1798 he was appointed Bampton lecturer and prebendary of Exeter. His Bampton lectures were published as *Fullness of Time* in 1799. He became rector of Kirk Bramwith, Yorkshire, in 1799 on the nomination of his former pupil Lord Hawkesbury (later Lord Liverpool), and from 1807 vicar of Luton, Bedfordshire, a preferment which he held until his death.

As a student of Christ Church, Hall had basked in Dean Jackson's favour, and in 1794 Jackson recommended him to the duke of Portland, then home secretary, for preferment in Ireland, as 'the very man to be brought forward hereafter. He has real learning, and real good qualities' (Bill, 78). In 1799 Hall became a canon of Christ Church, and in 1807, through the influence of Lord Liverpool, regius professor of divinity. Jackson's view of him now changed and he thought Hall's lectures as professor 'sadly sterile and jejune'. Within months of his promotion to the chair, Hall wrote to Liverpool for a bishopric, complaining of Jackson's hostility (Bill, 79). However, mainly through Liverpool's influence (Bill, 126, 233), Hall was in October 1809 'brought forward' to succeed Jackson as dean of Christ Church, thus becoming one of the few former students to achieve this ultimate triumph.

It was the not continuously resident Reginald Heber of All Souls College who made a telling but qualified contrast between Hall's rule and that of his predecessor: Jackson's rule 'was an absolute monarchy of the most ultra-oriental character, whereas [Hall] is as little attended to, to all appearances, as the peishwah of the Mahrattas; the whole ground resting on an oligarchy of tutors' under whom, Heber rightly thought, the college flourished as much as under Jackson ('Reginald Heber', Reminiscences of Oxford, by Oxford Men, ed. L. M. Quiller-Couch, 1892, 241). Hall's dependence on an oligarchy became painfully clear in 1817, when he failed to gain the support not only of the canons but also of the censors (and therefore of the common room) when he proposed George Canning as successor to Charles Abbott as MP for the university; such a rebuff was inconceivable under Jackson.

Frederick Oakeley, who resided at Christ Church from 1820, gives more detail: Hall cloaked his inferiority to Jackson by imitating his gait and dress (though there is no pictorial record of these in Hall's case), but Oakeley found Hall's manner 'haughty and overbearing', and had 'no pleasant recollections about him'. Wine parties were frequent and Oakeley found his surroundings and the attitudes of many of his contemporaries with their 'vice and loose conversation' not conducive to his own academic progress. Hall's own son fell into bad company there and had to be sent away without graduating. Under Hall, Christ Church did not fully maintain the high place in the class lists which had been foreshadowed under his predecessor; in the 29 honours examinations of Hall's time, Christ Church obtained 94 firsts, though 21 of these came in his earliest years, when candidates admitted by Jackson were involved. Few men who later distinguished themselves in politics were undergraduates under Hall, though several who proved sound tutors were selected, among whom C. T. Longley, Augustus Short, Charles Dodgson, and W. F. Hook were later to obtain promotion in the church. According to Hook, Hall was not interested in what undergraduates said to him (Bill, 223).

As dean, Hall presided at probably the most historic public function held in Christ Church, the dinner of 15 June 1814 during the visit of the allied sovereigns; he sat between the Prince Regent and the Duke of York, with Lord Grenville (chancellor of the university) and Prince Blücher in adjoining seats. Hall could greet foreign princes and conduct society weddings with appropriate dignity, but all was not well in the deanery itself. In 1824 Lord Liverpool wrote to George IV that 12 or 13 years earlier, just after he became dean, Hall might have become a bishop (as Hall himself had hoped), but this promotion was impossible because of his 'embarrassed circumstances' (letters of George IV, no. 1139, n. 2); these were explained by an observer in 1827: 'Bailiffs were continually in the House at Oxford' (S. Markham, *A Testimony of her Times*, 1990, 157) – a circumstance which cannot have enhanced Hall's standing among undergraduates richer than himself. Liverpool thought that Hall must be found a prosperous deanery; in 1824 the most suitable one, Durham, fell vacant, and Hall was appointed to it. Three years later, on 16 March 1827, Hall died at Edinburgh, where he had gone on medical advice. A month earlier a writ of sequestration read in Durham Cathedral (in Hall's presence) gave his debts as £35,800.

Hall's career did not fulfil its early promise; he never became a bishop. If it was an amusing chance that he was the only dean of Christ Church to have a brother-in-law nicknamed Poodle, it was by his own (or his wife's) mismanagement that he became the only dean who had bailiffs in the deanery – perhaps they were out of sight when the Prince Regent stayed there in mid-June 1814.

J. F. A. Mason

Index

List of Aircraft Flown *by John M'Kenzie-Hall*

Fixed-wing aircraft:

Miles Magister

DH 82A Tiger Moth (biplane)

PT-17 Stearman (biplane)

BT-13A Vultee Valiant

L4 Piper Cub

AT6 Harvard: types A,B & C

P-39 Airacobra

P-40 Tomahawk

P-51 Mustang

P-36 Mohawk

Airspeed Oxford twin engine

F6F Grumman Hellcat: types I & II

Typhoon

Corsair

Sea-fire

Fairey Firefly IV & V

Spitfire

Blackburn Firebrand I

Vampire Jet I (checkout)

Fairey Swordfish (checkout)

ME-109 F (checkout)

Lockheed Hudson (checkout)

D.H. Dove (checkout)

Auster Autocrat

Fairchild Argus (own private plane used in
    Tanganyika)

Fairey Barracuda

Anson I

Gloster Meteor (first British jet fighter)

Percival Prentice

Boulton Paul Balliol

D.H. Chipmunk

Helicopters:

Westland WS-51 Dragonfly

Bristol Sycamore

Westland Whirlwind S. 55
    (TQF: HAR 4, HCC8)

Abbreviations & Acronyms

AAFFTD	Army Air Forces Flying Training Detachment	MI5	Military Intelligence, Section 5
AFC	Air Force Cross	MVO	Member of the Royal Victorian Order
AOP	Airborne Observation Post	N3A	Fighter plane gunsight
ARAM	Associate of the Royal Academy of Music	NAAFI	Navy, Army and Air Force Institutes
ARCM	Associate of the Royal School of Music	NCO	Non-commissioned officer
AT6	Harvard aircraft	NFHA	National Federation of Housing Associations
BEA	British Europen Airways	OBE	Officer of the British Empire
BFTS	British Flying Training School	OC	Officer Commanding
BOAC	British Overseas Airway Corporation	P-36	Warhawk aircraft
		P-39	Airacobra aircraft
BT-13	Vultee Valiant aircraft	P-40	Tomahawk aircraft
CFI	Chief Flying Instructor	P-51	Mustang aircraft
Cpl.	Corporal	PT-17	Boeing Stearman aircraft
CTs	Communist terrorists	PX	Post Exchange (US Army base retail store)
CVO	Commander of the Royal Victorian Order	RAF	Royal Air Force
DFC	Distinguished Flying Cross	RCAF	Royal Canadian Air Force
DFM	Distinguished Flying Medal	RNAS	Royal Naval Air Service
DH82A	Tiger Moth aircraft	S-55	Westland Whirlwind helicopter
DTs	Delirium tremens	Sgt.	Sergeant
EFTS	Elementary Flying Traing School	S/Ldr.	Squadron Leader
EOKA	Ethniki Organosis Kyprion Agoniston	TQF	The Queen's Flight
		USAAF	United States Army Air Force
F/Lt.	Flight Lieutenant	V1	German WWII flying bomb
F/O	Flying Officer	V2	German WWII rocket flying bomb
GOC	General Officer Commanding	VIP	Very important person
HMS	His [Her] Majesty's Ship	VVIP	Very, very important person
HMT	His [Her] Majesty's Troopship	W/Cdr.	Wing Commander
ITW	Initial Training Wing		
JEHU	Joint Experimental Helicopter Unit		
KCB	Knight Commander of the Bath		
KL	Kuala Lumpur		
L4	Aircraft		
LVO	Lieutenant of the Royal Victorian Order		

Record of Service: John M'Kenzie-Hall

RAF World War Two
ITW Paignton, completed 2 April 1942
Student Pilot
EFTS Kingstown, Carlisle; 13 April to 8 May 1942
PDC Moncton, Canada; June 1942
USAAF Wings Over America student pilot course (Arnold Scheme)
Each course lasted nine weeks: divided into Preflight; Primary; Basic & Advanced.
Preflight: Turner Field, Georgia; July to 10 August 1942
Primary: Tuscaloosa, Alabama; 10 August 1942 to 7 October 1942
Basic: Gunter Field, Georgia; 12 October to 15 December 1942
Advanced: Craig Field, Alabama; 20 December 1942 to 31 January 1943, and gunnery course 1 –16 February 1943.
Qualified as pilot with award of American Army Air Force wings on 18 February 1943 with above average assessment and recommendation as Instructor, Single Day Fighter & Single Night Fighter.
Instructors Course
CFS Randolph Field, Texas; 23 March to 5 May 1943
Instructor
USAAF Eagle Pass, Texas; 6 May to 19 August 1943
No.1 BFTS, Terrell, Texas; 6 September 1943 to 17 May 1944
Return to England
No.29 EFTS, RAF Clyffe Pypard; 13-31 August 1944
No.20 (P) AFU, Kidlington; 29 September 1944 to 26 March 1945
Transfer to Fleet Air Arm
Naval Instrument Flying School Instrument course; 24–28 April 1945
891 Squadron Fleet Air Arm, Eglinton, Northern Ireland; 6 June to 15 August 1945

Post-War RAF
Biggin Hill, Kent; 8 July to 30 December 1949
FRS Finningley; 1 January to 3 February 1950
RAF College, Manby; 20 February to 20 March 1950
FTC ILC Brize Norton; 22 March to 1 April 1950
CFS Little Rissington; 1 May to 31 August 1950
No.6 FTS Ternhill 13 September; 1950 to 25 February 1953
Westland Aircraft Co Ltd; 2 March to 22 May 1953
Changi Creek, Singapore; 22 June to 26 June 1953
Benta Field 656 Squadron 1907 Flight AIR.OP; 2 to 8 July 1953
Taiping 656 Squadron 1914 Flight AIR.OP; 9 to 15 July 1953
194 Squadron, Kuala Lumpur; 23 July 1953 to 30 September 1954
155 Squadron, Kuala Lumpur; 5 October 1954 to 20 February 1956
JEHU, Middle Wallop 22; May to 16 June 1956
Nicosia, Cyprus; 18 June to 15 July 1956
JEHU, Middle Wallop; 16 July to 30 September 1956
HMS Theseus; 1–19 October 1956
JEHU, Middle Wallop; 20–24 October 1956
HMS Ocean 25 October to 7 November 1956
Gamil-Port Said, Egypt 7–28 November 1956
JEHU, Middle Wallop; 23 December 1956 to 3 June 1957
The Queens Flight, RAF Benson; 3 June 1957 to 19 June 1963